SPURGEON ON CHRIST

SPURGEON ON CHRIST

CHARLES H. SPURGEON

BRIDGE LOGOS

Alachua, Florida 32615

Bridge-Logos
Alachua, FL 32615 USA

Spurgeon on Christ
Charles H. Spurgeon

Copyright ©2014 Bridge-Logos, Inc.

All rights reserved. Under International Copyright Law, no part of this publication may be reproduced, stored, or transmitted by any means—electronic, mechanical, photographic (photocopy), recording, or otherwise—without written permission from the Publisher.

Unless otherwise indicated, the Scripture quotations in this publication are from the King James Version (KJV) of the Bible.

Printed in the United States of America.

Library of Congress Catalog Card Number: 2014942608
International Standard Book Number 978-1-61036-129-3

Researched and Updated by Harold J. Chadwick
Edited by Beverlee J. Chadwick

VP 07-01-14

Table of Contents

Preface 1

Biography 5

Chapter 1. Christ Crucified—
February 11, 1855 29

Chapter 2. Christ Our Passover—
December 2, 1855 57

Chapter 3. Christ in the Covenant—
August 31, 1856 81

Chapter 4. Christ the Power and
Wisdom of God—May 17, 1857 101

Chapter 5. Christ Lifted Up—
July 5, 1857 121

Chapter 6. Christ Glorified as the Builder
of His Church—May 2, 1858 143

Chapter 7. Christ—Our Substitute—
April 15, 1860 167

Chapter 8. Christ—Perfect Through Sufferings—
November 2, 1862 189

Chapter 9. Christ Is Glorious—Let Us Make
Him Known—March 20, 1864 215

Chapter 10. Christ the Conqueror of Satan—
November 26, 1876 243

Chapter 11. Christ's Resurrection and Our
Newness of Life—March 29, 1891 269

Study Guide 295

Preface

Charles Haddon Spurgeon was a God-given gift to the Church... boy preacher at the tender age of sixteen... the Prince of Preachers... inspired knowledge, interpretation and skillful teaching of Scripture readily understood by all with no age or education barriers, and accompanied by God-guided wisdom in its application.

The following selected chapters from Spurgeon's teachings on Christ will inspire, strengthen, motivate, captivate, educate, and produce a strong hunger within you to know and love Christ even more. As Spurgeon teaches, his personal relationship with Christ reveals a depth of love and knowledge that occurs only when one has constant fellowship and communion with Him.

The chapters, though they do not represent all the teachings Spurgeon did on Christ, have been carefully selected to reveal all that Christ has done for His Church—beginning with His crucifixion to His glorious resurrection and the life we are blessed to live in His righteousness, guidance, power and strength because of what He has done and to His glory and praise.

Spurgeon believed strongly that there has been much preaching done about Christ, but a definite lack of teaching on believing Christ and thereby pointing souls to Christ as our Savior, and the source of our life as He lives in and through us. Spurgeon said:

> "I become increasingly earnest that every preaching time should be a soul-saving time. I can deeply sympathize with Paul when he said, *"My heart's*

desire and prayer to God for Israel is, that they might be saved" (Romans 10:1). We have had so much preaching, but, comparatively speaking, so little believing in Jesus; and if there be no believing in Him, neither the law nor the gospel has answered its end, and our labor has been utterly in vain. Some of you have heard, and heard, and heard again, but you have not believed in Jesus. If the gospel had not come to your hearing you would not have been guilty of refusing it. "Have they not heard?" says the apostle. "Yes, verily:" but still "they have not all obeyed the gospel." Up to this very moment there has been no hearing with the inner ear, and no work of faith in the heart, in the case of many whom we love. Dear friends, is it always to be so? How long is it to be so? Shall there not soon come an end of this reception of the outward means and rejection of the inward grace? Will your soul not soon close in with Christ for present salvation? Break! Break, O heavenly day, upon those still in the darkness of unbelief, for our hearts are breaking over them. The reason why many do not come to Christ is not because they are not earnest, after a fashion, and thoughtful and desirous to be saved, but because they cannot accept God's way of salvation. *"They have a zeal for God, but not according to knowledge"* (Romans 10:2, NKJV). We get them by our exhortation far enough on the way that they become desirous to obtain eternal life, but *"they have not submitted themselves unto the righteousness of God"* (Romans 10:3).

I pray God will bless you with a deep yearning to learn more of Christ and a desire to commune and fellowship with Him more and more as you read this book on His holy Son, for as you learn more of the Son of God, you will also learn more of God the Father whom Christ came to reveal.

May God richly bless you,
Beverlee J. Chadwick, Senior Editor
Bridge-Logos, Inc.

*See *Spurgeon on God* and *Spurgeon on the Holy Spirit*—two of the excellent Pure Gold Classics published by Bridge-Logos, Inc.

BIOGRAPHY
REVEREND
CHARLES HADDON SPURGEON

Charles Haddon Spurgeon was born on June 19, 1834, in Kelvedon, Essex, England, 40 miles northeast of London. Early in his life it was obvious he was destined to be a preacher, like his father and grandfather, who were both independent ministers. The following is a story about him related by his biographer, W.Y. Fullerton.

When Charles was just six years of age, his Aunt Ann tells the story of how even at that early age he gave evidence of his vocation. During his first visit to Stambourne, he heard his grandfather lamenting time and again over the inconsistent life of one of his flock, and one day Charles suddenly declared his intention to kill "old Roads," the man in question. In spite of the warning his grandfather gave him about the awful fate of murderers, Charles persisted in his resolve. "I'll not do anything bad," he declared, "but I'll kill 'old Roads.'" Shortly afterwards he astonished them by asserting that he had done the deed. In answer to all their questions he declared he had done no wrong, but that he had been about the Lord's work, and killed "old Roads," who would never trouble his grandfather any more.

"The mystery was solved by the appearance of 'old Roads' himself, who shortly afterwards called at the manse, and told how he had been sitting in the public house, with his paper and mug of beer, when the boy entered and, pointing to him, said, "What doest thou here, Elijah, sitting with the ungodly, and you a member of the church, and breaking your pastor's heart? I'm ashamed of you. I wouldn't break my pastor's heart, I'm sure." The sermon in its brevity and simplicity and directness might also be put alongside that other which ten years later led the young preacher himself to surrender his life to Christ, as this one led "old Roads." During the four years that followed, the old man lived an exemplary life. He could not read, but he knew that the words of life were in the Bible, and with devoted love for the Book, he counted the very leaves of it."

Charles Spurgeon's own conversion took place on January 6, 1850, ten years after his encounter with "old Roads." He was fifteen years old at the time and here in his own words is how it happened.

"I sometimes think I might have been in darkness and despair now, had it not been for the goodness of God in sending a snowstorm one Sunday morning, when I was going to a place of worship. When I could go no further, I turned down a court and came to a little Primitive Methodist Chapel. There might be a dozen or fifteen people in that chapel. The minister did not come that morning: snowed in, I suppose. A poor man, a shoemaker, a tailor, or something of that sort, went up into the pulpit to preach. He was obliged to stick to his text, for the simple reason he had nothing else to say. The text was, *'Look unto me, and be ye saved, all the ends of the earth'* [Isaiah 45:22]. He did not even pronounce the words rightly, but that did not matter.

"There was, I thought, a glimpse of hope for me in the text. He began thus: 'My dear friends, this is a very simple text indeed. It says, "Look." Now that does not take a deal of effort. It ain't lifting your foot or your finger; it is just "look." Well, a man need not go to college to learn to look. You may be the biggest fool, and yet you can look. A man need not be worth a thousand a year to look. Anyone can look; a child can look. But this is what the text says. Then it says, "Look unto Me." 'Ay,' said he, in broad Essex, 'many of ye are looking to yourselves. No use looking there. You'll never find comfort in yourselves.' Then the good man followed up his text in this way: 'Look unto Me: I am sweating great drops of blood. Look unto Me; I am hanging on the Cross. Look: I am dead and buried. Look unto Me; I rise again. Look unto Me; I ascend; I am sitting at the Father's right hand. O, look to Me! Look to Me!' When he had got about that length, and managed to spin out ten minutes, he was at the length of his tether.

"Then he looked at me under the gallery, and I daresay, with so few present, he knew me to be a stranger. He then said, 'Young man, you look very miserable.' Well, I did; but I had not been accustomed to having remarks made on my personal appearance from the pulpit before. However, it was a good blow struck. He continued: 'And you will always be miserable—miserable in life and miserable in death—if you do not obey my text. But if you obey now, this moment, you will be saved.'

"Then he shouted, as only a Primitive Methodist can, 'Young man, look to Jesus Christ.' Then and there the cloud was gone, the darkness had rolled away, and in that moment I saw the sun. I had been waiting to do fifty things, but when I heard the word 'look,' I could have almost looked my eyes away. I could have risen that instant and sung with the most enthusiastic of them of the precious blood of Christ, and the simple faith that looks alone to Him.

"I thought I could dance all the way home and I now understand what John Bunyan meant when he declared he wanted to tell the crows on the plowed land all about his conversion. He was too full to hold it in. He must tell somebody. There was no doubt about his conversion; it went through every part of his being.

"As Richard Knill [a missionary] said, 'At such a time of the day, clang went every harp in Heaven, for Richard Knill was born again'; it was even so with me." Spurgeon later said if there had been a pile of blazing faggots [bundles of sticks] next to the church door, he could have stood in the midst of them without chains, happy to give his flesh and blood and bones to be burned, if only such action might have testified of the love he felt for Jesus. "Between half past ten, when I entered that chapel, and half past twelve, when I returned home, what a change had taken place in me!"

Spurgeon, who was soon to become known as "the boy preacher," was admitted to the church at Newmarket on April 4, 1850. At that time, he had not yet received the Lord's Supper, because though he had never heard of Baptists until he was fourteen, he had become convinced, by the Church of England catechism and by study of the New Testament, that believers in Christ should be baptized in His name after they received Him, and so he naturally desired baptism before his first communion.

He could not find a Baptist minister anywhere nearer than Isleham, where a Reverend W. W. Cantlow, who was a former missionary in Jamaica, ministered. Having decided to go there to be baptized, Charles first wrote to his parents to ask permission. They readily consented, although his father warned him that he must not trust in his baptism, and his mother reminded him that though she often prayed that her son would be a Christian, she had never asked that he would be a Baptist. Spurgeon playfully responded that the Lord had dealt with her in His usual bounty, and had given her exceedingly, abundantly, above all that she had asked.

It was on his mother's birthday, May 3, 1850, that Spurgeon "put on Christ," just short of his sixteenth birthday. He rose early in the morning, spent two hours in prayer and dedication, and walked eight miles to Isleham Ferry, on the river Lark, which is a beautiful stream that divides Suffolk from Cambridgeshire. Though there were not as many people at the baptism as there normally were on a Sunday baptism, there were a sufficient number watching to make Spurgeon, who had never seen a baptism before, a bit nervous. Here is his description of the scene.

"The wind blew down the river with a cutting blast as my turn came to wade into the flood; but after I had walked a few steps, and noted the people on the ferryboat, and in boats, and on either shore, I felt as if Heaven and Earth and hell might all gaze upon me, for I was not ashamed, then and there, to declare myself a follower of the Lamb. My timidity was washed away; it floated down the river into the sea, and must have been devoured by the fishes, for I have never felt anything of the kind since. Baptism also loosed my tongue, and from that day it has never been quiet."

That evening a prayer meeting was held in the Isleham vestry, at which time the newly baptized Spurgeon prayed openly—"And people wondered and wept for joy as they listened to the lad." In the morning he went back to Newmarket, and the next Sunday he had communion for the first time, and was appointed a Sunday school teacher.

Some years later he wrote, "I did not fulfill the outward

ordinance to join a party and to become a Baptist, but to be a Christian after the apostolic fashion; for they, when they believed, were baptized. It is now questioned whether John Bunyan was baptized, but the same question can never be raised concerning me. I, who scarcely belong to any sect, am nevertheless by no means willing to have it doubted in time to come whether or not I followed the conviction of my heart."

Later that year he moved to Cambridge. In the winter of 1850/1851, when he was just sixteen, he preached his first sermon in a cottage at Teversham, Cambridge. He hadn't planned on preaching there; in fact, he hadn't known he was going to, but he was tricked into it by a Mr. James Vinter in Cambridge, who was president of the Preachers' Association. Bishop Vinter, as he was generally known, called on Spurgeon one morning just as school was dismissed, and told him "to go over to Teversham the next evening, for a young man was to preach there who was not much used to services, and very likely would be glad of company."

Bishop Vinter apparently knew Spurgeon well, for a direct request for him to preach probably would have been refused. But Vinter knew that the young man had in him those qualities that make great preachers, and he only had to get started. Considering Vinter's reason for the ruse, it was excusable—it was also successful. Spurgeon and the other young man Vinter had mentioned started off in the early evening along the Newmarket Road to Teversham. After walking some distance in silence, Spurgeon expressed the hope that his companion, who was a bit older, would sense the presence of God when he preached. Horrified, the older man said he had never preached, could not preach, and would not preach.

The older man said there were be no sermon at all unless Spurgeon preached. Spurgeon hesitated at first, saying he did not know what he could preach. The older man replied that if Spurgeon would just give one of his Sunday school teachings it should do quite well. Spurgeon then agreed to preach, and reproached himself for his hesitation: "Surely I can tell a few poor cottagers of the sweetness and love of Jesus, since I feel them in my own soul." Now having settled the matter, it was as if the Lord himself walked with them as He did with the two men on the road to Emmaus.

Spurgeon's text that memorable evening was *"Unto you therefore which believe he is precious"* [1 Peter 2:7]. Then he expounded the praises of his Lord for nearly an hour, while those gathered in that thatched cottage listened attentively, enthralled with the eloquence of the young lad. When he finished, he was happy with the fact that he had been able to complete his sermon, which showed how little he thought of his preaching ability. Spurgeon then picked up a hymnbook to close out the service with praise and worship songs. Before he could start singing, however, an aged woman called out, "Bless your dear heart, how old are you?" Perhaps a bit prideful, or embarrassed to tell how young he was, Spurgeon replied, "You must wait until the service is over before making any such inquiries. Let us now sing." During the friendly conversation that followed the singing, the elderly woman asked Spurgeon again, "How old are you?"

To this Spurgeon replied, "I am under sixty."

"Yes," said the elderly woman, "and under sixteen."

"Never mind," Spurgeon said, "think of the Lord Jesus

Christ and His preciousness." Then upon the urging of several of the church members, he promised he would come back—if Bishop Vinter thought he was fit to preach again. From that small but notable beginning, Charles Spurgeon's fame as a preacher spread around the countryside, and he was invited to preach in Teversham both on Sundays and weekdays. Over the years in his writings and sermons, Spurgeon described his daily routine in those days. He would rise early in the morning for prayer and reading the Bible, and then he would attend to school duties until about five in the evening. Almost every evening he would visit the villages near Cambridge to tell the people what he had learned during the day. He found that those things took solid hold of him when he proclaimed them to others. He also said he made many blunders in those days, but he usually had a friendly audience and there were no reporters at that time writing down his every word.

Spurgeon promised to preach at the small Baptist church in October of 1851 in Waterbeach, six miles from Cambridge. This is the village where Rowland Hill (1744-1833) was said to have preached his first open air sermon. He had not, however, been licensed to preach, and so for preaching in the open air in and around Cambridge without a license, Hill was often opposed by the secular and church authorities and frequently assaulted by mobs. Finally, in 1773, after Hill had been refused ordination into the Church of England by six bishops, he was ordained by the bishop of Bath and Wells and offered the curacy of Kingston in Somerset, but was subsequently denied priest's orders and continued his ministry as an independent or nonconformist.

Later, having inherited considerable wealth from his father, Sir Rowland Hill, he built his own free chapel, Surrey

Chapel, which opened in 1783 on Blackfriars Road in London. Rowland Hill was also one of the founders, and chairman, of the Religious Tract Society, and an active promoter of the interests of the British and Foreign Bible Society and the London Missionary Society.

The chapel at Waterbeach was a primitive building with a thatched roof, which was common in those days. Spurgeon promised to preach for a few Sundays, but continued for more than two years. It was here that he published his first literary work: a gospel tract written in 1853. When Spurgeon took up the pulpit at Waterbeach, the village was notorious for its godlessness, public drunkenness and profanity, like many of the towns where Charles Finney preached during the Great American Awakening. And like those towns, Waterbeach was soon to come under the power of the gospel, for God had sent His chosen messenger there. Here is Spurgeon's account of the changes that took place.

"In a short time the little thatched chapel was crammed, the biggest vagabonds of the village were weeping floods of tears, and those who had been the curse of the parish became its blessing. I can say with joy and happiness that almost from one end of the village to the other, at the hour of eventide, one might have heard the voice of song coming from every rooftree, [a beam at the top of both sloping sides of a roof] and echoing from almost every heart."

Spurgeon's first convert in Waterbeach was a laborer's wife, and he said he prized that soul more than the thousands that came afterward. She received Christ at the Sunday service, and early the next morning the seventeen-year-old Spurgeon hurried down to see his first spiritual child. "If anybody had said to me, 'Somebody has left you twenty thousand pounds,' I would not have given a snap of my fingers for it compared with the joy I felt when I was told that God had saved a soul through my ministry. I felt like a boy who had earned his first guinea, or like a diver who had been down to the depth of the sea, and brought up a rare pearl."

Spurgeon's style and ability were considered to be far above the average from the beginning of his ministry. Of these early days, his brother James wrote, "When I drove my brother about the country to preach, I thought then, as I have thought ever since, what an extraordinary preacher he was. What wonderful unction and power I remember in some of those early speeches! The effect upon the people listening to him I have never known exceeded in after years. He seemed to have leaped full-grown into the pulpit. The breadth and brilliance of those early sermons, and the power that God's Holy Spirit evidently gave to him, made them perfectly marvelous. When he went to Waterbeach his letters came home, and were read as family documents, discussed, prayed over and wondered at. We were not surprised, however, for we all believed that it was in him."

It's a measure of how much Spurgeon ministered in the country where God had placed him that by the time he was called to London he had preached six hundred and seventy sermons.

While the young Spurgeon was busy in Waterbeach and content to stay there, the New Park Street Baptist Church in London was looking for a pastor who could revive its fallen condition. It was an influential church because of having probably the largest chapel of any Baptist church building—it could seat nearly 1200 people, and was one of only six churches that had a listed membership of over three hundred. For a number of years, however, the church had been unable to find pastors of any distinction and the active membership had dwindled to less than two hundred. At this time the pastorate had been vacant for three months, and then they discovered nineteen-year-old Charles Spurgeon.

It happened unexpectedly. George Gould, a deacon of the church at Loughton, Essex, was in Cambridge and attended the anniversary meeting of the Cambridge Sunday School Union. Charles Spurgeon was one of the speakers. During their speeches, the two older speakers scorned Spurgeon's youth. Spurgeon asked if he could reply. Both his speech and his reply so impressed Gould that when he returned to London one of the New Park Street deacons, Thomas Olney, complained to him that they had been unable to find a suitable pastor, Gould suggested young Spurgeon. The suggestion was ignored the first time it was made, but when it was made again at a later date, Olney spoke to another New Park Street deacon and they agreed "to try the experiment" and wrote to Waterbeach, which was the only address they had, and invited Spurgeon to preach one Sunday.

When the invitation reached Spurgeon on the last Sunday of 1853, he was certain it was a mistake and passed the letter to Robert Coe, one of his church deacons. Coe said he was certain it *wasn't* a mistake, and that what he had long dreaded had happened. But he was surprised at the invitation coming so soon and coming from London, which was "a great step from this little place." Spurgeon still wasn't convinced, but on November 28, he wrote a cautious answer to the invitation, and said that he was willing to go to London for a Sunday, but suggested that the invitation was probably a mistake since he was only nineteen, and was quite unknown outside of the Waterbeach area. A second letter from London, however, eased his mind and he arranged to preach at New Park Street on December 18, 1853.

When the reluctant Spurgeon reached London he was greeted with a total lack of hospitality. Rather than house him in the home of one of the affluent members, as was often the custom with visiting clergy, they sent him to a boarding house in Queen's Square, Bloomsbury, where he was given a bedroom barely large enough to hold a bed. The clothing he wore clearly showed his country breeding and upon hearing he was going to preach at New Park Street, the other boarders told him tall tales of London's wonderful preachers. By the time Spurgeon went to his small bedroom to sleep, he was thoroughly discouraged, which, added to the unaccustomed street noise, kept him awake most of the night.

When he went to New Park Street the next morning and saw the imposing building, he was amazed at his own recklessness at thinking he could preach there. If he hadn't been certain of his calling, he probably would have returned immediately to Waterbeach. But once in front of the sparse congregation that attended that morning—only about eighty people, he regained his normal confidence and delivered his sermon from James 1:17: *"Every good gift and every perfect gift is from above, and cometh down from the Father of lights, with whom is no variableness, neither shadow of turning."* His message so affected the congregation that after the meeting one of the deacons said that if Spurgeon was only with them for three months the church would be filled. News of the splendid young preacher from Waterbeach spread by word-of-mouth all Sunday afternoon, and that evening the congregation had more than tripled what it was in the morning. Among them was the young lady who was later to become Spurgeon's wife. His text that evening was from Revelation 14:5b: *"They are without fault before the throne of God."*

The people were so excited at the end the service that they would not leave until the deacons had convinced Spurgeon to come again, and before he left the building he agreed to return. Here is his account of that service. "The Lord helped me very graciously. I had a happy Sabbath in the pulpit, and spent the interval with warmhearted friends; and when at night I trudged back to the Queen's Square narrow lodging, I was not alone, and I no longer looked on Londoners as flinty-hearted barbarians. My tone was altered, I wanted no pity of anyone; I did not care a penny for the young gentlemen lodgers and their miraculous ministers, nor for the grind of the cabs, nor for anything else under the sun. The lion had been looked at all around, and his majesty did not appear to be a tenth as majestic as when I had heard his roar miles away."

No other preacher who had spoken at New Park Street during the three months when the pastorate was vacant had been invited a second time, but Spurgeon was invited back on the first, third, and fifth Sundays of January, 1854. His ministry was so successful that on January 25th, the Wednesday before the last Sunday, he was invited to occupy the pulpit for six months, with a view to becoming their new pastor. Spurgeon was in Cambridge when the invitation from the church reached him, and he immediately wrote back stating that he dared not accept an unqualified invitation for such a long time. "My objection is not to the length of the time of probation, but it ill becomes a youth to promise to preach to a London congregation so long until he knows them and they know him. I would engage to supply for three months of that time, and then, should the congregation fail or the church disagree, I would reserve to myself the liberty, without breach of engagement, to retire, and you on your part would have the right to dismiss me without seeming to treat me ill. Enthusiasm and popularity are often like the crackling of thorns, and soon expire. I do not wish to be a hindrance if I cannot be a help."

The suggested probation was cut short, however, when fifty of the men members signed a request to the deacons that a special meeting be called. The meeting was held on April 19, and a resolution was passed in which they expressed with thankfulness the esteem in which their new preacher was held and the extraordinary increase in attendance at all the church meetings. Thus they "consider it prudent to secure as early as possible his permanent settlement among us."

On April 28, just over four months after he arrived in London, the nineteen-year-old Spurgeon replied, "There is but one answer to so loving and candid an invitation. I accept it." Then he asked for their prayers, "Remember my youth and inexperience, and I pray that these may not hinder my usefulness. I trust also the remembrance of these will lead you to forgive mistakes I may make, or unguarded words that I may utter." Spurgeon was a man of great courage, especially when it came to spiritual matters and defense of the Bible. He once said, ""I have hardly ever known what the fear of man means." Along with this, God increasingly added courage to his faith, until there was literally nothing that could stop him from doing the work to which God had called him.

In his exposition of the ninety-first Psalm in The *Treasury of David*, perhaps one of his greatest works, he wrote this: "In the year 1854, when I had scarcely been in London twelve months, the neighborhood in which I lived was visited by Asiatic cholera, and my congregation suffered from its inroads. Family after family summoned me to the bedside of the smitten, and almost every day I was called to visit the grave. I gave myself up with youthful ardor to the visitation of the sick, and was sent for from all quarters of the district by persons of all ranks and religions. I became weary in body and sick at heart. My friends seemed falling one by one, and I felt or fancied that I was sickening like those around me. A little more work and weeping would have laid me low among the rest; I felt that my burden was heavier than I could bear, and I was ready to sink under it. As God would have it, I was returning mournfully from a funeral, when my curiosity led me to read a paper that was wafered [taped] up in a shoemaker's shop in the Dover Road. It did not look like a trade announcement, nor was it, for it bore in a good bold handwriting these words: *'Because thou hast made the LORD, which is my refuge, even the most High, thy habitation; There shall no evil befall thee, neither shall any plague come nigh thy dwelling.* [Psalm 91:9-10]. The effect on my heart was immediate. Faith appropriated the passage as her own. I felt secure, refreshed, girt with immortality. I went on with my visitation of the dying in a calm and peaceful spirit; I felt no fear of evil and I suffered no harm. The providence which moved the tradesman to place those verses on the window I gratefully acknowledge, and in the remembrance of its marvelous power I adore the Lord my God."

Though only about eighty people attended Spurgeon's first service at New Park Street, it soon became impossible to crowd into the building all the people who wanted to hear and see "the boy preacher," and the services moved to increasingly larger buildings. Soon the decision was made to enlarge the New Park Street chapel, and the services were moved to a public building, Exeter Hall. Although using a public place for churches services is common practice today, it was virtually unheard of in Spurgeon's day. However, even though Exeter Hall held several thousand more than the Park Street Chapel, it also wasn't large enough to contain the increasing crowds flocking to his meetings.

The work on the chapel took place from February 11 to May 27, 1855, and during this time Spurgeon became increasingly busy. Besides all his other ministerial duties and his writing, he was preaching as much as thirteen times a week. Soon his voice was overtaxed and the services in Exeter Hall were too much for him [keep in mind that there were no sound systems in those days and the preacher had to speak loudly enough for all in even the largest hall to hear him]. About his voice, his wife later wrote: "Sometimes his voice would almost break and fail as he pleaded with sinners to come to Christ, or magnified the Lord in His sovereignty and righteousness. A glass of chili vinegar always stood on a shelf under the desk before him, and I knew what to expect when he had recourse to that remedy.

"I remember with strange vividness the Sunday evening when he preached from the text, *'His name shall endure for ever'* [Psalm 72:17]. It was a subject in which he reveled, it was his chief delight to exalt his glorious Savior, and he seemed in that discourse to be pouring out his very soul and life in homage and adoration before his gracious King. However, I really thought he was going to die there, in the face of all those people. At the end he made a mighty effort to recover his voice; but utterance well nigh failed, and only in broken accents could the pathetic peroration [conclusion of the sermon] be heard—'Let my name perish, but let Christ's name last forever! Jesus! Jesus! JESUS! Crown Him Lord of all! You will not hear me say anything else. These are my last words in Exeter Hall for this time. Jesus! Jesus! JESUS! Crown Him Lord of all!' and then he fell back almost fainting in the chair behind him." Their return to the enlarged New Park Street Chapel on May 31 was disappointing for it was discovered that the money spent on it was almost wasted. Several hundred more could get into the chapel, however, the crowds were larger than before and thousands were disappointed. They remained there for about a year before it became necessary to rent Exeter Hall again.

In the meantime, like George Whitefield, Spurgeon preached in the open air whenever the opportunity was offered, once in a field to a crowd of almost twenty thousand. Writing on June 3 of the same year to the soon-to-be Mrs. Spurgeon, Spurgeon said: "Yesterday I climbed to the summit of a minister's glory. My congregation was enormous; I think ten thousand, but certainly twice as many as at Exeter Hall. The Lord was with me, and the profoundest silence was observed; but oh, the close—never did mortal man receive a more enthusiastic oration! I wonder I am alive! After the service five or six gentlemen endeavored to clear a passage, but I was borne along, amid cheers, and prayers, and shouts, for about a quarter of an hour—it really seemed more like a week! I was hurried round and round the field without hope of escape until, suddenly seeing a nice open carriage, with two occupants, standing near; I sprang in, and begged them to drive away. This they most kindly did, and I stood up, waving my hat, and crying, "The blessing of God be with you!" while from thousands of heads the hats were lifted and cheer after cheer was given. Surely amid these plaudits I can hear the low rumbling of an advancing storm of reproaches; but even this I can bear for the Master's sake."

As if on cue, the storms rumbled and rolled in. Spurgeon soon had almost as many detractors as he did admirers. On one occasion when his carriage was driven through a crowd in London, he was heartily hooted and booed. All throughout his ministry a portion of the press was scornfully critical of him. Spurgeon once said, "A true Christian is one who fears God, and is hated by the *Saturday Review*." But no matter how highly and often he was criticized, he never changed one dot of what he believed to be the truth of God. His Pauline Calvinism, his sturdy Puritanism, his old-fashioned apostolic gospel, remained unchanged to the end.

A criticism that followed him all his life was that he was conceited. His biographer, W. Y Fullerton, wrote about this:

As to the question of conceit, that criticism followed him all his life, and in later years he gave a sufficient answer. "A friend of mine was calling upon him some time ago," wrote one after his death, "and happened to say, 'Do you know, Mr. Spurgeon, some people think you conceited?' The great preacher smiled indulgently, and after a pause said, 'Do you see those bookshelves? They contain hundreds, nay, thousands of my sermons translated into every language under Heaven. Well, now, add to this that ever since I was twenty years old there never has been built a place large enough to hold the numbers of people who wished to hear me preach, and, upon my honor, when I think of it, I wonder I am not more conceited than I am.'" Upon which the writer remarks, "That is the kind of bonhomie [geniality] that disarms criticism."

Spurgeon became known through much of London, but not all its inhabitants had heard of him. Strangely, what quickly made him known in every part of the city was an accident. The owners of Exeter Hall said they could no longer rent it to one congregation, so plans were immediately formulated to build a larger structure that would hold the thousands the hall could not accommodate. In the meantime, some temporary building was needed. Fortunately, the Surrey Music Hall, which could hold 10- to 12,000 people, became available. The news that Spurgeon was to preach in the Music Hall spread like wildfire, and on Sunday evening, October 19, 1856, the hall was jammed with 10,000 people and another 10,000 in the gardens surrounding it.

The building was so crowded that the service began before its appointed time. A prayer was offered, then a hymn with the customary running commentary, then another hymn. Prayer before the sermon was being offered when suddenly a loud cry of "Fire!" rang throughout the hall. There was instant panic and bedlam. In the ensuing rush for the door, a stairway gave way and toppled people to the floor; others were knocked down and trampled underfoot. Seven were killed and twenty-eight were taken to the hospital seriously injured. There was, however, no fire; it was a false alarm.

In the midst of it all, Spurgeon was unaware of the extent of the disaster, and did not know there had been any fatal injuries. He attempted to quiet the people, and at the urging of repeated cries endeavored to preach. He told the crowd the text he had intended to use was the thirty-third verse of the third chapter of Proverbs, *"The curse of the LORD is in the house of the wicked: but he blesseth the habitation of the just,"* and asked the people to remain quiet or retire gradually if they felt they must leave. But there were more disturbances, and the service had to be discontinued. Spurgeon was so distressed by it all; he had to be carried from the pulpit.

The next day every newspaper in London carried vivid descriptions of the disaster and the deaths and injuries, and vilified Spurgeon for holding services in a public Music Hall. One leading newspaper said, "This hiring of places of amusement for Sunday preaching is a novelty, and a powerful one. It looks as if religion were at its last shift [a qualitative change]. It is a confession of weakness, rather than a sign of strength. It is not wrestling with Satan in his strongholds—to use the old earnest Puritan language—but entering into a very cowardly truce and alliance with the world." Within days every part of London was talking about the young preacher, and when he resumed preaching, after spending several days deeply depressed and discouraged, the crowds were larger than ever. Hoping to turn people against Spurgeon, the newspapers had done just the opposite, and made him the best-known preacher in all of London. What the enemy had intended for evil, God had turned to good.

Through all the years of his ministry, Spurgeon's popularity increased until he was known all over the civilized world. His sermons were reproduced by the millions in virtually every language. Even today they are read more than any other sermons ever printed.

On March 25, 1861, Spurgeon preached his first sermon in his newest and largest building, the Metropolitan Tabernacle at Elephant and Castle, Southwark. The building would seat 4,600 people, but often another 1,000 or more found some place to sit or stand. One of the deacons once claimed that on a special occasion they had crammed 8,000people into it. "We counted 8,000out of her," he said. "I don't know where she put 'em, but we did."

D. L. Moody had not yet arrived on the London scene,

but Spurgeon invited him to preach at the tabernacle, to which Moody replied, "In regard to coming to your tabernacle, I consider it a great honor to be invited; and, in fact, I should consider it an honor to black your boots, but to preach to your people would be out of the question. If they will not turn to God under your preaching, neither will they be persuaded though one rose from the dead." Moody did later preach for Spurgeon, and in writing to thank him, Spurgeon said, "I wish you could give us every night you can for the next sixty days. There are so few men who can draw on a weeknight."

That was the wonder of it. Spurgeon built a tabernacle seating between 5- and 6,000 persons, able to contain over 7,000, and for thirty-eight years he maintained that congregation there and elsewhere in London. Other great preachers, like Wesley and Whitefield, gathered as great crowds, but they traveled to various places to do so. Spurgeon remained rooted in London.

At a prayer meeting on May 26, 1890, Spurgeon looked around the Metropolitan Tabernacle and exclaimed, "How many thousands have been converted here! There has not been a single day but what I have heard of two, three or four having been converted; and that not for one, two, or three years, but for the last ten years!" It is an interesting note that additions to the church year by year were double the additions to New Park Street in the same periods of time, which shows that the number of new converts bears a relationship to the size of the congregation. With few exceptions, that great building was crowded every Sunday morning and evening for thirty years, and the attendance at the Thursday night meeting was usually even larger

Spurgeon once said, "Somebody asked me how I got my congregation. I never got it at all. I did not think it was my duty to do so. I only had to preach the gospel. Why, my congregation got my congregation. I had eighty, or scarcely a hundred, when I preached first. The next time I had two hundred. Everyone who heard me was saying to his neighbor, 'You must go and hear this young man!' Next meeting we had 400, and in six weeks, 800. That was the way in which my people got my congregation. Now the people are admitted by tickets. That does very well; a member can give his ticket to another person and say, 'I will stand in the aisle'; or 'I will get in with the crowd.' Some persons, you know, will not go if they can get in easily, but they will go if you tell them they cannot get in without a ticket. That is the way congregations ought to bring a congregation about a minister. A minister preaches all the better if he has a large congregation. It was once said by a gentleman that the forming of a congregation was like the beating-up of game, the minister being the sportsman. But there are some of our ministers that can't shoot! I really think, however, that I could shoot a partridge if I fired into the midst of a covey, though I might not do so if there were only one or two."

On October 26, 1891, Reverend Spurgeon, though he was feeling increasingly ill and weak from a combination of rheumatism, gout, and Bright's disease [chronic inflammation in the kidneys], which he had suffered from for many years, started out on a journey to Menton, France, where he often went to rest and recuperate. When he and Mrs. Spurgeon reached the Hotel Beau-Rivage, where they were staying, he enjoyed three months of "earthly paradise" without difficulty, and despite his weakness. By the middle of January, however, he began to weaken rapidly, though he conducted brief services in his room on January 10 and 17. These services were the last of his earthly work for his Lord. He died at the age of 58 on January 31, 1892. His wife and two sons outlived him, as did his father, who died at the age of almost ninety-two.

The news of his home-going flashed around the world. One London newspaper had the terse headline, "Death of Spurgeon." That day it was difficult to obtain a newspaper anywhere in England, the demand was so great. Spurgeon's coffin was brought back from Menton, France, and arrived at Victoria Station, London, on Monday, February 9, 1892. It was met by a small group of friends and taken to the Pastor's College, where it remained for the rest of the day. That night it was carried into the Metropolitan Tabernacle, and over 60,000 people passed by it to pay their homage. Four funeral services were held on Wednesday to accommodate the crowds. Ira D. Sankey, Moody's associate, was there and sang twice. Evan Herber Evans, a Welsh Nonconformist minister, spoke briefly and concluding said, "But there is one Charles Haddon Spurgeon whom we cannot bury; there is not earth enough in Norwood to bury him—the Spurgeon of history. The good works that he has done will live. You cannot bury them."

The funeral was on Thursday, and one newspaper said you could search all of London and not find three women who were not wearing black. At the graveside, Archibald G. Brown, a close friend and one of Spurgeon's most distinguished associates, gave a eulogy that some have said will be remembered forever. "Beloved President, faithful Pastor, Prince of Preachers, brother beloved, dear Spurgeon—we bid thee not 'Farewell,' but only for a little while 'Goodnight.' Thou shalt rise soon at the first dawn of the Resurrection day of the redeemed. Yet is the 'goodnight' not ours to bid, but thine; it is we who linger in the darkness; thou art in

God's holy light. Our night shall soon be passed, and with it all our weeping. Then, with thine, our songs shall greet the morning of a day that knows no cloud nor close; for there is no night there.

"Hard worker in the field, thy toil is ended. Straight has been the furrow thou hast ploughed. No looking back has marred thy course. Harvests have followed thy patient sowing, and Heaven is already rich with thine ingathered sheaves, and shall still be enriched through the years yet lying in eternity.

"Champion of God, thy battle, long and nobly fought, is over; thy sword, which clave to thy hand, has dropped at last: a palm branch takes it place. No longer does the helmet press thy brow, oft weary with its surging thoughts of battle; a victor's wreath from the great Commander's hand has already proved thy full reward.

"Here, for a little while, shall rest thy precious dust. Then shall thy Well-beloved come; and at His voice thou shalt spring from thy couch of earth, fashioned like unto His body, into glory. Then spirit, soul, and body shall magnify the Lord's redemption. Until then, beloved, sleep. We praise God for you and by the blood of the everlasting covenant, hope and expect to praise God with you. Amen."

Spurgeon's coffin was then lowered into the ground. On it was a Bible open to the text that led Spurgeon to the Lord and Savior he had served faithfully for more than forty years, *"Look unto me, and be ye saved, all the ends of the earth: for I am God, and there is none else"* [Isaiah 45:22].

CHAPTER 1

CHRIST CRUCIFIED

A Sermon
(No. 7-8)
Delivered on Sunday Morning, February 11, 1855,
by Reverend Charles H. Spurgeon,
at Exeter Hall, Strand, London, England

But we preach Christ crucified, unto the Jews a stumblingblock, and unto the Greeks foolishness; but unto them which are called, both Jews and Greeks, Christ the power of God, and the wisdom of God.
(1 Corinthians 1: 23-24)

What contempt has God poured upon the wisdom of this world! How He has brought it to failure, and made it appear as nothing! He has allowed it to work out its own conclusions, and prove its own folly. Men boasted that they were wise; they said that they could find out all about God and His secrets easily and to perfection. Therefore, in order that their folly might be refuted once and forever, God gave them the opportunity of doing so. He said, "Worldly wisdom, I will try you. You say that you are mighty, that your intellect is vast and comprehensive, that your eye is keen, and you can find all secrets; now, behold, I try you; I give you one great problem to solve. Here is the universe; stars make its canopy, fields and flowers adorn it, and the floods roll over its surface; my name is written therein; the invisible things of God may be clearly seen in the things which are made. (See Romans 1:19-20.) Philosophy, I give you this problem—find me out. Here are my works—find me out. Discover in the wondrous world that I have made, the way to worship me acceptably. I give you space enough to do it—there are data enough. Behold the clouds, the Earth, and the stars. I give you time enough; I will give you four thousand years, and I will not interfere; but you shall do as you will with your own world. I will give you men enough; for I will make many men with great minds whom you shall call lords of Earth; you shall have orators, and you shall have philosophers. Find me out, O reason; find me out, O wisdom; find me out, if you can; find me out unto perfection; and if you cannot, then close your mouth forever. Then I will teach you that the wisdom of God is wiser than the wisdom of man; yea, that the foolishness of God is wiser than men.

And how did the wisdom of man work out the problem? How did wisdom perform her feat? Look upon the heathen nations; there you see the result of wisdom's researches. In the time of Jesus Christ, you might have beheld the Earth covered with the slime of pollution, a Sodom on a large scale—corrupt, filthy, depraved; indulging in vices which we dare not mention; reveling in lust too abominable even for our imagination to dwell upon for a moment. We find the men prostrating themselves before blocks of wood and stone, adoring 10,000 gods more vicious than themselves.

We find, in fact, that reason wrote out her lines with a finger covered with blood and filth, and that she forever cut herself out from all her glory by the vile deeds she did. She would not worship God. She would not bow down to Him who is "clearly seen," but she worshiped any creature—the reptile that crawled, the viper—everything might be a god; but not the God of Heaven. Vice might be made into a ceremony, the greatest crime might be exalted into a religion; but true worship she knew nothing of. Poor reason! Poor wisdom! *How you are fallen from heaven; like Lucifer—you son of the morning you are lost.* (See Isaiah 14:12.) You have written out your conclusion, but a conclusion of consummate folly. *"For after that in the wisdom of God the world by wisdom knew not God, it pleased God by the foolishness of preaching to save them that believe"* (1 Corinthians 1:21).

WISDOM SHALL BE OVERCOME

Wisdom had its time, and it was time enough; and what it did was little enough, for it made the world worse than it was before it stepped upon it. God now says, "Foolishness shall overcome wisdom; now ignorance, as you call it, shall sweep away science; now, humble, childlike faith shall crumble to the dust all the colossal systems your hands have piled." God calls His armies. Christ puts His trumpet to His mouth and up come the warriors, clad in fishermen's garb, speaking with the accent of those from the area of Galilee—poor humble mariners. Here are the warriors, O wisdom, that are to confound you; these are the heroes who shall overcome your proud philosophers. These are the men who will plant their standard upon your ruined walls, and bid them to fall forever. These are the men and their successors who will exalt a gospel in the world which you may laugh at as absurd, and sneer at as folly, but which shall be exalted above the hills, and shall be glorious even to the highest heavens.

Since that day, God has always raised up successors of the apostles. Not by any lineal descent, but because I have the same roll and charter as any apostle, and am as much called to preach the gospel as Paul himself. If not as much owned by the conversion of sinners, yet, in a measure, blessed of God. Therefore, here I stand, foolish as Paul, Peter, or any of those fishermen might be; but still with the might of God I grasp the sword of truth, coming here to *"preach Christ crucified, unto the Jews a stumblingblock, and unto the Greeks foolishness; But unto them which are called, both Jews and Greeks, Christ the power of God, and the wisdom of God"* (1 Corinthians 1:23-24).

WHAT PREACHING CHRIST IS AND IS NOT

Before I enter upon our text, let me very briefly tell you what I believe preaching Christ crucified is *not*, and *is*. My friends, I do not believe it is preaching Christ crucified to give people a batch of philosophy every Sunday morning and evening, and neglect the truths of this Holy Book. I do not believe it is preaching Christ crucified to leave out the main cardinal doctrines of the Word of God, and preach a religion that is all a mist and a haze, without any definite truths whatever. I take it that a man does not preach Christ crucified, who can get through a sermon without mentioning Christ's name once; nor does that man preach Christ crucified who never says a word about the work of the Holy Ghost or of His Person, thereby prompting the hearers to say, *"We have not so much as heard whether there be any Holy Ghost"* (Acts 19:2).

And I have my own private opinion that there is no such thing as preaching Christ crucified, unless you preach what nowadays is called Calvinism. I have my own ideas, and those I always state boldly. It is a nickname to call it Calvinism. Calvinism is the gospel, and nothing else. I do not believe we can preach the gospel if we do not preach justification by faith without works, do not preach the sovereignty of God in His dispensation of grace, and do not exalt the electing, unchangeable, eternal, immutable, conquering love of Jehovah. I also do not think we can preach the gospel unless we base it upon the peculiar redemption that Christ made for His elect and chosen people. I cannot comprehend a gospel that lets saints fall away after they are called, and suffers the children of God to be burned in the fires of damnation after having believed. Such a gospel I abhor. The gospel of the Bible is not such a gospel as that. We preach Christ crucified in a different fashion, and to all gainsayers we reply, "[We] have not so learned Christ." (See Ephesians 4:20.)

I will discuss three things in this text:

First, *a gospel rejected, "Christ crucified, to the Jews a stumblingblock, and to the Greeks foolishness."*

Second, *a gospel triumphant, "unto those who are called, both Jews and Greeks."*

Third, *a gospel admired, "the power of God and the wisdom of God."*

1. A Gospel Rejected

First, we have here *a gospel rejected*. One would have imagined that when God sent His gospel to men, all men would meekly listen, and humbly receive its truths. We should have thought that God's ministers had but to proclaim that life is brought to light by the gospel and that Christ is come to save sinners, and every ear would be attentive, every eye would be fixed, and every heart would be wide open to receive the truth. We should have said, judging favorably of our fellow creatures, that there would not exist in the world a monster so vile, so depraved, and so polluted, as to put so much as a stone in the way of the progress of truth. We could not have conceived such a thing. Yet that conception is the truth.

When the gospel was preached, instead of being accepted and admired, a universal hiss went up to Heaven. Men could not bear it. They dragged its first preacher to the brow of the hill, and would have sent Him down headlong. Then they did more—they nailed Him to the Cross, and there they let Him languish out His dying life in agony such as no man has borne since. All His chosen ministers have been hated and abhorred by worldlings. Instead of being listened to they have been scoffed at. They have been treated as if they were the offscouring of all things and the very scum of mankind. (See 1 Corinthians 4:13.) Look at the holy men in the old times, how they were driven out of city after city, persecuted, afflicted, tormented, stoned to death, wherever the enemy had power to do so. Those friends of men, those real philanthropists, who came with hearts big with love, hands full of mercy, lips pregnant with celestial fire, and souls that burned with holy influence, were treated as if they were spies in the camp, deserters from the common cause of mankind, like enemies, and not, as they truly were, the best of friends. Do not suppose, my friends, that men like the gospel any better now than they did then.

Outwardly Better, Inwardly the Same

There is an idea going around that you are growing better. I do not believe it. You are growing worse. In many respects men may be better—outwardly better, but the heart within is still the same. The human heart of today dissected would be like the human heart a thousand years ago. The gall of bitterness within that breast of yours is just as bitter as the gall of bitterness in that of Simon of old. We have in our hearts the same latent opposition to the truth of God, and hence we find men, even as of old, who scorn the gospel. I shall, in speaking of the gospel rejected, endeavor to point out the two classes of persons who equally despise truth. The Jews make it a stumbling block, and the Greeks account it foolishness. Now I am not going to make these ancient individuals—the Jew and the Greek—the object of my condemnation, but I look upon them as members of a great parliament, representatives of a great constituency. I will attempt to show that if all the race of Jews were cut off, there would be still a great number in the world who would answer to the name of Jews, to whom Christ is a stumbling block; and that if Greece were swallowed up by some earthquake, and ceased to be a nation, there would still be the Greek unto whom the gospel would be foolishness. I will simply introduce the Jew and the Greek, and let them speak a moment to you, so you may see the persons who stand for many of you, who as yet are not called by divine grace.

The first is a Jew—to him the gospel is a stumbling block. The Jew was a respectable man in his day, all formal religion was concentrated in his person, he went up to the temple very devoutly, and he tithed all he had, even to the mint and the cumin. You would see him fast twice in the week, with a face all marked with sadness and sorrow. He wore the law between his eyes—the phylactery, and the borders of his garments were of amazing width that he might never be supposed to be a Gentile dog, that no one might ever conceive that he was not an Hebrew of pure descent. He had a holy ancestry; he came from a pious family, and was a good man. He did not like the Sadducees at all, who had no religion. He was thoroughly a religious man. He stood up for his synagogue, he would not have that temple on Mount Gerizim, and he could not bear the Samaritans and had no dealings with them. He was a religionist of the first order, a man of the very finest kind, and a specimen of a man who is a moralist, and loved the ceremonies of the law.

Accordingly, when he heard about Christ, he asked who Christ was. "The son of a carpenter," was the answer. "The son of a carpenter and His mother's name is Mary, and His father's name is Joseph."

"That of itself is presumption enough," said he. "It is, in fact, positive proof that He cannot be the Messiah."

And what does He say? Why, He says, *"Woe unto you, scribes and Pharisees, hypocrites"* (Matthew 23:13).

"That won't do."

Moreover, He says, "It is not by the works of the flesh that any man can enter into the Kingdom of Heaven."

The Jew tied a double knot in his phylactery at once—he

thought he would have the borders of his garment made twice as broad. He *bow* to the Nazarene? No, no, and if so much as a disciple of the carpenter crossed the street, he thought the place polluted, and would not tread in his steps. Do you think he would give up his old father's religion, the religion which came from Mount Sinai, that old religion that lay in the ark and the overshadowing cherubim? He give that up? Not he! A vile imposter—that is all Christ was in his eyes. He thought so. "A stumbling block to me, I cannot hear about it, and I will not listen to it." Accordingly, he turned a deaf ear to all the preacher's eloquence, and listened not at all. Farewell, old Jew! You sleep with your fathers, and your generation is a wandering race, still walking the Earth. Farewell! I have done with you. Poor wretch, that Christ, who was your stumbling block, shall be your judge, and on your head shall be that loud curse: *"His blood be on us, and on our children"* (Matthew 27:25).

But I am going to find Mr. Jew here in Exeter Hall—persons who answer to his description—to whom Jesus Christ is a stumbling block. Let me introduce you to yourselves, some of you. You were of a pious family too, were you not? Yes. And you have a religion which you love. You love it so far as the chrysalis of it goes, the outside, the covering, the husk. You would not have one rubric[1] altered, nor one of those dear old arches taken down, nor the stained glass removed, for all the world; and any man who should say a word against such things, you would set down as a heretic at once. Or, perhaps, you do not go to such a place of worship, but you love some plain old meetinghouse where your forefathers worshiped, called a dissenting chapel[2]. It is

---

1. An established rule, tradition or custom.
2. Disagrees doctrinally with the established or orthodox church.

a beautiful plain place. You love it, you love its ordinances, you love its exterior, and if anyone spoke against the place, how vexed you would feel. You think that what they do there, they ought to do everywhere. In fact, your church is a model one, the place where you go is exactly the sort of place for everybody, and if I were to ask you why you hope to go to Heaven, you would perhaps say, "Because I am a Baptist," or, "Because I am an Episcopalian," or whatever other sect you belong to. That is you, and I know Jesus Christ will be a stumbling block to you.

Loving Only the Externals of Religion

If I come and tell you that all your going to the house of God is good for nothing, that all those many times you have been singing and praying, all pass for nothing in the sight of God, that you are a hypocrite and a formalist, that your heart is not right with God, and unless it is so, all the external things are good for nothing, I know you will say, "I will not hear that preacher again." It is a stumbling block. If you had stepped into a church where you had heard formalism exalted, had been told, "this you must do, and this other you must do, and then you will be saved," you would highly approve of it. But how many of those who are externally religious, with whose characters you find no fault, have never had the regenerating influence of the Holy Ghost, never were made to lie prostrate on their face before Calvary's Cross, never turned a wistful eye to yonder Savior crucified, and never put their trust in Him that was slain for the sons of men? They have and love a superficial religion, but when a man talks about the deeper things of God; they turn away from it believing it to be pious and hypocritical.

You may love all that is external about religion, just as you may love a man for his clothes—caring nothing for the man himself. If so, I know you are one of those who reject the gospel. You will hear me preach, and while I speak about the externals you will hear me with attention. While I plead for morality, and argue against drunkenness, or show the heinousness of breaking the Sabbath, you will listen carefully. But if once I say, *"Except ye be converted, and become as little children, ye shall not enter into the kingdom of heaven"* (Matthew 18:3), if once I tell you that you must be elected of God, you must be purchased with the Savior's blood, or that you must be converted by the Holy Ghost, you say, "He is a fanatic! Away with him, away with him! We do not want to hear that any more." Christ crucified, is to the Jew—the ceremonialist—a stumbling block.

But there is another specimen of this Jew to be found. He is thoroughly orthodox in his sentiments. As for forms and ceremonies, he thinks nothing about them. He goes to a place of worship where he learns sound doctrine. He will hear nothing but what is true. He believes that we should have good works and morality. He is a good man, and no one can find fault with him. Here he is, regular in his Sunday pew. In the market he walks before men in all honesty—so you would imagine. Ask him about any doctrine, and he can give you an elaborate discussion on it. In fact, he could write a treatise upon anything in the Bible, and a great many things besides. He knows almost everything, and here, up in this dark attic of the head, his religion has taken up its abode. He has a "best parlor" down in his heart, but his religion never goes there—that is shut against it. He has money in there—Mammon, worldliness, or he has something else—self-love, pride. He loves to hear experimental preaching, he admires it all; in fact, he loves anything that is sound. But then, he has not any sound in himself; or rather, it is all sound and there is no substance.

He likes to hear true doctrine, but it never penetrates his inner man. You never see him weep. Preach to him about Christ crucified, a glorious subject, and you never see a tear roll down his cheek. Tell him of the mighty influence of the Holy Ghost—he admires you for it, but he never had the hand of the Holy Spirit on his soul. Tell him about communion with God, plunging in Godhead's deepest sea, and being lost in its immensity, and he does not understand what you're saying. The man loves to hear, but he never experiences. He has never communed with God. And so when you once begin to strike home, when you lay him on the table, take out your dissecting knife, begin to cut him up, and show him his own heart—let him see what it is by nature, and what it must become by grace—the man bolts, he cannot stand that, he wants none of that, none of Christ received in the heart and accepted. Even though he loves it enough in the head, to him it's a stumbling block, and he casts it away.

Do you see yourselves here, my friends? Do you see yourselves as *God* sees you? There are many to whom Christ is as much a stumbling block now as ever He was. O you formalists! I speak to you. O you, who have the nutshell, but abhor the kernel. O you who like the trappings and the dress, but care not for that fair virgin who is clothed in them. O you who like the paint and the tinsel, but abhor the solid gold, I speak to you. I ask you, does your religion give you solid comfort? Can you stare death in the face with it, and say, *"I know that my redeemer liveth?"* (Job 19:25). Can you close your eyes at night, singing as your vesper song, "I to the end must endure, as sure as the earnest is given?" Can you bless God for affliction? Can you plunge in, accounted as you are, and swim through all the floods of trial? Can you march triumphant through the lion's den, laugh at affliction, and bid defiance to hell? Can you? No! Your gospel is through the lion's den, laugh at affliction, and bid defiance to hell? Can you? No! Your gospel is an effeminate thing—a thing of words and sounds, and not of power. Cast it from you, I beseech you. It is not worth your keeping, and when you come before the throne of God, you will find it will fail you, and fail you so that you shall never find another. You shall be lost, ruined, destroyed, and you shall find that Christ, who is now "a stumbling block," will be your Judge.

I have reasoned out the Jew, and I have now to reason the Greek. He is a person of quite a different exterior from the Jew. As to the phylactery, to him it is all rubbish; and as to the broad-hemmed garment, he despises it. He does not care for the forms of religion; he has an intense aversion, in fact, to broad-brimmed hats, or to everything that looks like outward show. He likes eloquence, he admires a smart saying, he loves a quaint expression, and he likes to read the latest new book. He is a Greek, and to him the gospel is foolishness. The Greek is a gentleman found everywhere nowadays; manufactured sometimes in colleges, constantly made in schools, and produced everywhere. He is on the stock exchange, and the stock market. He keeps a shop, and rides in a carriage. He is noble, a gentleman. He is everywhere, even in court. He is thoroughly wise. Ask him anything, and he knows it. Ask for a quotation from any of the old poets, or anyone else and he can give it to you. If you are a

Muslim, and plead the claims of your religion, he will hear you very patiently. But if you are a Christian, and talk to him of Jesus Christ, he says, "Stop your nonsense. I don't want to hear anything about that."

This Grecian gentleman believes all philosophy except the true one. He studies all wisdom except the wisdom of God. He likes all learning except spiritual learning. And he loves everything except that which God approves. He likes everything that man makes, and nothing that comes from God; it is foolishness to him, confounded foolishness. You have only to discourse about one doctrine in the Bible, and he shuts his ears, and wishes no longer for your company—it is foolishness. I have met this gentleman a great many times. Once, when I saw him, he told me he did not believe in any religion at all. When I said I did, and had a hope that when I died I should go to Heaven, he said he dared say it was very comfortable, but he did not believe in religion, and that he was sure it was best to live as nature dictated.

Another time he spoke well of all religions, and believed they were very good in their place, and all true. He had no doubt that if a man were sincere in any kind of religion, he would be all right at last. I told him I did not think so, and that I believed there was but one religion revealed of God—the religion of God's elect, the religion which is the gift of Jesus. He then said I was a bigot, and wished me good morning. It was to him foolishness. He had nothing to do with me at all. He either liked no religion, or every religion. Another time I held him by the coat button, and I discussed with him a little about faith. He said, "It is all very well. I believe that is true Protestant doctrine." But presently I said something about election, and he said, "I don't like that. Many people have preached that and turned it to an inaccurate account." I then hinted something about free grace, but that he could not endure; it was to him foolishness.

He was a polished Greek, and thought that if he were not chosen, he ought to be. He never liked that passage, *"God hath chosen the foolish things of the world to confound the wise; . . . and things which are not, to bring to nought things that are"* (1 Corinthians 1:27-28). He thought it was very discreditable to the Bible, and when the book was revised he had no doubt it would be cut out. To such a man—for he is here this morning, very likely come to hear this reed shaken of the wind—I have to say this, "Ah! You wise man, full of worldly wisdom. Your wisdom will stand you here, but what will you do in the swelling floods of Jordan? Philosophy may do well for you to learn upon while you walk through this world, but the river is deep, and you will want something more than that. If you don't have the arm of the Most High to hold you up in the flood and cheer you with promises, you will sink, man. With all your philosophy, you will sink; with all your learning, you will sink, and be washed into that awful ocean of eternal torment, where you shall be forever. Ah! Greek, it may be foolishness to you, but you shall see the man your judge, and then you shall rue the day that you said that God's gospel was foolishness."

2. A Gospel Triumphant

Having spoken thus far upon the *gospel rejected*, I shall now briefly speak upon the *gospel triumphant*. *"Unto them which are called, both Jews and Greeks, Christ the power of God, and the wisdom of God."* (See 1 Corinthians 1:24.) A short distance away is a man who rejects the gospel, despises grace, and laughs at it as a delusion. Here is another man who also laughed at it, but God will put him down upon his knees. Christ shall not die for nothing. The Holy Ghost will not strive in vain. God has said, *"My word . . . shall not return unto me void, but it shall accomplish that which I please, and it shall prosper in the thing whereto I sent it"* (Isaiah 55:11). *"He shall see of the travail of his soul, and shall be satisfied"* (Isaiah 53:11). If one sinner is not saved, another shall be. The Jew and the Greek shall never depopulate Heaven. The choirs of glory shall not lose a single songster by all the opposition of Jews and Greeks, for God has said it—some shall be called, some shall be saved, some shall be rescued.

> *Perish the virtue, as it ought, abhorred,*
> *And the fool with it, who insults his Lord.*
> *The atonement a Redeemer's love has wrought*
> *Is not for you—the righteous need it not.*
> *See'st thou yon harlot wooing all she meets,*
> *The worn-out nuisance of the public streets*
> *Herself from morn till night, from night to morn,*
> *Her own abhorrence, and as much your scorn:*
> *The gracious shower, unlimited and free,*
> *Shall fall on her, when Heaven denies it thee.*
> *Of all that wisdom dictates, this the drift,*
> *That man is dead in sin, and life a gift.*[3]

If the righteous and good are not saved, if they reject the gospel, there are others who are to be called, others who shall be rescued, for Christ will not lose the merits of His agonies, or the purchase of His blood.

---

3. Poem written by William Cowper, poet and hymn writer.

THE GENERAL CALL AND THE SPECIAL CALL OF GOD

"Unto them which are called." I received a note this week asking me to explain that word *"called,"* because in one passage it says, *"Many are called, but few are chosen"* (Matthew 22:14), while in another it appears that all who are called must be chosen. Now, let me observe that there are two calls. As my old friend, John Bunyan, says, the hen has two calls, the common cluck, which she gives daily and hourly, and the special one, which she means for her little chickens. So there is a general call, a call made to every man—every man hears it. Many are called by it. All you are called this morning in that sense, but very few are chosen. The other is a special call, the children's call. You know how the bell sounds over the workshop, to call the men to work—that is a general call. A father goes to the door and calls out, "John, it is dinner time"—that is the special call.

Many are called with the general call, but they are not chosen; the special call is for the children only, and that is what is meant in the text, *"Unto them which are called, both Jews and Greeks, Christ the power of God, and the wisdom of God."* (See 1 Corinthians 1:24.) That call is always a special one. While I stand here and call men, nobody comes. While I preach to sinners universally, no good is done. It is like the sheet lightning you sometimes see on the summer's evening, beautiful, grand, but whoever heard of anything being struck by it? But the special call is the forked flash from Heaven; it strikes somewhere; it is the arrow sent in between the joints of the harness. The call which saves is like that of Jesus when He said, "Mary," and she said unto him, "Rabboni." (See John 20:16.)

Do you know anything about that special call, my beloved? Did Jesus ever call you by name? Can you recollect the hour when He whispered your name in your ear, when He said, "Come to me"? If so, you will grant the truth of what I am going to say next about it—that it is an effectual call, there is no resisting it. When God calls with His special call, there is no resisting that call. Ah! I know, I laughed at religion, I despised it, I abhorred it, but then that call came! Oh, I would not come. But God said, *"You shall come. All that the Father giveth me shall come."* (See John 6:37.) "Lord, I will not." "But you shall," said God. And I have gone up to God's house sometimes almost with a resolution that I would not listen, but listen I must. Oh, how the Word came into my soul! Was there a power of resistance? No! I was thrown down, each bone seemed to be broken, and I was saved by effectual grace.

I appeal to your experience, my friends. When God took you in hand, could you withstand Him? You stood against your minister many times. Sickness did not break you down, disease did not bring you to God's feet, and eloquence did not convince you, but when God puts His hand to the work, then what a change. Like Saul, with his horses going to Damascus, that voice from Heaven said, *"I am Jesus whom thou persecutest." "Saul, Saul, why persecutest thou me?"* (See Acts 9:4-5.). There was no going further then. That was an effectual call. Like that, again, which Jesus gave to Zaccheus, when he was up in the tree. Stepping under the tree, Jesus said, *"Zaccheus, make haste, and come down; for to day I must abide at thy house"* (Luke 19:5). Zaccheus was taken in the net, he heard his own name, the call sank into his soul, and he could not stay up in the tree, for an almighty impulse drew him down.

And I could tell you some singular instances of persons going to the house of God and having their characters described, traced out to perfection, so that they have said, "He is painting me, he is painting me." Just as I might say to that young man here, who stole his master's gloves yesterday, that Jesus calls him to repentance. It may be that there is such a person here, and when the call comes to a peculiar character, it generally comes with a special power. God gives His ministers a brush, and shows them how to use it in painting lifelike portraits, and thus the sinner hears the special call. I cannot give the special call, God alone can give it, and I leave it with Him. Some must be called. Jew and Greek may laugh, but still there are some who are called, both Jews and Greeks. Then, to close up this second point, it is a great mercy that many a Jew has been made to drop his self-righteousness, many a legalist has been made to drop his legalism and come to Christ, and many a Greek has bowed his genius at the throne of God's gospel. We have a few such. As William Cowper says:

> *We boast some rich ones, whom the gospel sways,*
> *And one who wears a coronet, and prays;*
> *Like gleanings of an olive tree they show,*
> *Here and there one upon the topmost bough.*

3. A Gospel Admired

Unto us who are called of God, it is the power of God, and the wisdom of God. Now, beloved, this must be a matter of pure experience between your souls and God. If you are called of God this morning, you will know it. I know there are times when a Christian has to say,

> *Tis a point I long to know,*
> *Oft it causes anxious thought;*
> *Do I love the Lord or no?*
> *Am I His, or am I not?*[4]

But if a man never in his life knew himself to be a Christian, he never was a Christian. If he never had a moment of confidence, when he could say, *"I know in whom I have believed"* (2 Timothy 1:12), I think I do not utter a harsh thing when I say that that man could not have been born again. For I do not understand how a man can be killed and then made alive again and not know it, how a man can pass from death unto life and not know it, and how a man can be brought out of darkness into marvelous liberty without knowing it. I am sure I know it when I shout out my old verse,

> *Now free from sin, I walk at large,*[5]
> *My Savior's blood's my full discharge;*
> *At His dear feet content I lay,*
> *A sinner saved, and homage pay.*

There are moments when the eyes glisten with joy and we can say, "We are persuaded, confident, certain." I do not wish to distress anyone who is under doubt. Often gloomy doubts will prevail; there are seasons when you fear you have

---

4. Hymn # 632 in the *Baptist Hymn Book* Published in 1903. 'Tis A Point I Long to Know" hymn written by John Newton.
5. Hymn #194 in *A Collection of Hymns: Intended for the Citizens of Zion* by Thomas Reed. Published by Applegate Publishers, New York, NY 1835.

not been called, when you doubt your interest in Christ. Ah! What a mercy it is that it is not your hold of Christ that saves you, but His hold of you! What a sweet fact that it is not how you grasp His hand, but His grasp of yours, that saves you. Yet I think you ought to know, sometime or other, whether you are called of God. If so, you will follow me in the next part of my discourse, which is a matter of pure experience; unto us who are saved, it is "Christ the power of God, and the wisdom of God."

The gospel is to the true believer a thing of power. It is Christ the power of God. Ay, there is a power in God's gospel beyond all description. Once, I, like Mazeppa,[6] bound on the wild horse of my lust, bound hand and foot, incapable of resistance, was galloping on with hell's wolves behind me, howling for my body and my soul, as their just and lawful prey. There came a mighty hand which stopped that wild horse, cut my bands, set me down, and brought me into liberty. Is there power, sir? Ay, there is power, and he who has felt it must acknowledge it. There was a time when I lived in the strong old castle of my sins, and rested in my works. There came a trumpeter to the door, and bade me open it. In anger I chided him from the porch, and said he never would enter. There came a goodly personage, with loving countenance; His hands were marked with scars where nails were driven, and His feet had nail-prints too. He lifted up His Cross, using it as a hammer. At the first blow the gate of my prejudice shook, at the second it trembled more, at the third down it fell, and in He came, and He said, "Arise, and stand upon thy feet, for I have loved thee with an everlasting love." A thing of power! Ah, it is a thing of power! I have felt it *here*, in this heart. I have the witness of

---

6. A poem written by Lord Byron in 1819.

the Spirit within, and know it is a thing of might, because it has conquered me, it has bowed me down.

> *His free grace alone, from the first to the last,*
> *Hath won my affection, and held my soul fast.*[7]

The gospel to the Christian is a thing of power. What is it that makes the young man devote himself as a missionary to the cause of God, to leave father and mother, and go into distant lands? It is a thing of power that does it—it is the gospel. What is it that constrains a minister, in the midst of the cholera, to climb up that creaking staircase, and stand by the bed of some dying creature who has that dire disease? It must be a thing of power that leads him to venture his life—it is love of the Cross of Christ which bids him do it. What is that which enables one man to stand up before a multitude of his fellows, all unprepared it may be, but determined that he will speak nothing but Christ and Him crucified? What is it that enables him to cry, like the warhorse of Job in battle, Aha! and move glorious in might? It is a thing of power that does it—it is Christ crucified.

And what emboldens that timid female to walk down that dark lane in the wet evening that she may go and sit beside the victim of a contagious fever? What strengthens her to go through that den of thieves, and pass by the profligate and profane? What influences her to enter into that charnel-house[8] of death, and there sit down and whisper words of comfort? Does gold make her do it? They are too poor to give her gold. Does fame make her do it? She shall never be known, nor written among the mighty women of this Earth. What makes her do it? Is it love of merit? No, she knows

---

7. Hymn: "Thy Mercy, My God" by John Stucker.
8. A burial vault.

she has no desert before high Heaven. What impels her to it? It is the power of the gospel on her heart; it is the Cross of Christ; she loves it, and she therefore says:

> *Were the whole realm of nature mine,*
> *That were a present far too small;*
> *Love so amazing, so divine,*
> *Demands my soul, my life, my all.*[9]

But I behold another scene. A martyr is going to the stake. The halberd[10] men are around him, the crowds are mocking, but he is marching steadily on. See, they bind him to the stake with a chain around his middle, they heap faggots[11] all about him, and the flame is lighted up. Listen to his words: *"Bless the LORD, O my soul: and all that is within me, bless his holy name"* (Psalm 103:1). The flames are kindling round his legs, the fire is burning him even to the bone, yet see him lift up his hands and say, *"I know that my Redeemer liveth, and though the fire devour this body, yet in my flesh shall I see the Lord."* (See Job 19:25.) Behold him clutch the stake and kiss it, as if he loved it, and hear him say, "For every chain of iron that man girdeth me with, God shall give me a chain of gold. For all these faggots, and this ignominy and shame, He shall increase the weight of my eternal glory." See all the under parts of his body are consumed, and still he lives in the torture. At last he bows himself, and the upper part of his body falls over, and as he falls you hear him say, *"Into thy hands I commend my Spirit"* (Luke 23:46). What wondrous magic was on him? What made that man strong? What helped him to bear that

---

9. Hymn: "When I Survey The Wondrous Cross." Words by Isaac Watts and music by Lowell Mason.
10. A long shaft with an axe on one side and spike on the other.
11. Brushwood used to build fires.

cruelty? What made him stand unmoved in the flames? It was the thing of power—it was the Cross of Jesus crucified. For *"unto us which are saved it is the power of God"* (1 Corinthians 1:18).

But behold another scene far different. There is no crowd there; it is a silent room. There is a poor pallet[12], a lonely bed, and a physician standing by. There is a young girl; her face is blanched by consumption. Long has the worm eaten her cheek, and though sometimes the flush came, it was the death flush of the deceitful consumption. There she lays, weak, pale, wan, worn, dying, and yet there is a smile upon her face as if she had seen an angel. She speaks, and there is music in her voice. Joan of Arc of old was not half as mighty as that girl. She is wrestling with dragons on her deathbed, but see her composure, and hear her dying sonnet:

> *Jesus, lover of my soul,*
> *Let me to thy bosom fly,*
> *While the nearer waters roll,*
> *While the tempest still is high!*
> *Hide me, O my Savior, hide,*
> *Till the storm of life is past,*
> *Safe into the haven guide,*
> *O receive my soul at last!*[13]

And with a smile she shuts her eyes on Earth and opens them in Heaven. What enables her to die like that? It is the thing of power—it is the Cross, it is Christ crucified. I have

---

12. A mattress filled with straw, or quilts folded to form a mattress.
13. Hymn: "Jesus Lover of My Soul." Words by Charles Wesley; Music by Joseph Parry.

little time to discourse upon the other point, and be it far from me to weary you by a lengthened and prosy sermon, but we must glance at the other statement: Christ is, to the called ones, the wisdom of God as well as the power of God. To a believer, the gospel is the perfection of wisdom, and if it does not appear so to the ungodly, it is because of the perversion of judgment, a consequence of their depravity.

An idea has long possessed the public mind that a religious man can scarcely be a wise man. It has been the custom to talk of infidels, atheists, and deists, as men of deep thought and comprehensive intellect, and to tremble for the Christian controversialist, as if he must surely fall by the hand of his enemy. But this is purely a mistake, for the gospel is the sum of wisdom, an epitome of knowledge, a treasure house of truth, and a revelation of mysterious secrets. In it we see how justice and mercy may be married. We behold inexorable law entirely satisfied, and sovereign love bearing away the sinner in triumph. Our meditation upon it enlarges the mind, and as it opens to our soul in successive flashes of glory, we stand astonished at the profound wisdom manifest in it.

Ah, dear friends, if you seek wisdom, you shall see it displayed in all its greatness. Not in the balancing of the clouds, nor the firmness of Earth's foundations. Not in the measured march of the armies of the sky, nor in the perpetual motions of the waves of the sea. Not in vegetation with all its fairy forms of beauty, nor in the animal with its marvelous tissue of nerve, and vein, and sinew. Nor even in man, that last and loftiest work of the Creator. But turn aside and see this great sight—an incarnate God upon the Cross, a substitute atoning for mortal guilt, a sacrifice satisfying the vengeance of Heaven, and delivering the rebellious sinner. Here is essential wisdom, enthroned, crowned, glorified. Admire, you people of Earth, if you are not blind. And you who glory in your learning bend your heads in reverence, and admit that all your skill could not have devised a gospel at once so just to God, so safe to man.

Remember, my friends, that while the gospel is in itself wisdom, it also confers wisdom on its students. It teaches young men wisdom and discretion, and gives understanding to the simple. A person who is a believing admirer and a hearty lover of the truth as it is in Jesus, is in a right place to follow with advantage any other branch of science. I confess I have a shelf in my head for everything now. Whatever I read I know where to put it; whatever I learn I know where to stow it away. Once when I read books, I put all my knowledge together in glorious confusion; but ever since I have known Christ, I have put Christ in the center as my sun, and each science revolves around it like a planet, while minor sciences are satellites to these planets. Christ is to me the wisdom of God. I can learn everything now. The science of Christ crucified is the most excellent of sciences; she is to me the wisdom of God. O, young person, build your studio on Calvary! There raise your observatory, and scan by faith the lofty things of nature. Take a hermit's cell in the Garden of Gethsemane, and wash your brow with the waters of Silo. Let the Bible be your standard classic—your last appeal in matters of contention. Let its light be your illumination, and you shall become wiser than Plato, more truly learned than the seven sages of antiquity.

And now, my dear friends, solemnly and earnestly, as in the sight of God, I appeal to you. You are gathered here this morning, I know, from different motives. Some of you have come from curiosity; others of you are my regular hearers. Some have come from one place and some from another. What have you heard me say this morning? I have told you of two classes of persons who reject Christ—the religionist who has a religion of form and nothing else, and the man of the world who calls our gospel foolishness. Now, put your hand upon your heart, and ask yourself this morning, "Am I one of these?" If you are, then walk the Earth in all your pride, and then go as you came in. But know that for all this the Lord shall bring you unto judgment; your joys and delights shall vanish like a dream, "and, like the baseless fabric of a vision," be swept away forever.

Know this, moreover, that one day in the halls of Satan, down in hell, I perhaps may see you among those myriad spirits who revolve forever in a perpetual circle with their hands upon their hearts. If your hand is transparent, and your flesh is transparent, I shall look through your hand and flesh and see your heart within. And how shall I see it? Set in a case of fire—in a case of fire! And there you shall revolve forever with the worm gnawing within your heart, which never shall die—a case of fire around your never-dying, ever-tortured heart. Good God! Let not these still reject and despise Christ, but let this be the time when they shall be called. To the rest of you who are called, I need say nothing. The longer you live, the more powerful you will find the gospel to be, the more deeply Christ-taught you will be, the more you will live under the constant influence of the Holy Spirit, the more you will know the gospel to be a thing of power, and the more you will understand it to be a thing of wisdom. May every blessing rest upon you, and may God come up with us in the evening!

Let men or angels dig the mines
Where nature's golden treasure shines;
Brought near the doctrine of the cross,
All nature's gold appears but dross.
Should vile blasphemers with disdain
Pronounce the truths of Jesus vain,
We'll meet the scandal and the shame,
And sing and triumph in his name.[14]

---

14. Hymn by Isaac Watts.

CHAPTER 2

CHRIST OUR PASSOVER

A Sermon
(No. 54)
Delivered on Sunday Evening, December 2, 1855,
by Reverend Charles H. Spurgeon,
at New Park Street Chapel, Southwark,
London, England

For even Christ our passover is sacrificed for us.
(1 Corinthians 5:7)

The more you read the Bible, and the more you meditate upon it, the more you will be astonished with it. Those who are but casual readers of the Bible do not know the height, the depth, the length and breadth of the mighty meanings contained in its pages. There are certain times when I discover a new vein of thought, and I put my hand to my head and say in astonishment, "Oh, it is wonderful, I never saw this before in the Scriptures." You will find the Scriptures enlarge as you enter them. The more you study them the less you will appear to know of them, for they *widen[1] out as we approach them. You will especially find this the case with the typical parts of God's Word. Most of the historical books were intended to be types either of dispensations, or experiences, or offices of Jesus Christ. Study the Bible with this as a key,*

---

1. Broaden and extend the boundaries of one's understanding of Scripture.

and you will not blame Herbert[2] when he calls it "not only the book of God, but the God of books." One of the most interesting points of the Scriptures is their constant tendency to display Christ, and perhaps one of the most beautiful figures under which Jesus Christ is ever exhibited in sacred writ is the Passover Paschal Lamb. It is Christ of whom we are about to speak tonight.

Israel was in Egypt, in extreme bondage. The severity of their slavery had continually increased till it was so oppressive that their incessant groans went up to Heaven. God who avenges His own elect, though they cry day and night unto him (see Luke 18:7.), at last determined that He would direct a fearful blow against Egypt's king and Egypt's nation, and deliver His own people. We can picture the anxieties and the anticipations of Israel, but we can scarcely sympathize with them, unless we as Christians have had the same deliverance from spiritual Egypt. Let us, beloved, go back to the day in our experience, when we abode in the land of Egypt, working in the brickkilns of sin, toiling to make ourselves better, and finding it to be of no avail. Let us recall that memorable night, the beginning of months, the commencement of a new life in our spirit, and the beginning of an altogether new era in our soul.

The Word of God struck the blow at our sin. He gave us Jesus Christ our sacrifice, and in that night we went out of Egypt. Though we have passed through the wilderness since then, and have fought the Amalekites, have trodden on the fiery serpent, have been scorched by the heat and frozen by the snows, yet we have never since that time

---

2. George Herbert, 1593-1633, English writer and devotional poet.

gone back to Egypt. Although our hearts may sometimes have desired the leeks, the onions, and the *fleshpots*[3] *of Egypt, yet we have never been brought into slavery since then. Come; let us keep the Passover this night, and think of the night when the Lord delivered us out of Egypt. Let us behold our Savior Jesus as the Paschal Lamb on which we feed. Let us not only look at Him as such, but let us sit down tonight at His table, let us eat of His flesh and drink of His blood, for His flesh is meat indeed, and His blood is drink indeed. In holy solemnity let our hearts approach that ancient supper. Let us go back to Egypt's darkness, and by holy contemplation behold, instead of the destroying angel, the angel of the covenant, at the head of the feast,—"the Lamb of God, which taketh away the sin of the world"* (John 1:29).

I shall not have time tonight to enter into the whole history and mystery of the Passover. You will not hear me preach tonight concerning *the whole of it,* but a few prominent points therein as a part of them. It would require a dozen sermons to do so.

Two Points We Shall Look At:

First of all look at the Lord Jesus Christ, and show how He corresponds with the Paschal Lamb.

Second, we shall endeavor to bring you to the two points—of having His blood sprinkled on you, and having fed on Him.

---

3. A place of lewd entertainment.

1. How the Lord Jesus Christ Corresponds with the Paschal Lamb

First, then, *Jesus Christ is typified here under the Paschal Lamb.* And should there be one of the seed of Abraham here who has never seen Christ to be the Messiah, I beg his special attention to that which I am to bring forward for consideration, when I speak of the Lord Jesus as none other than the Lamb of God slain for the deliverance of His chosen people. Follow me with your Bibles, and open first at the 12th chapter of Exodus. We commence, first of all, with the victim—*the lamb.* How fine a picture of Christ is the lamb. No other creature could so well have typified Him who was holy, harmless, undefiled, and separate from sinners. Being also the emblem of sacrifice, it most sweetly portrayed our Lord and Savior Jesus Christ. Search natural history through, and though you will find other emblems that set forth different characteristics of His nature, and admirably display Him to our souls, yet there is none that seems as appropriate to the person of our beloved Lord as that of the Lamb. A child would at once perceive the likeness between a lamb and Jesus Christ, so gentle and innocent, so mild and harmless, neither hurting others, nor seeming to have the power to resent an injury. "A humble man before his foes, a weary man and full of woes."

What tortures the sheepish race has received from us! How, though innocent, they are continually slaughtered for our food! Their skin is dragged from their backs; their wool is shorn to give us a garment. And so the Lord Jesus Christ, our glorious Master, gives us His garments that we may be clothed with them. He is rent asunder for us; His very blood is poured out for our sins, harmless and holy, a glorious sacrifice for the sins of all His children. Thus the Paschal Lamb might well convey to the pious Hebrew the person of a suffering, silent, patient, harmless Messiah.

Look further down. It was a lamb *without blemish!* (See Exodus 12:5.) A blemished lamb, if it had the smallest speck of disease, the least wound, would not have been allowed for a Passover. The priest would not have allowed it to be slaughtered, nor would God have accepted the sacrifice at his hands. It must be a lamb without blemish. And was not Jesus Christ even such from His birth? Unblemished, born of the pure Virgin Mary, begotten of the Holy Ghost, without a taint of sin. His soul was pure, and spotless as the driven snow, white, clear, perfect, and His life was the same. In Him was no sin. He took our infirmities and bore our sorrows on the Cross. He was in all points tempted as we are, but there was that sweet exception, *"yet without sin"* (Hebrews 4:15). He was a lamb without blemish. You who have known the Lord, who have tasted of His grace, who have held fellowship with Him, does not your heart acknowledge that He is a lamb without blemish? Can you find any fault with your Savior? Have you anything to lay to His charge? Has His truthfulness departed? Have His words been broken? Have His promises failed? Has He forgotten His engagements? And, in any respect, can you find in Him any blemish? Ah, no! He is the unblemished lamb, the pure, the spotless, the immaculate, *"the Lamb of God, which taketh away the sin of the world,"* and in Him there is no sin. (See John 1:29.)

Go on further down the chapter. "Your lamb shall be without blemish, *a male of the first year."* I need not stop to consider the reason why the male was chosen; we only note that it was to be a male of the first year. Then it was in its prime; then its strength was unexhausted; then its power was just ripened into maturity and perfection—God would not have an untimely fruit. God would not have that offered which had not come to maturity. And so our Lord Jesus Christ had just come to the ripeness of manhood when He was offered. At 34 years of age He was sacrificed for our sins. He was then hale and strong, although his body may have been emaciated by suffering, and His face more marred than that of any other man (see Isaiah 52:14), yet He was then in the perfection of manhood.

I think I see Him then, His goodly beard flowing down upon His breast. I see him with His eyes full of genius, His form erect, His manner majestic, His energy entire, His whole frame in full development—a real man, a magnificent man—fairer than the sons of men. He was a Lamb not only without blemish, but with all His powers fully brought out. Such was Jesus Christ—a Lamb of the first year—not a boy, not a lad, not a young man, but a full man, that He might give His soul unto us. He did not give himself to die for us when He was a youth, for He would not then have given all He was to be. He did not give himself to die for us when He was in old age, for then would He have given himself when He was in decay. But just in his maturity, in His very prime, then Jesus Christ our Passover was sacrificed for us.

INCOMPARABLE OBEDIENCE

And, moreover, at the time of His death, Christ was full of life, for we are informed by one of the evangelists that *He "cried with a loud voice, and gave up the ghost"* (Mark 15:37). This is a sign that Jesus did not die through weakness, or through decay of nature. His soul was strong within Him. He was still the Lamb of the first year. He was still mighty. He could, if He pleased, even on the Cross, have unlocked His hands from their iron bolts, and descending from the tree of infamy, have driven His astonished foes before Him, like deer scattered by a lion, yet did He meekly yield obedience unto death.

My soul, can you not see your Jesus here, the unblemished Lamb of the first year, strong and mighty? And, O my heart! Does not the thought rise up—if Jesus consecrated himself to you when He was in all His strength and vigor, should not I in youth dedicate myself to Him? And if I am in manhood, am I not doubly bound to give my strength to Him? And if I am in old age, I should still seek while the little remains, to consecrate that little to Him. If He gave His all to me, which was much, should I not give my little all to Him? Should I not feel bound to consecrate myself entirely to His service, to lay body, soul, spirit, time, talents and my all upon His altar? And though I am not an unblemished lamb, yet I am happy that as the leavened cake was accepted with the sacrifice, though never burned with it—I, though a leavened cake, may be offered on the altar with my Lord and Savior, the Lord's burnt offering. And so, though impure, and full of leaven, I may be accepted in the beloved, an offering of a sweet savor, acceptable unto the Lord my God. (See Ephesians 1:6.) Here is Jesus, beloved, a Lamb without blemish, a Lamb of the first year!

The subject now expands and the interest deepens. Let me have your very serious consideration to the next point, which has much gratified me in its discovery and will instruct you in the relation. In the 6th verse of the 12th chapter of Exodus we are told that this lamb which should be offered at the Passover was to be selected four days before its sacrifice, and to be kept apart:

> *"In the tenth day of this month they shall take to them every man a lamb, according to the house of their fathers, a lamb for an house: And if the household be too little for the lamb, let him and his neighbour next unto his house take it according to the number of the souls; every man according to his eating shall make your count for the lamb" (Exodus 12:3-4). The 6th verse says, "And ye shall keep it up until the fourteenth day of the same month."*

For four days this lamb, chosen to be offered, was taken away from the rest of the flock and kept alone by itself, for two reasons: partly that by its constant bleating they might be put in remembrance of the solemn feast that was to be celebrated, and, moreover, that during the four days they might be quite assured that it had no blemish, for during that time it was subject to constant inspection, in order that they might be certain that it had no hurt or injury that would render it unacceptable to the Lord.

THE LAMB OF GOD... FOUR MEMORABLE DAYS BEFORE HIS CRUCIFIXION

And now, brethren, a remarkable fact flashes before you—just as this lamb was separated four days, the ancient allegories used to say that Christ was separated four years. *Four* years after He left his father's house He went into the wilderness, and was tempted of the devil. *Four* years after His baptism He was sacrificed for us. But there is another, better than that. About *four* days before His crucifixion, Jesus Christ rode in triumph through the streets of Jerusalem. He was thus openly set apart as being distinct from mankind. He, on the donkey, rode up to the temple, that all might see Him to be Judah's Lamb, chosen of God, and ordained from the foundation of the world. And what is more remarkable still, during those four days, you will see, if you turn to the Evangelists, at your leisure, that as much is recorded of what He did and said as through all the other part of His life. During those four days, He upbraided the fig tree, and immediately it withered. It was then that He drove the buyers and sellers from the temple. It was then that He rebuked the priests and elders, by telling them the similitude of the two sons, one of whom said he would go, and did not, and the other who said he would not go, and went.

It was then that He narrated the parable of the husbandmen (see Mark 12.), who slew those who were sent to them. Afterwards He gave the parable of the marriage of the king's son. Then comes His parable concerning the man who went unto the feast, not having on a wedding garment. And then also, the parable concerning the ten virgins, five of whom were very wise, and five of whom were foolish. Then comes the chapter of very striking denunciations against the Pharisees: *"Woe unto you O ye blind Pharisees! cleanse first that which is within the cup and platter"* (see Matthew 23:26). And then also comes that long chapter of prophecy concerning what should happen at the siege of Jerusalem, and an account of the dissolution of the world: *"Learn a parable of the fig tree; When his branch is yet tender, and putteth forth leaves, ye know that summer is nigh"* (Matthew 24:32).

But I will not trouble you by telling you here that at the same time He gave them that splendid description of the Day of Judgment, when the sheep shall be divided from the goats. In fact, the most splendid utterances of Jesus were recorded as having taken place within these *four* days. Just as the lamb separated from its fellows, did bleat more than ever during the four days, so did Jesus during those four days speak more, and if you want to find a choice saying of Jesus, turn to the account of the last four days' ministry to find it. There you will find that chapter, *"Let not your heart be troubled"* (John 14:1). There also His great prayer, *"Father, I will"* (John 17: 1-26), and so on. *The greatest things He did, He did in the last four days when He was set apart.*

No Blemish. . . .

And there is one more thing to which I beg your particular attention, and that is, that during those four days I told you that the lamb was subject to the closest scrutiny, so, also, during those four days, it is singular to relate, that Jesus Christ was examined by all classes of persons. It was during those four days that the lawyer asked Him which was the greatest commandment. And He said, *"Thou shalt love the Lord thy God with all thy heart, and with all thy soul, and with all thy mind . . . and thou shalt love thy neighbour as thyself."* (See Matthew 22:37-39.) It was then that the Herodians came and questioned Him about the tribute money; it was then that the Pharisees tempted Him, and it was then that the Sadducees tried Him upon the subject of the resurrection.

He was tried by all classes and grades—Herodians, Pharisees, Sadducees, lawyers, and the common people. It was during these four days that He was examined. How did He come forth? An immaculate Lamb! The officers said, *"Never man spake like this man"* (John 7:46). His foes found none who could even bear false witness against Him, such as agreed together, and Pilate declared, *"I find no fault in him"* (John 19:4). He would not have been fit for the Paschal Lamb had a single blemish been discovered, but "I find no fault in him," was the utterance of the great chief magistrate, who thereby declared that the Lamb might be eaten at God's Passover, the symbol and the means of the deliverance of God's people. O beloved! You have only to study the Scriptures to find out wondrous things in them; you have only to search deeply, and you will stand amazed at their richness. You will find God's Word to be a very precious word; the more you live by it and study it, the more it will be endeared to your minds.

Location of the Place of Killing

But the next thing we must mark is *the place where this lamb was to be killed,* which peculiarly sets forth that it must be Jesus Christ. The first Passover was held in Egypt, the second Passover was held in the wilderness, but we do not read that there were more than these two Passovers celebrated until the Israelites came to Canaan. And then, if you turn to a passage in Deuteronomy, the 16th chapter, you will find that God no longer allowed them to slay the Lamb in their own houses but appointed a place for its celebration. In the wilderness, they brought their offerings to the tabernacle where the lamb was slaughtered, but at its first appointment in Egypt, they had no special place to which they took the lamb to be sacrificed. Afterwards, we read in the 16th of Deuteronomy, and verses 5-6,

> *"Thou mayest not sacrifice the passover within any of thy gates, which the Lord thy God giveth thee: but at the place which the Lord thy God shall choose to place his name in, there thou shalt sacrifice the Passover at even, at the going down of the sun, at the season that thou camest forth out of Egypt."*

It was in Jerusalem that men ought to worship, for salvation was of the Jews; there was God's palace, there His altar smoked, and there only might the Paschal Lamb be killed. So was our blessed Lord led to Jerusalem. The infuriated throng dragged Him along the city. In Jerusalem our Lamb was sacrificed for us. It was at the precise spot where God had ordained that it should be. Oh! If that mob who gathered round Him at Nazareth had been able to push Him headlong down the hill, then Christ could not have died at Jerusalem, but as He said, *"a prophet cannot perish out of Jerusalem."* (See Luke 13:33.) So was it true that the King of all prophets could not do otherwise—the prophecies concerning Him would not have been fulfilled. *"Thou shalt kill the lamb in the place the Lord thy God shall appoint."* (See Deuteronomy 16:2.) He was sacrificed in the very place. Thus, again you have an incidental proof that Jesus Christ was the Paschal Lamb for His people.

Manner of His Death

The next point is *the manner of his death*. I think the manner in which the lamb was to be offered so peculiarly sets forth the crucifixion of Christ, that no other kind of death could by any means have answered all the particulars set down here. First, the lamb was to be slaughtered, and its blood caught in a basin. Usually blood was caught in a golden basin. Then, as soon as it was taken, the priest standing by the altar on which the fat was burning threw the blood on the fire or cast it at the foot of the altar. You may guess what a scene it was. Ten thousand lambs sacrificed, and the blood poured out in a purple river. Next, the lamb was to be roasted, but it was not to have a bone of its body broken.

Now I do say that nothing but crucifixion can answer all these three things. Crucifixion has in it the shedding of blood—the hands and feet were pierced. It has in it the idea of roasting, for roasting signifies a long torment, and as the lamb was for a long time before the fire, so Christ, in crucifixion, was for a long time exposed to a broiling sun, and all the other pains that crucifixion engenders. Moreover not a bone was broken, which could not have been the case with any other punishment. Suppose it had been possible to put Christ to death in any other way. Sometimes the Romans put criminals to death by decapitation, but by such a death the neck is broken. Many martyrs were put to death by having a sword pierced through them, but, while that would have been a bloody death, and not a bone broken necessarily, the torment would not have been long enough to have been pictured by the roasting. So take whatever punishment you will. Take hanging, which sometimes the Romans practiced in the form of strangling, that mode of punishment does not involve shedding of blood, and consequently the requirements would not have been answered.

I do think any intelligent Jew reading through this account of the Passover, and then looking at the crucifixion, must be struck by the fact that the penalty and death of the

Cross by which Christ suffered, must have taken in all these three things. There was blood-shedding, the long continued suffering—the roasting of torture, and then added to that, singularly enough, by God's providence not a bone was broken, but the body was taken down from the Cross intact. Some may say that burning might have answered the matter; but there would not have been a shedding of blood in that case and the bones would have been virtually broken in the fire; besides the body would not have been preserved entire. Crucifixion was the only death which could answer all of these three requirements.

My faith receives great strength from the fact, that I see my Savior not only as a fulfillment of the type, but the only one. My heart rejoices to look on Him whom I have pierced, and see His blood, as the lamb's blood, sprinkled on my lintel and my doorpost, and see His bones unbroken, and to believe that not a bone of His spiritual body shall be broken hereafter. I rejoice, also, to see Him roasted in the fire, because thereby I see that He satisfied God for that roasting which I ought to have suffered in the torment of hell forever and ever.

Christian! I wish I had words to depict in better language, but, as it is, I give you the undigested thoughts, which you may take home and live upon during the week. For you will find this Paschal Lamb to be an hourly feast, as well as supper, and you may feed upon it continually, until you come to the mount of God, where you shall see Him as He is, and worship Him in the Lamb in the midst thereof. (See Revelation 5:6.)

2. HOW WE DERIVE BENEFIT FROM THE BLOOD OF CHRIST

Christ our Passover is slain for us. The Jew could not say that. He could say *a* lamb, but *"the Lamb,"* even "Christ our Passover," had not yet become a victim. And here are some of my hearers within these walls tonight who cannot say "Christ our Passover is slain for us." But glory be to God, some of us can! There are not a few here, who have laid their hands upon the glorious Scapegoat, and now they can put their hands upon the Lamb also, and they can say, "Yes, it is true, He is not only slain, but Christ our Passover is slain for us."

We derive benefit from the death of Christ in two modes: first, by having His blood sprinkled on us for our *redemption;* second, by our eating His flesh for our *regeneration and sanctification.* The first aspect in which a sinner views Jesus is that of a lamb slain, whose blood is sprinkled on the doorpost and on the lintel. Note the fact, that the blood was never sprinkled on the threshold. It was sprinkled on the lintel, the top of the door and on the side posts, but never on the threshold, for woe unto him who tramples underfoot the blood of the Son of God! Even the priest of Dagon trod not on the threshold of his god; much less will the Christian trample underfoot the blood of the Paschal Lamb. But His blood must be on our right hand to be our constant guard, and on our left to be our continual support. We want to have Jesus Christ sprinkled on us.

As I told you before, it is not only the blood of Christ poured out on Calvary that saves a sinner; it is the blood of Christ sprinkled on the heart. Let us turn to the land of Egypt. Let us behold the scene together. It is evening. The Egyptians are going homeward—little thinking of what is coming. But just as soon as the sun is set, a lamb is brought into every Hebrew house. The Egyptian strangers passing by, say, "These Hebrews are about to keep a feast tonight," and they retire to their houses utterly careless about it. The father of the Hebrew house takes his lamb, and examining it once more with anxious curiosity, looks it over from head to foot, to see if it has a blemish. He finds none. "My son," he says to one of them, "bring hither the basin." It is held. He stabs the lamb, and the blood flows into the basin. Do you not think you see the sire, as he commands his matronly wife to roast the lamb before the fire! "Take heed," he says, "that not a bone be broken." Do you see her intense anxiety, as she puts it down to roast, lest a bone should be broken? Now, says the father, "bring a bunch of hyssop." A child brings it. The father dips it into the blood. "Come here, my children, wife and all, and see what I am about to do." He takes the hyssop in his hands, dips it in the blood, and sprinkles it across the lintel and the doorposts. His children say, "What does this ordinance mean?" He answers, "This night the Lord God will pass through to smite the Egyptians, and when He sees the blood upon the lintel and on the two side posts, the Lord will pass over the door, and will not suffer the destroyer to come into your houses to smite you."

The thing is done, the lamb is cooked, the guests are set down to it, the father of the family has prayed a blessing, and they are sitting down to feast upon it. And mark how the old man carefully divides joint from joint, lest a bone should be broken, and he is particular that the smallest child of the family should have some of it to eat, for so the Lord has commanded. Let us listen as he tells them, "it is a solemn night—make haste—in another hour we shall all go out of Egypt." He looks at his hands; they are rough with labor, and clapping them, he cries, "I am not to be a slave any longer." Perhaps his eldest son has been suffering pain from lashes he received. His father says, "Son, you have had the taskmaster's lash upon you this afternoon, but it is the last time you shall feel it." He looks at them all, with tears in his eyes and says, "This is the night the Lord God will deliver you."

Do we see them with their hats on their heads, with their loins girt, and their staves in their hands? It is the dead of the night. Suddenly they hear a shriek! The father says, "Keep within doors, my children; you will know what it is in a moment." Now another shriek—another shriek—shriek succeeds shriek—they hear perpetual wailing and lamentation. "Remain within," he says, "the angel of death is flying abroad." A solemn silence is in the room, and they can almost hear the wings of the angel flap in the air as he passes their blood-marked door. "Be calm," says the sire, "that blood will save you." The shrieking increases. "Prepare quickly, my children," he says again, and in a moment the Egyptians come close by saying, "Get out of here! Get out! We are not after the jewels that you have borrowed. You have brought death into our houses." "Oh!" says a mother, "Go! For the sake of our children, go! My eldest son lies dead!" "Go!" says a father, "Go! And peace go with you. It was an ill day when your people came into Egypt, and our king began to slay your firstborn, for God is punishing us for our cruelty." Ah! See the Hebrews leaving the land, the shrieks are still heard, and the Egyptians are busy tending to their dead. As they go out, a son of Pharaoh is taken away to be buried in one of the pyramids. Presently they see one of their taskmaster's sons taken away. A happy night for the Hebrews—when they escape!

And do you see, my hearers, a glorious parallel? They had to sprinkle the blood, and also to eat the lamb. My soul, have you ever had the blood sprinkled on you? Can you say that Jesus Christ is yours? It is not enough to say *"He loved the world, and gave His Son"* (see John 3:16). You must say, "He loved *me*, and gave himself for *me*." There is another hour coming, dear friends, when we shall all stand before God's judgment bar, and then God will say, "Angel of death, you once smote Egypt's firstborn. You know your prey. Unsheathe your sword." I behold the great gathering; you and I are standing among them. It is a solemn moment. All men stand in suspense. There is neither hum nor murmur. The very stars cease to shine lest the light should disturb the air by its motion. All is still. God says, "Have you sealed those that are mine?"

"I have," says Gabriel, "they are sealed by blood every one of them." Then God says, "Sweep with your sword of slaughter! Sweep the Earth! And send the unclothed, the unpurchased, and the unwashed ones to the pit." How shall we feel beloved when for a moment we see that angel flap his wings? He is just about to fly. "But," will the doubt cross our minds, "perhaps he will come to me?" No, we shall stand and look the angel full in his face.

> *Bold shall I stand in that great day!*[4]
> *For who aught to my charge shall lay*
> *While through thy blood absolved I am*
> *From sin's tremendous curse and shame.*

If we have the blood on us, we shall see the angel coming,

---

4. Hymn # 103, The Gadsby Hymnal: "The Imputed Righteousness of Christ" Verse 3, Written by Count Zinzendorf, Translated by John Wesley.

we shall smile at him. We shall dare to come even to God's face and say, "Great God! I'm clean! Through Jesus' blood, I'm clean!"

But if, my hearer, your unwashed spirit shall stand unshriven[5] before its maker, if your [6]guilty soul shall appear with all its black spots upon it, unsprinkled with the purple tide, how will you speak when you see flash from the scabbard the angel's sword swift for death, and winged for destruction, and when it shall cut asunder? I think I see you standing now. The angel is sweeping away a thousand there. There is one of your drinking companions. There one with whom you did dance and swear. There another, who after attending the same chapel as you was a despiser of religion. Now death comes nearer to you. Just as when the reaper sweeps the field and the next ear trembles because its turn shall come next, I see a brother and a sister swept into the pit. Have I no blood upon me? Then, oh rocks, it would be kind of you to hide me. You have no benevolence in your arms. Mountains, let me find in your caverns some little shelter. But it is all in vain, for vengeance shall cleave the mountains and split the rocks open to find me out. Have I no blood? Have I no hope? No! He smites me. Eternal damnation is my horrible portion. The depth of the darkness of Egypt for you, and the horrible torments of the pit from which none can escape! Ah, my dear hearers, could I preach as I could wish, could I speak to you without my lips and with my heart, then I would beg you to seek that sprinkled blood, and urge you by the love of your own soul, by everything that is sacred and eternal, to labor to get this blood of Jesus sprinkled on your souls. It is the blood sprinkled that saves a sinner.

---

5. Unforgiven.
6. Not sprinkled with Christ's blood.

But when the Christian gets the blood sprinkled, that is not all he wants. *He wants something to feed upon.* And, O sweet thought! Jesus Christ is not only a Savior for sinners, but He is food for them after they are saved. The Paschal Lamb by faith we eat. We live on it. You may tell, my hearers, whether you have the blood sprinkled on the door by this: do you eat the Lamb? Suppose for a moment that one of the old Jews had said in his heart, "I do not see the use of this feasting. It is quite right to sprinkle the blood on the lintel or else the door will not be known, but what good is all this inside? We will have the lamb prepared, and we will not break his bones, but we will not eat of it." And suppose he went and stored the lamb away. What would have been the consequence? Why, the angel of death would have smitten him as well as the rest, even if the blood had been upon him. And if, moreover, that old Jew had said, "There, we will have a little piece of it, but we will have something else to eat. We will have some unleavened bread, we will not turn the leaven out of our houses, but we will have some leavened bread."

If they had not consumed the lamb, but had reserved some of it, then the sword of the angel would have found the heart out as well as that of any other man. Oh, dear hearer, you may think you have the blood sprinkled, you may think you are just, but if you do not live *on* Christ as well as *by* Christ, you will never be saved by the Paschal Lamb. "Ah!" say some, "we know nothing of this." Of course you don't. When Jesus Christ said, *"Except ye eat the flesh of the Son of man, and drink his blood, ye have no life in you"* (John 6:53), there were some that said, *"This is an hard saying; who can hear it?"* (John 6:60), and many from that time went back and walked no more with Him. They could not understand Him, but, Christian, do you not understand it?

Is Jesus Christ your daily food? And even with the bitter herbs, is He not sweet food?

Some of you, my friends, who are true Christians, live too much on your changing frames and feelings, on your experiences and evidences. Now, that is all wrong. That is just as if a worshiper had gone to the tabernacle and began eating one of the coats that were worn by the priest. When a man lives on Christ's righteousness, it is the same as eating Christ's dress. When a man lives on his frames and feelings, that is as much as if the child of God should live on some tokens that he received in the sanctuary that never were meant for food, but only to comfort him a little. What the Christian lives on is not Christ's righteousness, but Christ. He does not live on Christ's pardon, but on Christ, and on Christ he lives daily, on nearness to Christ. Oh, I do love preaching Christ. It is not the doctrine of justification that does my heart good, it is Christ, the justifier. It is not pardon that so much makes the Christian's heart rejoice, it is Christ the pardoner. It is not election that I love half so much as my being chosen in Christ before worlds began. It is not final perseverance that I love so much as the thought that in Christ my life is hid, and that since He gives unto His sheep eternal life, they shall never perish, neither shall any man pluck them out of his hand. (See John 10:28.)

Take care, Christian, to eat the Paschal Lamb and nothing else; if you eat that alone, it will be like bread to you—your soul's best food. If you live on anything else but the Savior, you are like one who seeks to live on some weed that grows in the desert, instead of eating the manna that comes down from Heaven. Jesus is the manna. *In* Jesus as well as *by* Jesus we live. Now, dear friends, in coming to this table, we will keep the Paschal Supper. Once more, by faith, we will eat the Lamb, by holy trust we will come to a crucified Savior, and feed on His blood, and righteousness, and atonement.

And now, in concluding, let me ask you, are you hoping to be saved my friends? One says, "Well, I don't hardly know; I hope to saved, but I do not know how." Do you imagine I tell you a lie when I tell you that people are hoping to be saved by works, but it is not so, it is a truth. In traveling through the country I meet with all sorts of characters, but most frequently with self-righteous persons. How often I meet with a man who thinks himself quite godly because he attends the church once on a Sunday, and who thinks himself quite righteous because he belongs to the establishment; as a churchman said to me the other day, "I am a rigid churchman."

"I am glad of that," I said to him, "because then you are a Calvinist, if you hold to the '*Articles*[7].'"

He replied "I don't know about the 'Articles,' I go more by the '*Rubric*[8].'"

And so I thought he was more of a formalist than a Christian. There are many persons like that in the world. Another says, "I believe I shall be saved. I don't owe anybody anything, I have never been bankrupt, I pay everybody twenty shillings in the pound, I never get drunk; and if I wrong anybody at any time, I try to make up for it by giving a pound a year to such-and-such a society. I am as religious as most people, and I believe I shall be saved." That will not do. It is as if some old Jew had said, "We don't want the blood on the lintel, we have a mahogany lintel. We don't want the

---

7. Doctrinal Statements.
8. Rules for religious procedures.

blood on the doorpost, we have a mahogany doorpost." Ah, whatever it was, the angel would have smitten it if it had not had the blood upon it. You may be as righteous as you like, but if you do not have the blood sprinkled, all the goodness of your doorposts and lintels will be of no avail whatever.

"Yes," says another, "I am not trusting exactly there. I believe it is my duty to be as good as I can, but then I think Jesus Christ's mercy will make up the rest. I try to be as righteous as circumstances allow, and I believe that whatever deficiencies there may be, Christ will make them up." That is as if a Jew had said, "Child, bring me the blood," and then, when that was brought, he had said, "bring me a vessel of water," and then he had taken it and mixed it together, and sprinkled the doorpost with it. Why, the angel would have smitten him as well as anyone else, for it is *blood, blood, blood, blood* that saves. It is not blood mixed with the water of our poor works; it is *blood, blood, blood, blood* and nothing else. And the only way of salvation is by blood. For, without the shedding of blood there is no remission of sin (see Hebrews 9:22). Have the precious blood of Christ sprinkled upon you, my hearers. Trust in precious blood, let your hope be in a salvation sealed with an atonement of precious blood, and you are saved. But having no blood, or having blood mixed with anything else, you are as damned as you are alive—for the angel shall slay you, however good and righteous you may be. Go home, then, and think of this: *"Christ our passover is sacrificed for us"* (1 Corinthians 5:7).

CHAPTER 3

CHRIST IN THE COVENANT

A Sermon
(No. 103)
Delivered on Sunday Morning, August 31, 1856,
by Reverend Charles H. Spurgeon,
at New Park Street Chapel, Southwark,
London, England

I will . . . give thee for a covenant of the people.
(Isaiah 49:8)

We all believe that our Savior has very much to do with the covenant of eternal salvation. We have been accustomed to regard Him as the mediator of the covenant, as the surety of the covenant, and as the scope or substance of the covenant. We have considered Him to be the *mediator* of the covenant (see 1 Timothy 2:5), for we were certain that God could make no covenant with man unless there were a mediator—a man who could stand between them both. And we have hailed Him as the mediator who, with mercy in His hands, came down to tell to sinful man the news that grace was promised in the eternal counsel of the most High. We have also loved our Savior as the *surety* of the covenant (see Hebrews 7:22.) who, on our behalf, undertook to pay our debts, and on His Father's behalf undertook, also, to see that all our souls should be secure and safe, and ultimately presented unblemished and complete before Him. And I doubt not that we have also rejoiced in the thought that Christ is the *sum and substance* of the covenant; we believe that if we would sum up all spiritual blessings, we must say, "Christ is all" (Colossians 3:11). He is the matter, He is the substance of it, and although much might be said concerning the glories of the covenant, yet nothing could be said that is not to be found in that one name, "Christ." But this morning I shall dwell on Christ, not as the mediator, nor as the surety, nor as the scope of the covenant, but as one great and glorious article of the covenant that God has given to His children.

It is our firm belief that Christ is ours, and is given to us of God; we know that *"he freely delivered him up for us all,"* and we, therefore, believe that He will, *"with him, freely give us all things"* (see Romans 8:32). We can say, with the spouse, *"My beloved is mine"* (Song of Solomon 2:16). We feel that we have a personal property in our Lord and Savior Jesus Christ, and it will therefore delight us for a while this morning, in the simplest manner possible, without the garnishing of eloquence or the trappings of oratory, just to mediate upon this great thought, that Jesus Christ in the covenant is the property of every believer.

Points We Will Examine:

First, we shall declare that Christ Jesus is the property of every believer and we will *examine this property* in all its senses.

Second, we shall notice *the purpose* for which it was conveyed to us.

Third, we shall give *one precept*, which may well be affixed upon so great a blessing as this, and is indeed an inference from it.

1. Christ, a Great Possession

In the first place here is a *great possession*—Jesus Christ by the covenant is the property of every believer. By this we must understand Jesus Christ in many different senses. We will begin, first of all, by declaring that Jesus Christ is ours *in all His attributes*. He has a double set of attributes, seeing that there are two natures joined in glorious union in one person. He has the attributes of very God, and He has the attributes of perfect man. Whatever these may be, they are each the perpetual property of every believing child of God. I need not dwell on His attributes as God. You all know how infinite His love is, how vast His grace, how firm His faithfulness, how unswerving His veracity. You know He is omniscient, you know He is omnipresent, you know He is omnipotent, and it will console you if you will but think that all these great and glorious attributes which belong to God are also yours.

Has He power? That power is yours—yours to support and strengthen you, yours to overcome your enemies, yours to keep you immutably secure. Has He love? Well, there is not a particle of His love in His great heart that is not yours. All His love belongs to you. You may dive into the immense, bottomless ocean of His love, and you may say of it all, "It is mine." Does He have justice? It may seem a stern attribute, but even that is yours, for He will by His justice see to it that all which is covenanted to you by the oath and promise of God shall be most certainly secured to you.

Mention whatever you please that is a characteristic of Christ as the ever glorious Son of God, and O faithful one, you may put your hand upon it and say, "It is mine." Your arm, O Jesus, upon which the pillars of the Earth do hang, is mine. Those eyes, O Jesus, which pierce through the thick darkness and behold the future, your eyes are mine, to look on me with love. Those lips, O Christ, which sometimes speak words louder than ten thousand thunders, or whisper syllables sweeter than the music of the harps of the glorified, those lips are mine. And that great heart which beats high with such impartial, pure, and unaffected love, that heart is mine. The whole of Christ, in all His glorious nature as the Son of God, as God over all, blessed forever, is yours, positively, actually, not symbolically, but in reality yours.

Consider Him as man, too. All that He has as perfect man is yours. As a perfect man He stood before His Father, *"full of grace and truth"* (John 1:14), full of favor, and accepted by God as a perfect being. O believer, God's acceptance of Christ is your acceptance, for do you not know that the love the Father set on a perfect Christ, He sets on you now? For all that Christ did is yours. That perfect righteousness that Jesus wrought when through His stainless life He kept the law and made it honorable, is yours. There is not a virtue that Christ ever had that is not yours. There is not a holy deed that He ever did that is not yours. There is not a prayer He ever sent to Heaven that is not yours. There is not one solitary thought towards God that it was His duty to think, and which He thought as man serving His God, that is not yours.

All His righteousness, in its vast extent, and in all the perfection of His character, is imputed to you. Oh, can you think what you have gotten in the word "Christ?" Come, believer, consider that word "God," and think how mighty it is, and then meditate upon that word "perfect man," for all that the man-God Christ, and the glorious God-man Christ, ever had, or ever can have as the characteristic of either of His natures, all that is yours. It all belongs to you. It is out of pure free favor, beyond the fear of revocation, passed over to you to be your actual property—and that forever.

Then consider, believer, that not only is Christ yours in all His attributes, but He is yours *in all His offices*. Great and glorious these offices are; we have scarce time to mention them all. Is He a prophet? Then He is *your* prophet. Is He a priest? Then He is *your* priest. Is He a king? Then He is *your* king. Is He a redeemer? Then He is *your* redeemer. Is He an advocate? Then He is *your* advocate. Is He a forerunner? Then He is *your* forerunner. Is He a surety of the covenant? Then He is *your* surety. In every name He bears, in every crown He wears, in every vestment in which He is arrayed, He is the believer's own. Oh, child of God, if you had grace to gather up this thought into your soul it would comfort you marvelously, to think that everything Christ is in office, He is most assuredly yours.

Do you see Him yonder, interceding before His Father, with outstretched arms? Do you see His ephod—His golden miter on His brow, inscribed with "holiness unto the Lord"? (See Exodus 29:6, 39:30.) Do your see Him as He lifts up His hands to pray? Hear you not that marvelous intercession such as man never prayed on Earth, that authoritative intercession such as He himself could not use in the agonies of the Garden of Gethsemane? For,

> *With sighs and groans, He offered up*[1]
> *His humble suit below;*
> *But with authority He pleads,*
> *Enthroned in glory now.*

---

1. Verse two a hymn on intercession written by Augustus Toplady.

Do you see how He asks, and how He receives, as soon as His petition is put up? And can you, dare you, believe that that intercession is all your own? That on His breast your name is written, that in His heart your name is stamped in marks of indelible grace? That all the majesty of that marvelous, surpassing intercession is your own, and would all be expended for you if you require it? That He has not any authority with His Father that He will not use on your behalf if you need it, and that He has no power to intercede that He would not employ for you in all times of necessity? Come now, words cannot set this forth, it is only your thoughts that can teach you this, it is only God the Holy Spirit bringing home the truth that can set this ravishing, transporting, thought in its proper position in your heart—that Christ is yours in all He is and has.

Do you see Him on Earth? There He stands, the priest offering His bloody sacrifice. See Him on the tree, His hands are pierced, His feet are gushing gore! Oh, do you see that pallid countenance, and those languid eyes flowing with compassion? Do you see that crown of thorns? Do you behold that mightiest of sacrifices, the sum and substance of them all? Believer, that is *yours,* those precious drops plead and claim *your* peace with God. That open side is *your* refuge; those pierced hands are *your* redemption; that groan He groans for *you.* That cry of a forsaken heart He utters for *you;* that death He dies for *you.* Come, I beseech you, consider Christ in any one of His various offices, but when you do consider Him lay hold of this thought: that in all these things He is *your* Christ, given unto *you* to be one article in the eternal covenant—*your* possession forever.

Then note next, Christ is the believer's in every one of His *works.* Whether they are works of suffering or of duty, they are the property of the believer. As a child, He was circumcised, and is that bloody rite mine? Yes, *"Circumcised in Christ"* (see Colossians 2:11). As a believer He is buried, and is that watery sign of baptism mine? Yes, *"Buried with Christ in baptism unto death"* (see Romans 6:4). Jesus' baptism I share when I lie interred with my best friend in the selfsame watery tomb. See there, He dies, and it is a master work to die. But is His death mine? Yes, I die in Christ. He rises. See Him startling His guards, and rising from the tomb!

And is that resurrection mine? Yes, we are *"risen together with Christ"* (see Colossians 3:1). Look again, He ascends up on high, and leads *"captivity captive"* (Ephesians 4:8). Is that ascension mine? Yes, for He has "raised us up together" (Ephesians 2:6). And see, He sits on His Father's throne. Is that deed mine? Yes, He has made us, "sit together in heavenly places" (ibid). All He did is ours.

By divine decree, there existed such an union between Christ and His people that all Christ did His people did, all Christ has performed His people performed in Him, for they were in His loins when He descended to the tomb, and in His loins they have ascended up on high. With Him they entered into bliss, and with Him they sit in heavenly places. Represented by Him, their head, all His people even now are glorified in Him—even in Him who is the head over all things to His Church (see Ephesians 1:22). In all the deeds of Christ, both in His humiliation and His exaltation, remember, O believer, you have a covenant interest, and all those things are yours.

I would for one moment hint at a sweet thought, which is this: you know that in the person of Christ *"dwelleth all the fulness of the Godhead bodily"* (Colossians 2:9). Ah, believer,

"And of his fulness have all we received, and grace for grace" (John 1:16). *All the fullness of Christ!* Do you know what that is? Do you understand that phrase? I guarantee you do not know it, and shall not, just yet. But all that fullness of Christ, the abundance of which you may guess by your own emptiness—all that fullness is yours to supply your multiplied necessities. All the fullness of Christ to restrain you, to keep you and preserve you; all that fullness of power, of love, and of purity, that is stored up in the person of the Lord Jesus Christ is yours. Do treasure that thought, for then your emptiness need never be a cause of fear—how can you be lost while you have all fullness to fly to?

But I come to something sweeter than this—*the very life of Christ* is the property of the believer. Ah, this is a thought into which I cannot dive, and I feel I have outdone myself in only mentioning it. The life of Christ is the property of every believer. Can you conceive what Christ's life is? "Sure," you say, "He poured it out upon the tree." He did, and it was His life that He gave to you then. But He took that life again. Even the life of His body was restored, and the life of His great and glorious Godhead had never undergone any change, even at that time. But now, you know He has immortality: *"he only hath immortality"* (see 1 Timothy 6:16). Can you conceive what kind of life it is that Christ possesses? Can He ever die? No! Far sooner may the harps of Heaven be stopped and the chorus of the redeemed cease forever; far sooner may the glorious walls of paradise be shaken and the foundations thereof be removed, than that Christ, the Son of God, should ever die.

Immortal as His Father, now He sits, the great eternal one. Christian, that life of Christ is yours. Hear what He says: *"Because I live, ye shall live also"* (John 14:19). *"Ye are dead, and your life"*—where is it? It *"is hid with Christ in*

God" (Colossians 3:3). The same blow that smites us dead, spiritually, must slay Christ, too. The same sword that can take away the spiritual life of a regenerate man, must take away the life of the Redeemer also, for they are linked together—they are not two lives, but one. We are but the rays of the great *"Sun of righteousness"* (see Malachi 4:2), our Redeemer—but sparks that must return to the great orb again. If we are indeed the true heirs of Heaven, we cannot die until He from whom we take our "rise" dies also. We are the stream that cannot stop until the fountain is dry. We are the rays that cannot cease until the sun ceases to shine. We are the branches, and we cannot wither until the trunk itself shall die. "Because I live, ye shall live also." The very life of Christ is the property of every one of the children of God.

And best of all, *the person of Jesus Christ* is the property of the Christian. I am persuaded, beloved, we think a great deal more of God's gifts than we do of God; and we preach a great deal more about the Holy Spirit's influence than we do about the Holy Spirit. And I am also assured that we talk a great deal more about the offices, and works, and attributes of Christ than we do about the person of Christ. Therefore, that is why there are few of us who can often understand the figures that are used in Song of Solomon concerning the person of Christ, because we have seldom sought to see Him or desired to know Him. But, O believer, you have sometimes been able to behold your Lord. Have you not seen *"him, who is white and ruddy,* "*the chief amongst ten thousand, and the altogether lovely?"* (See Song of Solomon 5:10.)

Have you not been sometimes lost in pleasure when you have seen His feet, which are like much fine gold, as if they burned in a furnace? Have you not seen Him in the double character, the white and the red, the lily and the rose, the

God yet the man, the dying yet the living; the perfect, and yet bearing about with Him a body of death? Have you even beheld that Lord with the nail=print in His hands, and the mark still on His side? And have you ever been ravished at His loving smile, and been delighted at His voice? Have you never had love visits from Him? Has He never put His banner over you? Have you never walked with Him to the villages and the garden of fruit trees? Have you never sat under His shadow? Have you never found His fruit sweet to your taste? Yes, you have. His *person* then is yours.

The wife loves her husband; she loves his house and his property; she loves him for all he gives her, for all the bounty he has, and all the love he bestows; but his person is the object of her affections. It is the same with the believer: he or she blesses Christ for all He does and all He is. But oh! it is Christ that is everything. The believer does not care so much about Christ's office, as he does about *the Man* Christ.

See the child on his father's knee—the father is a professor in the university; he is a great man with many titles, and perhaps the child knows that these are honorable titles, and esteems him for them; but he does not care so much about his father the professor and his dignity, as about the person of his father. It is not the college square cap, or the gown that the child loves. Moreover, if it is a loving child it will not be so much the meal the father provides or the house in which it lives, as the father which it loves; it is his dear person that has become the object of true and hearty affection. I am sure it is so with you, if you know your Savior; you love His mercies, you love His offices, you love His deeds, but oh! you love His person best. Reflect, then that the person of Christ is in the covenant conveyed to you: "I will give thee to be a covenant for the people."

2. Now we come to the second: *For what purpose God put Christ in the Covenant.*

Well, in the first place, Christ is in the covenant in order *to comfort every coming sinner.* "Oh," says the sinner who is coming to God, "I cannot lay hold on such a great covenant as that. I cannot believe that Heaven is provided for me. I cannot conceive that the robe of righteousness and all these wondrous things can be intended for such a wretch as I am." Here is a thought for you to dwell on, sinner: Christ is in the Covenant. Sinner, can you lay hold on Christ? Can you say,

> "*Nothing in my hand I bring,*
> *Simply to thy cross I cling*"?[2]

Well, if you have understood that, it was put in on purpose for you to hold fast to. All God's covenant mercies go together, and if you have laid hold on Christ, you have gained every blessing in the covenant. That is one reason why Christ was put there. Why, if Christ were not there, the poor sinner would say, "I dare not lay hold on that mercy. It is a God-like and divine one, but I dare not grasp it; it is too good for me. I cannot receive it, it staggers my faith." But he sees Christ with all His great atonement in the covenant; and Christ looks so lovingly at him, and opens His arms so wide, saying, in Matthew 11:28, "*Come unto me, all ye that labour and are heavy laden, and I will give you rest,*"

---

2. Hymn: "Rock of Ages, Cleft for Me" verse 3, written by Augustus Toplady in 1776. Music by Thomas Hastings.

that the sinner comes and throws his arms around Christ, and then Christ whispers, "Sinner, in laying hold of me, you have laid hold of all." Why, Lord, I dare not think I could have the other mercies. I dare trust you, but I dare not take the others. Ah, sinner, but because you have taken me you have taken all, for the mercies of the covenant are like links in the chain. This one link is an enticing one. The sinner lays hold of it; and God has purposely put it there to entice the sinner to come and receive the mercies of the covenant.

For when he has once got hold of Christ—here is the comfort—he has everything that the covenant can give.

Christ is put also *to confirm the doubting saint*. Sometimes he cannot read his interest in the covenant. He cannot see his portion among them that are sanctified. He is afraid that God is not *his* God, that the Spirit hath no dealings with *his* soul; but then,

> "Amid temptations, sharp and strong,[3]
> His soul to that dear refuge flies;
> Hope is his anchor, firm and strong,
> When tempests blow and billows rise."

So he lays hold of Christ, and were it not for that, even the believer dare not come at all. He could not lay hold on any other mercy than that with which Christ is connected. "Ah," says he, "I know I am a sinner, and Christ came to save sinners." So he holds fast to Christ. "I can hold fast here," he says, "my sin-blackened hands will not soil Christ, my filthiness will not make Him unclean." So the saint holds hard to Christ, as hard as if it were the death grasp of a

---

3. Hymn 139 from *Psalms and Hymns of Isaac Watts* (1674-1748).

drowning man. And what then? Why, he has got every mercy of the covenant in his hand. It is the wisdom of God that He has put Christ in, so that a poor sinner, who might be afraid to lay hold of another, knowing the gracious nature of Christ, is not afraid to lay hold of Him, and therein he grasps the whole, but often times unconsciously to himself.

Again, it was necessary that Christ should be in the covenant, because *there are many things there that would be nothing without Him.* Our great redemption is in the covenant, but we have no redemption except through *His* blood. It is true that my righteousness is in the covenant, but I can have no righteousness apart from that which Christ has wrought out, and which is imputed to me by God. It is very true that my eternal perfection is in the covenant, but the elect are only perfect in Christ. They are not perfect in themselves, nor will they ever be, until they have been washed, and sanctified, and perfected by the Holy Ghost. And even in Heaven their perfection consists not so much in their sanctification, as in their justification in Christ.

"Their beauty this, their glorious dress,[4]
Jesus the Lord their righteousness."

In fact, if you take Christ out of the covenant, you have just done the same as if you should break the string of a necklace: all the jewels, or beads, or corals, drop off and separate from each other. Christ is the golden string whereon the mercies of the covenant are threaded, and when you lay hold of Him, you have obtained the whole string of pearls. But if Christ is taken out, true there will be the pearls, but we cannot wear them, we cannot grasp them; they are separated,

---

4. Hymn # 490, on Christ's Righteousness. Written in 1739 by Count Zinzendorf, and translated by John Wesley in 1740.

and poor faith can never know how to get hold of them. It is a mercy worth worlds that Christ is in the covenant.

But note this once more; as I told you when preaching concerning God in the covenant, Christ is in the covenant *to be used*. There are some promises in the Bible which I have never yet used; but I am well assured that there will come times of trial and trouble when I shall find that poor despised promise, which I thought was never meant for me, will be the only one on which I can float. I know that the time is coming when every believer shall know the worth of every promise in the covenant. God has not given him any part of an inheritance which he did not mean him to use. Christ is given to us to use. Believer, use Him! I tell you again, as I told you before; you do not use your Christ as you should. Why, man, when you are in trouble, why do you not go and tell Him? Has He not a sympathizing heart, and can He not comfort and relieve you? Why are you gadding around to all your friends instead of your best friend? Why are you telling your tale of woe everywhere except into the bosom of your Lord? Oh, use Him, use Him.

Are you black with yesterday's sins? Here is a fountain filled with blood; use it, saint, use it. Has your guilt returned again? Well, His power has been proved again and again; come use Him! Use Him! Do you feel naked? Come here, soul, put on the robe. Don't stand staring at it; put it on. Strip off your own righteousness and your fears, too. Put this on and wear it, for it was meant to *wear*. Do you feel sick? What, will you not go and pull the night-bell of prayer, and tell your Great Physician? I beseech you to go and tell Him, and He will give the medicine that will revive you. Are you sick, with such a physician next door to you, a present help in time of trouble, and will not go to Him? Oh, remember you are poor, but then you have *"a kinsman, a mighty man of wealth."* (See Ruth 2:1.) What! Will you not go to Him and ask Him to give you of His abundance, when He has given you this promise, that as long as He has anything He will give it to you, for all He is and all He has is yours?

Oh, believer, do use Christ, I beseech you. There is nothing Christ dislikes more than for His people to make a show thing of Him and not to use Him. He loves to be worked. He is a great laborer; He always was for His Father, and now He loves to be a great laborer for His brethren. The more burdens you put on His shoulders the better He will love you. Cast your burden on Him. You will never know the sympathy of Christ's heart and the love of His soul so well as when you have heaved a very mountain of trouble from yourself to His shoulders, and have found that He does not stagger under the weight. Are your troubles like huge mountains of snow upon your spirit? Bid them rumble like an avalanche upon the shoulders of the Almighty Christ. He can bear them all away, and carry them into the depths of the sea. Do use your Master, for it is for this very purpose He was put into the covenant, that you might use Him whenever you need Him.

3. NOW, LASTLY, HERE IS A PRECEPT.

What shall the precept be? *Christ is ours; then you are Christ's, beloved.* You *are* Christ's, you know right well. You are His by your Father's donation when He gave you to the Son. You are His by His bloody purchase, when He counted down the price for your redemption. You are His by dedication, for you have dedicated yourselves to Him.

You are His by adoption, for you are brought to Him and made one of His brethren and joint-heirs with Him. I beseech you, labor, dear brethren, to show the world that you are His in practice. When tempted to sin, reply, "I cannot do this great wickedness. I cannot, for I am one of Christ's." When wealth is before you to be won by sin, touch it not; say that you are Christ's, or else you would take it; but now you cannot.

Tell Satan that you would not gain the world if you had to love Christ less. Are you exposed to difficulties and dangers in the world? Stand fast in the evil day, remembering that you are one of Christ's. Are you in a field where much is to be done, and others are sitting down idly and lazily, doing nothing? Go at your work, and when the sweat stands upon your brow and you are bidden to stop, say, "No, I cannot stop; I am one of Christ's. He had a baptism to be baptized with, and so have I, and I am staying until it is accomplished. I am one of Christ's. If I was not one of His, and purchased by blood, I might be like Issachar, crouching between two burdens; but I am one of Christ's." When the siren song of pleasure would tempt me from the path of right, reply, "Hush your strains, O temptress; I am one of Christ's. Your music cannot affect me; *I am not my own, I am bought with a price.*" (See 1 Corinthians 6:20 and 7:23.)

When the cause of God needs you, give yourself to it, for you are Christ's. When the poor need you, give yourself away, for you are one of Christ's. When, at any time there is much to be done for His Church and for His Cross, do it, remembering that you are one of Christ's. I beseech you, never misrepresent your profession. Do not go where others could say of you, "He cannot be Christ's"; but always be one whose speech is Christian, whose very expressions are Christ-like, whose conduct and conversation are so fragrant of Heaven, that all who see you may know that you are one of the Savior's and may recognize in you His features and His lovely countenance.

And now, dearly beloved hearers, I must say one word to those of you to whom I have not preached, for there are some of you who have never truly understood the vital importance of the covenant and the need to trust in it. I sometimes hear it whispered, and sometimes read that there are men who trust to the uncovenanted[5] mercies of God. Let me solemnly assure you that there is no such thing in Heaven as uncovenanted mercy; there is no such thing beneath God's sky or above it, as uncovenanted grace towards men. All you can receive, and all you ever ought to hope for, must be through the covenant of free grace, and that alone.

Perhaps, poor convinced sinner you do not dare accept the covenant today because you say it is not yours. Perhaps you are afraid it can never be yours because you are such an unworthy wretch. Let me ask you, can you lay hold on Christ? Do you dare do that? "Oh," you say, "I am too unworthy." No, dear soul, do you dare to touch the hem of His garment today? Do you dare to come close enough to Him to just touch the very hem of His garment that is trailing on the ground? Oh no, you say, "I dare not." "Why not, poor soul, why not? Can you not trust in Christ? Are not His mercies rich and free? Then say, poor soul, why not for thee?" *"I dare not come; I am so unworthy,"* you say. Hear, then; my Master bids you come, and will you be afraid after that?

---

5. Not bound by, promised, or guaranteed by a covenant.

> *"Come unto me, all ye that labour and are heavy laden, and I will give you rest" (Matthew 11:28).*
> *"This is a faithful saying, and worthy of all acceptation, that Christ Jesus came into the world to save sinners" (1 Timothy 1:15).*

Why do you dare not come to Christ? Oh, you are afraid He will turn you away! Listen carefully to what He says; *"Whosoever cometh unto me, I will in nowise cast out."* (See John 6:37.) You say, "I know He would cast me out." Come, then, and see if you can prove Him a liar. I know you cannot, but come and try. He has said *"whosoever."* *"But,"* you say, *"I am the blackest with sin."*

Nevertheless, He has said "whosoever": come along, blackest of the black. *"Oh,"* you say, *"but I am filthy."* Come along, filthy one, come and try Him, come and prove Him; remember He has said He will cast out none that come to Him by faith. Come and try Him. I do not ask you to lay hold on the whole covenant, you will do that by-and-by; but lay hold on Christ, and if you will do that, then you have the covenant. *"Oh, I cannot lay hold of Him,"* saith one poor soul. Well, then, lie prostrate at His feet, and beg of Him to lay hold of you. Do groan one groan, and say, "Lord, have mercy on me, a sinner!" Do sigh one sigh, and say, "Lord, save me, or I perish." Do let your heart say it, if your lips cannot. If grief, long smothered, burns like a flame within your bones, at least let one spark out. Now pray one prayer, and truly I say unto you, one sincere prayer shall most assuredly prove that He will save you. One true groan, where God has put it in the heart, is an earnest of His love; one true wish after Christ, if it is followed by sincere and earnest seeking of Him, shall be accepted of God, and you will be saved.

Come, soul, once more. Lay hold on Christ. *"Oh, but I dare not do it."* Now I was about to say a foolish thing; I was going to say that "I wish I was a sinner like you at this moment, and I think I would run before, and lay hold on Christ, and then say to you,

> *"Venture on Him, (tis no venture,) venture wholly,*
> *Let no other trust intrude;*
> *None but Jesus*
> *Can do helpless sinners good."*[6]

He can do you all the good you want; trust my Master. Oh yes, trust my Master; He is a precious Lord Jesus, He is a sweet Lord Jesus, He is a loving Savior, He is a kind and condescending forgiver of sin. Come, you filthy, black with sin; come, you poor; come, you dying; come, you lost—you who have been taught to feel your need of Christ, come all of you—come now for Jesus bids you come; come quickly. Lord Jesus, draw them, draw them by the Spirit! Amen.

---

6. Hymn: "Come Ye Sinners, Poor and Wretched." Lyrics by Joseph Hall, Music by Wm L. Viner.

CHAPTER 4

CHRIST—THE POWER AND WISDOM OF GOD

A Sermon
(No. 132)
Delivered on Sunday Morning, May 17, 1857,
by Reverend C. H. Spurgeon,
at the Music Hall, Royal Surrey Gardens,
London, England

"Christ the power of God, and the wisdom of God."
—1 Corinthians 1:24

Unbelief toward the Gospel of Jesus Christ is the most unreasonable thing in all the world, because the reason which the unbeliever gives for his unbelief is fairly met by the character and constitution of the Gospel of Jesus Christ. Notice that before this verse we read—*"The Jews required a sign, and the Greeks seek after wisdom."* (See 1 Corinthians 1:22.) If you met the Jew who believed not on Christ in the apostle's day, he would have said, "I cannot believe, because I want a sign;" and if you met the Greek, he would have said, "I cannot believe, because I want a philosophic system, one that is full of wisdom." "Now," says the apostle, "both these objections are *untenable*[1] and unreasonable. If you suppose that the Jew requires a sign, that sign is given him: Christ is the power of God. The

---

1. Incapable of being defended or justified.

miracles that Christ wrought upon Earth were signs more than sufficiently abundant; and if the Jewish people had but the will to believe, they would have found abundant signs and reasons for believing in the personal acts of Christ and His apostles." And let the Greeks say, "I cannot believe, because I require a wise system." O Greek, Christ is the wisdom of God. If you would but investigate the subject, you would find in it profoundness of wisdom—a depth where the most gigantic intellect might be drowned. It is no shallow gospel, it is a deep, and a great deep too, a deep which passes understanding. Your objection is ill founded; for Christ is the wisdom of God, and His gospel is the highest of all sciences. If you wish to find wisdom, you must find it in the word of revelation.

Now, this morning, we shall try to bring out these two thoughts of the gospel; and it may be that God shall bless what we say to the removing of the objection of either Jew or Greek; that the one requiring a sign may see it in the *power* of God in Christ, and that he who requires wisdom may behold it in the *wisdom* of God in Christ.

We shall understand our text in a threefold manner:

First—Christ, that is, *Christ personally*, is "the power of God and the wisdom of God."

Second—Christ, that is, *Christ's gospel*, is "the power of God and the wisdom of God."

Third—Christ, that is, *Christ in the heart—true religion*, is "the power of God and the wisdom of God."

1. CHRIST PERSONALLY

Christ considered as God and man, the Son of God equal with His Father, and yet the man, born of the Virgin Mary. Christ, in His complex person, is "the power of God and the wisdom of God." *He is the power of God from all eternity.* "By His word were the heavens made, and all the host of them." (See Psalm 33:6.) "The Word was God, and the Word was with God. . . . All things were made by him; and without him was not any thing made that was made." (See John 1:1-3.) The pillars of the Earth were placed in their everlasting sockets by the omnipotent right hand of Christ; the curtains of the heavens were drawn upon their rings of starry light by Him who was from everlasting the All-glorious Son of God. The orbs that float aloft in *ether*[2], those ponderous planets, and those mighty stars, were placed in their positions or sent rolling through space by the eternal strength of Him who is "the first and the last." "The Prince of the kings of the Earth." Christ is the power of God, for He is the Creator of all things, and by Him all things exist.

But *when He came to Earth*, took upon himself the fashion of a man, tabernacled in the inn, and slept in the manger, He still gave proof that He was the Son of God; not so much so when, as a newborn infant, long the immortal was the mortal and the infinite became a babe; not so much so in His youth, but afterward when He began His public ministry, He gave abundant proofs of His power and Godhead. The winds hushed by His finger uplifted, the waves calmed by His voice, so that they became solid as marble

---

2. Archaic: ancient Greek word meaning "upper air."

beneath Him. The tempest, cowering at His feet, as before a conqueror whom it knew and obeyed; these things, these stormy elements, the wind, the tempest, and the water, gave full proof of His abundant power. The lame man leaping, the deaf man hearing, the dumb man singing, the dead rising, these, again, were proofs that He was, the "power of God."

When the voice of Jesus startled the shades of Hades, and rent the bonds of death, with "Lazarus, come forth!" and when the carcass rotten in the tomb woke up to life, there was proof of His divine power and Godhead. A thousand other proofs He afforded; but we need not stay to mention them to you who have Bibles in your houses, and who can read them every day. At last He yielded up His life, and was buried in the tomb. Not long, however, did He sleep; for He gave another proof of His divine power and Godhead, when waking from His slumber, He frightened the guards with the majesty of His grandeur, not being held by the bonds of death, they being like green twigs before our conquering Samson, who had meanwhile pulled up the gates of hell, and carried them on His shoulders far away.

That He is the *power* of God *now*, Scripture very positively affirms, for it is written, *"he sitteth on the right hand of God."* (See Colossians 3:1.) He has the reins of Providence gathered in His hands; the fleet coursers of Time are driven by Him who sits in the chariot of the world, and bids its wheels run round; and He shall bid them stop when it shall please Him. He is the great umpire of all disputes, the great Sovereign Head of the Church, the Lord of Heaven, and death, and hell; and by-and-by we shall know that He shall come, "On fiery clouds and wings of wind, Appointed Judge of all mankind"; and then the quickened dead, the startled myriads, the divided firmaments, the "Depart, ye cursed," and the "Come, ye blessed," shall proclaim Him to be the power of God, who has power over all flesh, to save or to condemn, as it pleases Him.

But He is equally "the *wisdom* of God." The great things that He did *before all worlds* were proofs of His wisdom. He planned the way of salvation; He devised the system of atonement and substitution; He laid the foundations of the great plan of salvation. There was wisdom. But He built the heavens by wisdom, and He laid the pillars of light, upon which the firmament is balanced, by His skill and wisdom. Look at the world; and learn, as you see all its multitudinous proofs of the wisdom of God, and there you have the wisdom of Christ; for He was the creator of it. And *when He became a man*, He gave proofs enough of wisdom. Even in childhood, when He made the doctors sit abashed by the questions that He asked, He showed that He was more than mortal. (See Luke 2:46-47.)

And when the Pharisee and Sadducee and Herodian were all at last defeated, and their nets were broken, He proved again the superlative wisdom of the Son of God. And when those who came to take Him in the Garden of Gethsemane, stood transfixed by His eloquence, spell-bound by His marvelous oratory, there was again a proof that He was the wisdom of God, who could so bind the minds of men. And now that He intercedes before the throne of God, now that He is our Advocate before the throne, the pledge and surety for the blessed, now that the reins of government are in His hands, and are ever wisely directed, we have abundant proofs that the wisdom of God is in Christ, as well as the power of God.

Bow before Him, you that love Him; bow before Him,

you that desire Him! Crown Him, crown Him, crown Him! He is worthy of it, unto Him is everlasting might; unto Him is unswerving wisdom. Bless His name; exalt Him; clap your wings, you seraphs; cry aloud, you cherubim; shout, shout, shout, to His praise, you ransomed host above. And you, O men that know His grace, extol Him in your songs forever; for He is Christ, the power of God and the wisdom of God.

2. Christ's Gospel Is the Power and Wisdom of God

Christ's gospel is *a thing of divine power*. Do you want proofs of it? You shall not go far. How could Christ's gospel have been established in this world as it was, if it did not have in itself intrinsic might? By whom was it spread? By mitered prelates, by learned doctors, by fierce warriors, by caliphs, by prophets? No; by fishermen, untaught, unlettered; except as the Spirit gave them utterance, not knowing how to preach or speak. How did they spread it? By the bayonet, by their swords, by the keen metal of their blades? Did they drive their gospel into men at the point of the lance, and with the scimitar[3]? Say, did myriads rush to battle, as they did when they followed the crescent of Mohammed, and did they convert men by force, by law, by might? Ah, not so. Nothing but their simple words, their unvarnished eloquence, their rough declamation, their unpolished oratory; these it was, which, by the blessing of God's Spirit, carried the gospel around the world within a century after the death of its founder.

---

3. A curved oriental saber.

CHRIST—THE POWER AND WISDOM OF GOD

But what was this gospel which achieved so much? Was it a thing palatable to human nature? Did it offer a paradise of present happiness? Did it offer delight to the flesh and to the senses? Did it give charming prospects of wealth? Did it give licentious ideas to men? No; it was a gospel of strict morality, it was a gospel with delights entirely spiritual—a gospel which abjured[4] the flesh, which, unlike the coarse delusion of Joseph Smith[5], cut off every prospect from men of delighting themselves with the joys of lust. It was a gospel holy, spotless, clean as the breath of Heaven; it was pure as the wing of angel; not like that which spread of old, in the days of Mohammed, a gospel of lust, of vice, and wickedness, but pure, and consequently not palatable to human nature. And yet it spread. Why? My friends, I think the only answer I can give you is, because it has in it the power of God.

But do you want another proof? How has it been maintained since then? The gospel has had no easy path. The good ship of the Church has had to plow her way through seas of blood, and those who have manned her have been spattered with the bloody spray; yes, they have had to man her and keep her in motion, by laying down their lives unto the death. Read about the bitter persecution of the Church of Christ from the time of Nero to the days of Mary, and further on, through the days of Charles the Second, and of those kings of unhappy memory, who had not as yet learned how to spell "toleration." From the dragoons [6]of Claverhouse, to the gladiatorial shows of Rome, what a long series of persecutions has the gospel had! But, as the old divines used

---

4. Renounced.
5. Founder of the Latter Day Saint Movement and author of the Book of Mormon.
6. A European military unit of heavily armed cavalrymen in Claverhouse, an area of Dundee, Scotland.

to say, "The blood of the martyrs" has been "the seed of the Church." It has been, as the old herbalists had it, like the herb chamomile, the more it is trodden on, the more it grows; and the more the Church has been ill-treated, the more it has prospered. Behold the mountains where the Albigenses[7] walk in their white garments; see the stakes of Smithfield[8], not yet forgotten; behold the fields among the towering hills, where brave hands kept themselves free from despotic tyranny. Never forget the Pilgrim Fathers, driven by a government of persecution across the briny deep. See what vitality the gospel has. Plunge her under the wave, and she rises purer for her washing; thrust her in the fire, and she comes out brighter for her burning; cut her in sunder, and each piece shall make another church; behead her, and like the hydra[9] of old, she shall have a hundred heads for every one you cut away. She cannot die; she must live; for she has the power of God within her.

Do you want another proof? I give you a better one than the last. I do not wonder that the Church has outlived persecution so much as I wonder she has outlived the unfaithfulness of her professed teachers. Never was a church so abused as the Church of Christ has been, all through her history; from the days of Diotrephes mentioned in 3 John 1:9-12, who sought to have the pre-eminence, even to these later times, we can read of proud, arrogant prelates, and supercilious, haughty lords over God's inheritance. Bonners's, Dunstans's, and men of all sorts, have come into her ranks, and done all they could to kill her; and with their lordly

---

7. A Christian religious sect in France during the 12th and 13th centuries. Exterminated during the Inquisition.
8. Smithfield Fires, near Oxford in England. More than 300 persons burned at the stake in Smithfield during the Reformation in England.
9. A nine-headed snake in Greek mythology.

priest craft they have tried to turn her aside. And what shall we say to that huge apostasy of Rome? A thousand miracles that ever the Church outlived that! When her pretended head became apostate, and all her bishops disciples of hell, and she had gone far away, wonder of wonders, that she should come out, in the days of the glorious Reformation, and should still live. And, even now, when I mark the passiveness of many of my brethren in the ministry, and their utter and entire inefficiency of doing anything for God. When I see their waste of time, preaching now and then on the Sunday, instead of going to the highways and hedges and preaching the gospel everywhere to the poor. When I see the need of unction in the Church itself, and the need of prayerfulness. When I see wars and fighting, factions and disunions, and the hot blood and pride, even in the meetings of the saints, I say it is a thousand miracles that the Church of God should be alive at all, after the unfaithfulness of her members, ministers, and bishops. She has the power of God within her, or else she would have been destroyed; for she has enough within her own loins to work her destruction.

"But," someone says, "you have not yet proved it is the power of God to my understanding." Sir, I will give you another proof. There are those of you now present, who would be ready, I know, if it were necessary, to rise in your seats and bear me witness that I speak the truth. There are some who, not many months ago, were drunkards; some who lived loosely; men who were unfaithful to every vow which should keep man to truth, right, chastity, honesty, and integrity. Yes, I repeat, there are some here who look back to a life of detestable sin. You tell me, some of you, that for thirty years even (there is one such present now) you never listened to a gospel ministry, nor ever entered the house of God at all.

You despised the Sabbath, you spent it in all kinds of evil pleasures, you plunged headlong into sin and vice, and the only wonder is that God has not counted you out long ago; but here you are now, as different as light from darkness. I know your characters, and have watched you with a father's love; for, child though I am, I am the spiritual father of some here whose years outnumber mine by four times the number. I have seen some of you honest who were thieves, and some sober who were drunkards. I have seen the wife's glad eye sparkling with happiness; and many a woman has grasped me by the hand, shed her tears upon me, and said, "I bless God; I am a happy woman now; my husband is reclaimed, my house is blessed; our children are brought up in the fear of the Lord." Not one or two, but scores of such are here. And, my friends, if these are not proofs that the gospel is the power of God, I say there is no proof of anything to be had in the world, and everything must be conjecture.

Moreover, there worships with you this day (and if there be a secularist here, my friend will pardon me for alluding to him for a moment), there is in the house of God this day one who was a leader in your ranks, one who despised God, and ran very far away from right. And here he is! It is his honor this day to call himself a Christian; and I hope, when this sermon is ended, to grasp him by the hand, for he has done a valiant deed; he has bravely burned his papers in the sight of all the people, and has turned to God with full purpose of heart. I could give you proofs enough, if proofs were wanted, that the gospel has been to men the power of God and the wisdom of God. More proofs I could give, yes, thousands, one upon the other.

CHRIST'S GOSPEL IS THE WISDOM OF GOD

But we must notice the other points. Christ's gospel is the *wisdom* of God. Look at the gospel itself and you will see it to be wisdom. The man who scoffs and sneers at the gospel does so because he does not understand it and for no other reason. We have two of the richest books of theology still existing that were written by professed infidels before they wrote the books. You may have heard the story of Lord Lyttelton and Gilbert West; they were lawyers who determined to refute Christianity. One of them took up the subject of Paul's conversion, and the other, the subject of Christ's resurrection; they proceeded to write books to ridicule those two events, and the effect was, that in studying the subject, they both became Christians, and wrote books which are now a strong defense to the Church they hoped to have overthrown.

Every man who looks the gospel fairly in the face, and studies it as it should be studied, will discover that it is no false gospel, but a gospel that is replete with wisdom, and full of the knowledge of Christ. If any man finds objection to anything in the Bible, let him object. There are some men who can find no wisdom anywhere, except in their own heads. Such men, however, are no judges of wisdom. We should not send a mouse to explain the phenomena of astronomy, nor should we send a man who is so foolish as to do nothing but object and refuse to understand the wisdom of the gospel. A man should at least be honest, and have some share of sense, or we cannot dispute with him at all. Christ's gospel, to any man who believes it, is the wisdom of God.

Believing God's Word Honors One's Intellect

Allow me just to hint that to be a believer in the gospel is no dishonor to a man's intellect. While the gospel can be understood by the poorest and the most illiterate, there are shallows in it where a lamb may wade, there are depths where leviathan may swim. The intellect of the Philosopher John Locke found ample space in the gospel; the mind of Sir Isaac Newton submitted to receive the truth of inspiration as a little child, and found something in its majestic being higher than itself, unto which it could not attain. The rudest and most untaught have been enabled, by the study of the Holy Scripture of God's truth to enter the kingdom; and the most scholarly have said of the gospel, it surpasses thought.

I was thinking the other day what a vast amount of literature would be lost if the gospel were not true. No book was ever so suggestive as the Bible. Large, heavy books we have in our libraries which takes all our strength to lift, all upon holy Scripture; myriads upon myriads of smaller volumes, tens of thousands of every shape and size, all written about the Bible. I have thought that the very suggestiveness of Scripture, the supernatural suggestiveness of holy Writ, may be in itself a proof of its divine wisdom, since no man has ever been able to write a book which could have so many commentators and so many writers upon its text as the Bible has received.

3. CHRIST IN THE HEART IS THE POWER AND WISDOM OF GOD

Christ in a man, the gospel in the soul, is the power of God and the wisdom of God. We will picture the Christian from his beginning to his end. We will give a short map of his history. He begins there in that prison house, with huge iron bars he cannot file; in that dark, damp cell, where pestilence and death are bred. There, in poverty and nakedness, without a cup to put to his thirsty lips, without a mouthful even of dry crust to satisfy his hunger, that is where be begins—in the prison chamber of conviction, powerless, lost and ruined. I thrust my hand to him between the bars and give to him in God's name the name of Christ to plead. Look at him; he has been filing away at these bars many and many a day, without their yielding an inch; but now he has got the name of Christ upon his lips; he puts his hands upon the bars, and one of them is gone, and another, and another; and He makes a happy escape, crying, "I am free, I am free, I am free! Christ has been the power of God to me, in bringing me out of my trouble."

No sooner is he free, however, than a thousand doubts meet him. This one cries, "You are not elect"; another cries, "You are not redeemed"; another says, "You are not called"; another says, "You are not converted." "Go away" says he, "Go away! Christ died for me;" and he just pleads the name of Christ as the power of God, and the doubts flee away, and he walks straight on. He comes soon into the furnace of trouble; he is thrust into the innermost prison, and his feet are made fast in the stocks. God has put His hand upon him. He is in deep trouble; at midnight he begins to sing of

Christ; and the walls begin to totter, and the foundation of the prison starts to shake. Then the man's chains are taken off, and he comes out free; for Christ has delivered him from trouble.

Here is a hill to climb, on the road to Heaven. Wearily he pants up the side of that hill, and thinks he will die before he can reach the summit. The name of Jesus is whispered in his ear; he leaps to his feet, and pursues his way, with fresh courage, until the summit is gained, where he cries out, "Jesus Christ is the strength of my song; He also has become my salvation." See him again. All of a sudden he is set upon by many enemies; how shall he resist them? With this true sword, this true Jerusalem blade, Christ, and Him crucified. With this he keeps the devil at arm's length; with this he resists and fights against temptation, against lust, and against spiritual wickedness in high places. Now, he has come to his last struggle; the river Death rolls black and sullen before him; dark shapes rise upward from the flood and howl and fright him. How shall he cross the stream? How shall he find a landing place on the other side? Dread thoughts perplex him for a moment; he is alarmed; but he remembers, Jesus died for him; and catching up that watchword he ventures to the flood. Before his feet the Jordan flies apart; like Israel of old, he walks through, dry shod, singing as he goes to Heaven, "Christ is with me, Christ is with me, passing through the stream! Victory, victory, victory, to Him that loveth me!"

To the Christian in his own experience, Christ is forever the power of God. As for temptation he can meet that with Christ; as for trouble he can endure that through Christ who strengthens him; yes, he can say with Paul, *"I can do all things through Christ who strengthens me"* (see Philippians 4:13). Have you ever seen a Christian in trouble, a true

Christian? I have read a story of a man who was converted to God by seeing the conduct of his wife in the hour of trouble. They had a lovely child, their only offspring.

The father's heart doted on the child perpetually, and the mother's soul was knit up in the heart of the little one. The child lay sick upon its bed, and the parents watched it night and day. At last it died. The father had no God: he rent his hair; he rolled upon the floor in misery, wallowed upon the earth, cursing his being, and defying God in the utter casting down of his agony. There sat his wife, as fond of the child as he ever could be; and though tears would come, she gently said, "The Lord gave, and the Lord has taken away; blessed be the name of the Lord." "What," said he, starting to his feet, "do you not love that child? I thought that when that child died it would break your heart. Here am I, a strong man. I am mad: here are you, a weak woman, and yet you are strong and bold; tell me what possesses you?" Said she, "Christ is my Lord, I trust in Him; surely I can give this child to Him who gave himself for me." From that instant the man became a believer. "There must," he said, "be some truth and some power in the gospel, which could lead you to believe in such a manner, under such a trial." Christians, try to exhibit that spirit wherever you are, and prove to the world that in your experience at least "Christ is the power of God and the wisdom of God."

And now the last point. In the *Christian's experience*, Christ is wisdom, as well as power. If you want to be a thoroughly learned man the best place to begin, is to begin with the Bible, to begin with Christ. It is said that even children learn to read more quickly from the Bible than from any other book; and this I am sure of, that we, who are but grownup children will learn better and learn faster by beginning with Christ than we could by beginning with anything else. I remember saying once, and as I cannot say it better I will repeat it, that before I knew the gospel I gathered up a mixed mass of all kinds of knowledge from here, there, and everywhere; a bit of chemistry, a bit of botany, a bit of astronomy, and a bit of this, that, and the other. I put them altogether, in one great confused chaos.

When I learned the gospel, I got a shelf in my head to put everything away upon just where it should be. It seemed to me as if, when I had discovered Christ and Him crucified, that I got the center of the system, so that I could see every other science revolving around in order. From the Earth the planets appear to move in a very irregular manner—they are progressive, retrograde, stationary; but if you could get upon the sun, you would see them marching around in their constant, uniform, circular motion. It is the same with knowledge. Begin with any other science you like, and truth will seem to be awry. Begin with the science of Christ crucified, and you will begin with the sun, you will see every other science moving around it in complete harmony.

The greatest mind in the world will be evolved by beginning at the right end. The old saying is, "Go from nature up to nature's God"; but it is hard work going uphill. The best thing is to go from nature's God down to nature; and if you once get to nature's God, and believe Him and love Him, it is surprising how easy it is to hear music in the waves, and songs in the wild whisperings of the winds. You will start to see God everywhere, in the stones, in the rocks, in the rippling brooks, and hear Him everywhere, in the lowing of cattle, in the rolling of thunder, and in the fury of tempests. Get Christ first, put Him in the right place, and you will find Him to be the wisdom of God in your own experience.

But wisdom is not knowledge; and we must not confound the two. Wisdom is the right use of knowledge; and Christ's gospel helps us, by teaching us the right use of knowledge. It directs us. When a Christian has lost his way in dark woods, God's Word is a compass to him, and a lantern, too: he finds his way by Christ. He comes to a turn in the road. Which is right, and which is wrong? He cannot tell. Christ is the great signpost, telling him which way to go. Every day He sees new difficulties to attend to; he does not know which way to steer. Christ is the great pilot who puts His hand on the tiller, and makes him wise to steer through the shoals of temptation and the rocks of sin. Get the gospel, and you are a wise man. *"The fear of the Lord is the beginning of wisdom, and right understanding have they who keep his commandments"* (see Psalm 111:10). Ah! Christian, you have had many doubts, but you have had them all solved, when you have come to the Cross of Christ. You have had many difficulties; but they have been all explained in the light of Calvary. You have seen mysteries, when you have brought them to the face of Christ, made clear and manifest, which once you never could have known.

Allow me to remark here, that some people make use of Christ's gospel to illuminate their heads, instead of making use of it to illuminate their hearts. They are like the farmer Rowland Hill once described. The farmer is sitting, by the fire with his children; the cat is purring on the hearth, and they are all in great comfort. The plowman rushes in and cries, "Thieves! thieves! thieves!" The farmer rises up in a moment, grasps the candle, holds it up to his head, rushes after the thieves, and, says Rowland Hill, "he tumbles over a wheelbarrow, because he holds the light to his head, instead of holding it to his feet." So there are many who just hold religion up to illuminate their intellect, instead of holding it down to illuminate their practice; and so they make a sad tumble of it, and cast themselves into the mire, and do more hurt to their Christian profession in one hour than they will ever be able to retrieve. Take care that you make the wisdom of God, by God's Holy Spirit, a thing of true wisdom, directing your feet into His statutes, and keeping you in His ways.

And now a practical appeal and we will be done. I have been putting my arrow on the string; and if I have used any light similes, I have done so, just as the archer tips his arrow with a feather, to make it fly the better. I know that a rough quaint saying often sticks, when another thing is entirely forgotten. Now let us draw the bow, and send the arrow right at your hearts. Men, brethren, fathers, how many of you have felt in yourselves that Christ is the power of God, and the wisdom of God? Internal evidence is the best evidence in the world for the truth of the gospel. No Paley[10] or Butler[11] can prove the truth of the gospel as well as Mary, the servant girl yonder, that has got the gospel in her heart, and the power of it manifest in her life. Say, has Christ ever broken your bonds and set you free? Has He delivered you from your evil life, and from your sin? Has he given you "a good hope through grace," and can you now say, "On him I lean; on my beloved I stay myself?" If so, go away and rejoice: you are a saint; for the apostle has said, *"He is unto us who are saved, Christ the power of God and the wisdom of God."*

But if you cannot say this, allow me affectionately to warn you. If you do not want this power of Christ, and this wisdom of Christ now, you will want them in a few short

---
10. William Paley, English clergyman 1743-1805.
11. George Butler, Clergyman 1819-1890.

moments, when God shall come to judge the quick and the dead, when you shall stand before His judgment bar, and when all the deeds that you have done shall be read before an assembled world. You will want religion then. O that you had grace to tremble now; grace to *"kiss the Son, lest he be angry, and you perish from the way, when his wrath is kindled but a little"* (see Psalm 2:12). Hear how to be saved, and I will be done. Do you feel that you are a sinner? Are you conscious that you have rebelled against God? Are you willing to acknowledge your transgressions, and do you hate and abhor them, while at the same time you feel you can do nothing to atone for them? Then hear this. Christ died for you; and if He died for you, you cannot be lost. Christ died in vain for no man for whom He died.

If you are a penitent and a believer He died for you, and you are safe; go your way: rejoice "with joy unspeakable, and full of glory"; for He who has taught you your need of a Savior, will give you that Savior's blood to be applied to your conscience, and you shall before long be, with the yonder blood-washed host, praising God and the Lamb saying, "Hallelujah, forever, Amen!" Do you feel that you are a sinner? If not, I have no gospel to preach to you; I can but warn you. But if you feel your lost estate, and come to Christ, come, and welcome, for He will never cast you away.

CHAPTER 5

CHRIST LIFTED UP

A Sermon
(No. 139)
Delivered on Sunday Morning, July 5, 1857,
by Reverend Charles H. Spurgeon,
at the Music Hall, Royal Surrey Gardens,
London, England

"And I, if I be lifted up... will draw all men unto me."
—John 12:32

It was an extraordinary occasion upon which the Savior uttered these words. It was the crisis of the world. We very often speak of the "present crisis of affairs," and it is very common for persons of every period to believe their own age to be the crisis and turning point of the whole world's history. They rightly imagine that very much of the future depends upon their present exertions; but they wrongly stretch the thought, and imagine that the period of their existence is the very hinge of the history of the world: that it is the crisis. Now, however it may be correct, in a modified sense that every period of time is in some sense a crisis, yet there never was a time which could be truly called a crisis, in comparison with the season when our Savior spoke.

The Greatest Turning Point in the World's History

In the 31st verse, immediately preceding my text, we find in the English translation, "*Now is the judgment of this world*"; but we find in the Greek, "Now is the crisis of this world." The world had come to a solemn crisis: now was the great turning point of all the world's history. Should Christ die, or should He not? If He would refuse the bitter cup of agony, the world is doomed; if He should pass onward, do battle with the powers of death and hell and come off a victor, then the world is blessed, and her future shall be glorious. Will He succumb? Then the world would be crushed and ruined beneath the trail of the old serpent. Will He conquer? Will He lead captivity captive and receive gifts for men? Then this world shall yet see times when there shall be "*a new heaven and a new earth, wherein dwelleth righteousness.*" (See 2 Peter 3:13.) "Now is the crisis of this world!" "The crisis," He says, "is two-fold. Dealing with Satan and men. I will tell you the result of it. '*Now shall the prince of this world be cast out*' (John 12:31). Fear not that hell shall conquer. I shall cast him out; and, `on the other hand doubt not but that I shall be victorious over the hearts of men. '*I, if I be lifted up, will draw all men unto me*'" (see John 12:32). Remembering the occasion upon which these words were uttered, we shall now proceed to a discussion of them.

We have three things to notice.

First—Christ crucified, Christ's glory. He calls it a lifting Him up.

Second—Christ crucified, the minister's theme. It is the minister's business to lift Christ up in the gospel.

Third—Christ crucified, the heart's attraction. *"I, if I be lifted up, will draw all men unto me."*

His own glory—the minister's theme—the heart's attraction.

1. Christ's Crucifixion Is Christ's Glory

He uses the word "lifted up" to express the manner of His death. *"I, if I be lifted up, will draw all men unto me. This He said, signifying what death He should die"* (see John 12:32-33). But notice the choice of the word to express His death. He does not say, I, if I be crucified; I, if I be hanged on the tree; no, but "I, if I be lifted up": and in the Greek there is the meaning of exaltation. "I, if I be exalted—I if I be lifted on high." He took the outward and visible fashion of the Cross, it being a lifting of Him up, to be the type and symbol of the glory with which the Cross would give to Him. *"I, if I be lifted up."*

Now, *the Cross of Christ is Christ's glory.* We will show you how. Man seeks to win his glory by the slaughter of others—Christ by the slaughter of himself; men seek to get crowns of gold—He sought a crown of thorns; men think that glory lies in being exalted over others—Christ thought that His glory laid in becoming *"a worm and no man,"* a scoff and reproach amongst all that beheld Him. (See Psalm 22:6.) He stooped when He conquered; and He knew that the glory lay as much in the stooping as in the conquest.

Christ was glorified on the Cross, we say, first, *because love is always glorious*. If I might prefer any glory, I would ask to be beloved by men. Surely, the greatest glory that a man can have among his fellows is not that of mere admiration, when they stare at him as he passes through the street, and throng the avenues to behold him as he rides in his triumph; the greatest fame, the greatest glory of a patriot is the love of his country—to feel that young men and maidens, old men and sires, are prepared to fall at his feet in love, to give up all they have to serve him who has served them.

Now, Christ won more love by the Cross than He did ever win elsewhere. O Lord Jesus, you would never have been so much loved if you had sat in Heaven forever, as you are now loved since you have stooped to death. Not cherubim and seraphim, and angels clad in light, could ever have loved with hearts so warm as your redeemed above, or even your redeemed below. You won love more abundantly by the nail than by your scepter. Your open side brought you no emptiness of love, for your people love you with all their hearts. Christ won glory by His Cross. He was never so lifted up as when He was cast down; and the Christian will bear witness, that though he loves his Master everywhere, yet nothing moves his heart to the rapture and intensity of love, like the story of the crucifixion and the agonies of Calvary.

Christ's Fortitude

Christ at this time won much glory *by fortitude*. The Cross was a trial of Christ's fortitude and strength, and it was a garden in which His glory was planted. The laurels of His crown were sown in a soil that was saturated with His own blood. Sometimes the ambitious soldier pants for battle, because in days of peace he cannot distinguish himself. "Here I sit," he says, "and rust my sword in my scabbard, and win no glory; let me rush to the cannon's mouth; though some call honor a faded trinket, it may be so, yet I am a soldier, and I want it "and he pants for the encounter that he may win glory. Now, in an infinitely higher sense than that poor glory which the soldier gets, Christ looked upon the Cross as being His way to honor. "Oh!" He said, "now shall be the time of my endurance: I have suffered much, but I shall suffer , and then shall the world see what a strong heart of love I have; how patient is the Lamb, how mighty to endure. Never would Christ have had such glorious praise and such songs of honor as He has now won, if He had avoided the conflict, the battle, and the agony. We might have blessed Him for what He is and for what He wished to do. We might have loved Him for the very longings of His heart but we never could have praised Him for His strong endurance, His intrepid spirit, His unconquerable love, if we had not seen Him put to the severe test of crucifixion and the agonies of that awful day. Christ won glory by being crucified.

THE WORK OF GRACE COMPLETED

Christ looked upon His crucifixion *as the completion of all His work,* and therefore He looked upon it as an exaltation. The completion of an enterprise is the harvest of its honor. Though thousands have perished in the arctic regions, and have obtained fame for their intrepid conduct, yet, my friends, the man who at last discovers the passage is the most of all honored. We shall forever remember those bold men who pushed their way through winter in all its might, and dared the perils of the deep, yet the man who accomplishes the deed wins more than his share of the glory. Surely the accomplishment of an enterprise is just the point where the honor hangs. And, my hearers, Christ longed for the Cross, because He looked for it as the goal of all His exertions. It was to be the place upon which He could say, *"It is finished"* (John 19:30). He could never say *"It is finished"* on His throne: but on His Cross He did cry it.

He preferred the sufferings of Calvary to the honors of the multitude that crowded round about Him; for, preach as He might, and bless them as He might, and heal them as He might, still His work was not done. He was determined; He had a baptism to be baptized with, and He longed for His glorious work to be accomplished. "But," He said, "now I pant for my Cross, for it is the cornerstone of my labor. I long for my sufferings, because they shall be the completion of my great work of grace." Brethren, it is the end that brings the honor; it is the victory that crowns the warrior rather than the battle. And so Christ longed for this, His death, that He might see the completion of His labor. "And I," He said, "when I am crucified, I am exalted, and lifted up."

Christ's Hour of Triumph

And, once again, Christ looked upon His crucifixion with the eye of firm faith *as the hour of triumph*. His disciples thought that the Cross would be a degradation; Christ looked through the outward and visible, and beheld the spiritual. "The Cross," He said, "the gallows of my doom may seem to be cursed with shame and the world shall stand round and hiss at the crucified; my name forever dishonored as one who died upon the tree; and unbelievers and scoffers may forever throw this in the teeth of my friends that I died with the malefactor; but I look not at the Cross as you do. I know its disgrace, but I despise the shame—I am prepared to endure it all. I look upon the Cross as the gate of triumph, as the portal of victory. Oh, shall I tell you what I shall behold upon the Cross?—just when my eye is swimming with the last tear, and when my heart is palpitating with its last pang; just when my body is rent with its last shudder of anguish, then my eye shall see the head of the dragon broken, it shall see hell's towers dismantled and its castle fallen.

"My eye shall see my seed eternally saved, I shall behold the ransomed coming from their prison houses. In that last moment of my doom, when my mouth is just preparing for its last cry of 'It is finished; I shall behold the year of my redeemed come, I shall shout my triumph in the delivery of all my beloved! Yes, and I shall then see the world, my own Earth conquered, and usurpers all dethroned, and I shall behold in vision the glories of the latter days, when I shall sit upon the throne of my father, David, and judge the Earth, attended with the pomp of angels and the shouts of my beloved!" Yes, Christ saw in His Cross the victories of it, and therefore He did pant and long for it as being the place of victory and the means of conquest. "I," said Jesus, "if I be lifted up, if I be exalted," He puts His crucifixion as being His glory. This is the first point of our text.

2. CHRIST CRUCIFIED, THE MINISTER'S THEME

Not shameful, but truly honorable; there is a lifting of Him upon the pole of the gospel, in the preaching of the Word. Christ Jesus is to be lifted up every day; for that purpose He came into the world: *"That like as Moses lifted up the serpent in the wilderness,"* even so He might by the preaching of the truth be lifted up, *"that whosoever believeth in him should not perish, but have everlasting life."* (See John 3:14-15.).

In opposition to a thousand other things which most men choose, I would prefer that the most prominent feature in my ministry would be the preaching of Christ Jesus. Christ should be most prominent, *not hell and damnation*. God's ministers must preach God's terrors as well as God's mercies; we are to preach the thunder of God's law. If men sin, we are to tell them that they must be punished for it. If they transgress, woe unto the watchman who is ashamed to say, "The Lord comes who takes vengeance." We would be unfaithful to the solemn charge which God has given us if we were to wickedly stifle all the threatening of God's Word.

Does God say, "The wicked shall be cast into hell, with all the nations that forget God?" It is our business to say so. Did the loving Savior talk of the pit that burns, of the worm that never dies, and of the fire that can never be extinguished? It is ours to speak as He spoke, and not to soften the matter. It is no mercy to men to hide their doom. But, my brethren, terrors never ought to be the prominent feature of a minister's preaching. Many old divines thought they would do a great deal of good by preaching this. I do not believe it. Some souls are awakened and terrified by such preaching; they however, are but few.

Sometimes, right solemnly, the sacred mysteries of eternal wrath must be preached, but far oftener let us preach the wondrous love of God. There are more souls won by wooing than by threatening. It is not hell, but Christ, we desire to preach. O sinners, we are not afraid to tell you of your doom, but we do not choose to be forever dwelling on that doleful theme. We would rather love to tell you of Christ, and Him crucified. We want to have our preaching full of the frankincense of the merits of Christ than of the smoke, and fire, and terrors of Mount Sinai, we are not come unto Mount Sinai, but unto Mount Zion—where milder words declare the will of God, and rivers of salvation are abundantly flowing.

PREACH CHRIST FIRST... THEN DOCTRINE

Again, the theme of a minister should be Christ Jesus in opposition to *mere doctrine*. Some of my good brethren are always preaching doctrine. Well, they are right in so doing, but I would not care myself to have as the characteristic of my preaching, doctrine only. I would rather have it said, "He dwelt much upon the person of Christ, and seemed best pleased when he began to tell about the atonement and the sacrifice. He was not ashamed of the doctrines, he was not afraid of threatening, but he seemed as if he preached the threatening with tears in his eyes. He preached the doctrine solemnly as God's own Word; but when he preached of Jesus his tongue was loosed, and his heart was at liberty."

Brethren, there are some men who preach the doctrine

only, who are an injury, I believe to God's Church rather than a benefit. I know of men who have set themselves up as umpires over all spirits. They are *the* men. Wisdom will die with them. If they were once taken away the great standard of truth would be removed. We do not wonder that they hate the Pope, two of a trade never agree, for they are far more popish than he, they being themselves infallible. I am afraid that very much of the soundness of this age, is but a mere sound, and is not real; does not enter into the eye of the heart, nor affect the being. Brethren, we would rather preach Christ than election. We love election, we love predestination, we love the great doctrines of God's Word, but we would rather preach Christ than preach these. We desire to put Christ over the head of the doctrine, we make the doctrine the throne for Christ to sit on, but we dare not put Christ at the bottom, and then press Him down, and overload Him with the doctrines of His own Word.

Preach Christ... Then Morality

And again, the minister ought to preach Christ in opposition to *mere morality*. How many ministers in London could preach as well out of Shakespeare as the Bible, for all they want is a moral maxim. The good man never thinks of mentioning regeneration. He sometimes talks of moral renovation. He does not think of talking about perseverance by grace. No, continuance in doing well is his perpetual cry. He does not think of preaching "believe and be saved." No; his continual exhortation is, "Good Christian people, say your prayers, and behave well, and by these means you shall enter the Kingdom of Heaven." The sum and substance of his gospel is that we can do very well without Christ, that although certainly there is a little amiss in us, yet if we just mend our ways in some little degree, that old text, *"except a man be born again"* (John 3:3), need not trouble us.

If you want to be made drunkards, if you want to be made dishonest, if you want to be taught every vice in the world, go and hear a moral preacher. These gentlemen, in their attempts to reform and make people moral, are the men that lead them from morality. Hear the testimony of holy Bishop Lavington[1], "We have long been attempting to reform the nation by moral preaching. With what effect! None. On the contrary, we have dexterously preached the people into downright infidelity. We must change our voice; we must preach Christ and Him crucified; nothing but the gospel is the power of God unto salvation."

PREACH CHRIST...
THEN ENCOURAGE LEARNING

And yet one more remark. The minister ought to preach Christ in opposition to some who think they ought to preach *learning*. God forbid we should ever preach against learning. The more of it a man can get, the better for him; and the better for his hearers if he has grace enough to use it well, but there are some who have so much learning, that if in the course of their readings they find a very hard word, out comes the pencil case: they note it down, to be glorified in the next Sunday morning's sermon. Do they find out some outlandish German expression, which, if pulled to pieces,

---

1. Bishop George Lavington, 1684-1762, Episcopal Bishop of Exeter.

would mean nothing, but looks as if it must be something wonderful, that must always come out, even if the gospel is secondary? You ought to pray to God that the preacher may never be allowed to read anything but their Bibles all the week because then you might hear something you could understand. However, this would not suit his reference, if he could be understood; he would not be a great preacher, for a great preacher, according to the opinion of some, is a man who is called intellectual. An intellectual is one who knows more about the Bible than the Bible knows about itself, a person who can explain all mysteries by intellect merely, who smiles at anything like unction and savor, or the influence of God's Spirit as being mere fanaticism.

Intellect with him is everything. You sit and listen to him, then you go out and say, "Dear me, what a remarkable man he is. I suppose he made something out of the text, but I did not know what it was. He seemed to me to be in a fog himself although I admit it was an extremely luminous haze." Then people will go again, and be sure to take a pew in that church, because they say he is such a clever man. The only reason is because they cannot understand him. I read a book on advice to ministers the other day, it stated, and very gravely too, by some good old tutor of a college, "Always have one part of your sermon which the vulgar cannot comprehend, because in that way you will have a name for learning, and what you say that they can understand, will impress them the more, for by putting in a sentence or two which is incomprehensible, you at once strike their minds as being a superior person, and they believe in the weight and the authority of your learning, and therefore, give credence to the rest which they can comprehend."

Now, I believe that is all wrong. Christ wants us not to

preach *learning,* but to preach the good word of life in the simplest manner possible. Why, if I could only get lords and ladies to listen to me, by preaching to them so that they alone could understand me, there they might go, and I would not so much as snap my finger for them all. I would desire to preach so that the servant maid can understand, that the coachman can understand, that the poor and illiterate may hear readily and gladly receive the Word. This is an important truth, very little good will come to the ministry until it is simplified, and until our brethren learn one language, which they do not seem to know. Latin, Greek, French, Hebrew, and twenty other languages they know. There is one I would recommend to their very serious study—it is called Anglo-Saxon. If they would just try and learn that, it is astonishing what a mighty language they would find it to move the hearts of men. Saxon before every language in the world. When every other has died out for want of power, Saxon will live, and triumph with its iron tongue, and its voice of steel. We must have the common, plain language in which to address the people. And moreover, we must have Christ lifted up, Christ crucified, without the embellishment and words of little value and significance, and without the trappings of attempted eloquence or oratory. If Christ Jesus is earnestly preached He will draw all men unto Him.

3. The Essence of the Text, the Attracting Power of the Cross of Christ

If Christ is thus preached, thus fully held forth, thus simply proclaimed to the people, the effect will be that He will draw all men unto Him. Now, I will show the attracting power of Christ in three or four ways. Christ draws *like a trumpet* attracting men to hear the proclamation. Christ draws *like a net* bringing men out of the sea of sin. Christ draws, also, *with bonds of love*. In the next place, Christ attracts *like a standard,* bringing all the soldiers around Him, and, in the last place, Christ draws *like a chariot.* "I, if I be lifted up, I will draw all men unto me."

CHRIST DRAWS AS A TRUMPET

First, I said that Christ draws *as a trumpet.* Men have always sounded a trumpet to attract an audience to the reading of a proclamation. The people come from their houses at the well-known sound, to listen to what they desire to know. Now, my brethren, part of the attractive power of the gospel lies in the attracting people to hear it. You cannot expect people to be blessed by the preaching of the gospel if they do not hear it. One part of the battle is to get them to listen to its sound. Now, the question is asked in these times, "How are we to get the working class to listen to the Word?" The answer is, Christ is His own attraction, and Christ himself is the only trumpet you need. Preach the gospel, and the people of the congregation will come on their own. The only infallible way of getting a good congregation, is to do this. "Oh!" said a Socinian[2] once, to a good Christian minister, "I cannot make it out; my chapel is always empty, and yours always crammed full. And yet, I am sure mine is the more rational doctrine, and

---
2. Socinian belief influenced the development of the Unitarian theology.

you are not by any means so talented a preacher as I am." "Well," said the other, "I will tell you the reason why your chapel is empty, and mine full. The people have a conscience, and that conscience tells them that what I preach is true and that what you preach is false, so they will not hear you." You may look through the history of this realm ever since the commencement of the days of Protestantism, and I will dare to say it without fear of contradiction, that you will almost in every case find that the men who have attracted the greatest mass of people to hear them, have been men who were the most evangelical—who preached the most about Christ and Him crucified.

What was there in Whitefield to attract an audience, except the simple gospel preached with a vehement oratory that carried everything before it? Oh, it was not his oratory, but the gospel that drew the people. There is a something about the truth that always makes it popular. If someone were to you tell me that if a man preaches the truth his chapel will be empty. I would say, "Sir, I defy you to prove that." Christ preached His own truth, and the common people heard Him gladly, and the multitude flocked to listen to Him.

My good ministering brother, have you got an empty church? Do you want to fill it? I will give you a good recipe, and if you will follow it, you will, in all probability, have your chapel full to the doors. Burn all your manuscripts, that is number one. Give up your notes, that is number two. Read your Bible and preach it as you find it in the simplicity of its language. And give up all your Latinized English. Begin to tell the people what you have felt in your own heart, and beseech the Holy Spirit to make your heart as hot as a furnace for zeal. Then go out and talk to the people. Speak to them like their brother. Be a man amongst men. Tell them what you have felt and what you know, and tell it heartily with a good, bold face; and, my dear friend, I do not care who you are, you will get a congregation.

But if you say, "Now, to get a congregation, I must buy an organ." That will not serve you a bit. "But we must have a good choir." I would not care to have a congregation that comes because of a good choir. "No," says another, "but really I must alter my style of preaching." My dear friend, it is not the style of preaching, it is the style of feeling. People sometimes begin to mimic other preachers, because they are successful. Why, the worst preachers are those who mimic others, whom they look upon as standards. Preach naturally. Preach out of your hearts just what you feel to be true, and the old soul-stirring words of the gospel will soon draw a congregation. *"Where the body is, thither will the eagles be gathered together."* (See Luke 17:37.)

CHRIST IS THE NET THAT DRAWS MEN

But if it ended there, what would be the good of it? If the congregation came and listened to the sound, and then went away unsaved, of what use would it be? But in the next place, Christ acts *as a net* to draw men unto Him. The gospel ministry is, in God's Word, compared to a fishery; God's ministers are the fishermen, they go to catch souls, as fishermen go to catch fish. How shall souls be caught? They shall be caught by preaching Christ. Just preach a sermon that is full of Christ, and throw it unto your congregation, as you throw a net into the sea—you need not look where they are, nor try to fit your sermon to different cases; but, throw it in, and as sure as God's Word is what it is, it shall not return to Him void. It will accomplish that which He pleases, and prosper in the thing whereto He has sent it. The gospel has never been unsuccessful yet, when it was preached with the demonstration of the Spirit and of power. It is not fine orations upon the death of princes, or the movements of politics that will save souls. If we wish to have sinners saved and to have our churches increased; if we desire the spread of God's Kingdom, the only thing whereby we can hope to accomplish the end, is the lifting up of Christ; for, "I, if I be lifted up, will draw all men unto me."

CHRIST DRAWS MAN WITH CORDS OF LOVE

In the next place, Christ Jesus draws *as the cords of love*. After men are saved, they are still apt to go astray; it needs a cord to reach all the way from a sinner to Heaven; and it needs to have a hand pulling at him all the way. Now, Christ Jesus is the bead of love that draws the saint to Heaven. O child of God, you would go astray again if Jesus did not hold you fast; if He did not draw you to himself you would still wander. Christian people are like our Earth. Our world has two forces, it has one tendency to run off at a tangent from its orbit; but the sun draws it by a centripetal power and attracts it to itself, and so between the two forces it is kept in a perpetual circle. Oh! Christian, you will never walk right, and keep in the orbit of truth, if it were not for the influence of Christ perpetually attracting you to the center. You feel, and if you do not always feel, it is still there, —you feel an attraction between your heart and Christ, and Christ is perpetually drawing you to himself, to His likeness, to His character, to His love, to His bosom, and in that way you are kept from your natural tendency to fly off and be lost in the wide fields of sin. Bless God, that Christ lifted up draws all His people unto Him in that fashion.

Christ Is the Center of Attraction

And now, in the next place Christ Jesus is the center of attraction; even *as a standard* is the center of gathering. We want unity in these days; we are now crying out, "away with sectarianism." O for unity! There are some of us who truly pant after it. We do not talk about an evangelical alliance; alliances are made between men of different countries. We believe that the phrase "Evangelical Alliance" is a faulty one,—it should be "Evangelical Union,"—knit together in Union. Why! I am not in alliance with a brother of the Church of England; I would not be in alliance with him if he were ever so good a man! I would be in union with him, I would love him with all my heart, but I would not make a mere alliance with him. He never was my enemy, he never will be; and, therefore, it is not an alliance I want with him,—it is a union.

And so with all God's people, they do not care about alliances; they love real union and communion one with another. Now, what is the right way to bring all the churches to union? "We must revise the prayer book," says one. You may revise it, and revise it as long as you like, you will never bring some of us to agree to it, for we hate Prayer Books as such, however close to perfection they may be. "Well then, we must revise the doctrines, so that they may meet all classes." You cannot; that is impossible. "Well then, we must revise the discipline." Yes, sweep the dirt from the stable. And then after that, the majority of us will stand as much aloof as ever. "No, but each of us must make mutual concession." Indeed, I wonder who will, except the Vicars of Bray[3], who have no principle at all. For if we have to make mutual concession, who can guarantee that I must not concede a part of what I believe to be true? And that I cannot do, nor can my brother on the opposite side. The only standard of union that can ever be lifted up in England is the Cross of Christ.

As soon as we shall begin to preach Christ and Him crucified, we shall all be one. We can fight anywhere except at the foot of the Cross,—there it is that the order goes forth": sheath swords." And those that were bitter combatants before, come and prostrate themselves there, and say, "You dear Redeemer, you have melted us into one." Oh my brethren, let us all preach the gospel mightily, and there will be union. The Church of England is becoming more united with dissenters. Our good friends at Exeter Hall have gone a very long way to bless the world, and uproot the exclusiveness of their own system. As sure as they are alive they have taken the most excellent step in the world to pull down the absurd pretensions of some of their own brethren, to the exclusive claim of being "the Church." I glory and rejoice in it! I bless God for that movement, and I pray that the day may come when every bishop may do the same. And I do not glory in it merely because I look upon it as the beginning of union, but because of the preaching of the gospel.

But, at the same time, I know this, let their example be followed, and the barriers between dissenters and the Church of England are not tenable. Even the nationality of

---

3. Satirical men with no firm principles.

Episcopacy[4] must yet come down. If my lord, the bishop of so and so, is to have so many thousands a year for preaching to a number of people in Exeter Hall, I have as much right as he has to a State grant, for I serve as many Englishmen as he does. There is no one church in the world that has any right to take a farthing of national money any more than I have. And if there are ten thousand gathered here, it is an unrighteous thing that we should have no subsidy from the State, when a paltry congregation of thirteen and a half in the City of London is to be supported out of national money. The thing cannot be held long, it is impossible; Christ's Church will one day reject the patronage of the State. Let all of us begin to preach the gospel, and we shall soon see that the gospel is self-supporting; and that the gospel does not want entrenchments of bigotry and narrow-mindedness, in order to make it stand. No, we shall say, "brother, there is my pulpit for you. You are an Episcopalian; preach in my pulpit, you are welcome."

The Episcopalian will say, "You are a Baptist, and my brother, there is the parish church for you." And I just announce that the first chance I get to preach in a parish church, I will do it, and risk the consequence. They are our structures, they all belong to England, we can give them to whom we please, and if tomorrow the will of the sovereign people should transfer those edifices to another denomination, there is nothing in the world that can prevent it. But if not, by what law of Christian love is one denomination to shut its pulpit doors against every other?

Many of my dear friends in the Episcopal Church are willing to lend their edifices, but they dare not. But remember

---

4. The collective body of bishops.

this, when the gospel is preached fully, all those things will be broken down. For one brother will say, "My dear friend, you preach Christ and so do I, I cannot shut you out of my pulpit." And another will cry, "I am anxious for the salvation of souls, and so are you. Come into my house, come into my heart. I love you." The only means of unity we shall ever get will be all of us preaching Christ crucified; when that is done, when every minister's heart is in the right place, full of anxiety for souls. When every minister feels that, whether he is called to be a bishop, presbyter, or preacher—all he wants to do is to glorify God and win souls to Jesus, then, my dear friends, we can maintain our denominational distinctions, but the great bugbear of bigotry and division will have ceased and schism will no more be known.

For that day I anxiously pray, may God send it in His own time. As far as I am concerned there is my hand for every minister of God in creation, and my heart with it, I love all them that love the Lord Jesus Christ. And I feel persuaded that the nearer we all come to the one point of putting Christ first, Christ last, Christ midst, and Christ without end—the nearer we shall come to the unity of the one Church of Christ in the bond of holy permanence.

CHRIST'S ARMS ARE THE CHARIOT THAT BRINGS ALL MEN TO HEAVEN

And now I close by noticing the last sweet thought—*"I, if I be lifted up, will draw all men unto me."* Then Christ Jesus will draw all His people to Heaven; He says He will draw them unto himself. He is in Heaven; then *Christ is the chariot* in which souls are drawn to Heaven. The people of the Lord are on their way to Heaven, they are carried in everlasting arms; and those arms are the arms of Christ. Christ is carrying them up to His own house, to His own throne; by His prayer—*"Father, I will that they, whom thou hast given me be with me where I am,"* shall be wholly fulfilled. (See John 17:24.) And it is fulfilling now, for He is like a strong courser drawing His children in the chariot of the covenant of grace unto himself. Oh blessed be God, the Cross is the plank on which we swim to Heaven; the Cross is the great covenant transport which will weather out the storms, and reach its desired Heaven. This is the chariot, the pillars are of gold, and the bottom is silver; it is lined with the purple of the atonement of our Lord Jesus Christ.

And now, poor sinner, I pray to God Christ would pardon you; remember His death on Calvary, remember His agonies and bloody sweat—all this He did for you; if you feel yourself to be a sinner. Does this not draw you to Him?

*"Though thou art guilty he is good,
He'll wash thy soul in Jesus' blood."*

You have rebelled against Him, and revolted, but He says, "return, backsliding children." Will His love not draw you? I pray that both may have their power and influence that you may be drawn to Christ now and at last be drawn to Heaven. May God give a blessing for Jesus' sake. Amen.

CHAPTER 6

CHRIST GLORIFIED AS THE BUILDER OF HIS CHURCH

A Sermon
(No. 191)
Delivered on Sunday Morning, May 2, 1858,
by Reverend Charles H. Spurgeon,
at the Music Hall, Royal Surrey Gardens,
London, England

"He shall build the temple of the Lord; and he shall bear the glory."—Zechariah 6:13

*"There's music in all things, if men had ears;
The earth is but the music of the spheres."*
—Lord George G. Byron

Heaven sings eternally. Angels and redeemed saints before the throne of God extol His name. And this world is singing too; sometimes with the loud noise of the rolling thunder, the boiling sea, the dashing waterfall, and the lowing cattle; and often with that still, solemn harmony that flows from the vast creation, when in its silence it praises God. Such is the song that gushes in silence from the mountain lifting its head to the sky, covering its face sometimes with the wings of mist, and at other times unveiling its snow-white brow before its Maker. It reflects His sunshine back to Him, gratefully thanking Him for the light with which it has been made to glisten, and for the gladness of which it is the solitary spectator, as in its grandeur it looks down upon the laughing valleys. The tune to which Heaven and Earth are set, is the same. In Heaven they sing, "The Lord be exalted; let His name be magnified forever." And the Earth sings the same: "Great are you in your works, O Lord and unto you be glory!" It would seem, therefore, a strange anomaly if the Church, the temple of the living God, were without song, and we bless God that such an anomaly does not exist, for *"day and night they serve God in his temple."* (See Revelation 7:15.) And while it is true the ceaseless circles of the starry heavens are praising Him without ceasing, it is also true that the stars of Earth, the churches of the Lord Jesus Christ, are each of them eternally singing their hymns of praise to Him.

Today, in this house, thousands of voices shout His name, and when the sun of today shall set, it shall rise upon another land, where Christian hearts awakened, will begin to praise as we have just concluded. And tomorrow when we enter upon the business of the week, we will praise Him when we rise, we will praise Him when we retire to rest, and we will solace ourselves with the sweet thought, that when the link of praise here is covered with darkness after the setting sun, another golden link is sparkling in the sunshine in the lands where the sun is just rising.

Notice how the music of the Church is set to the same tune as that of Heaven and Earth—"Great God, thou art to be magnified." Is this not the unanimous song of all the redeemed below? When we sing, is this not the sole burden of our hosannas and hallelujahs?—*"Unto him that liveth and sitteth upon the throne, unto him be glory, world without end."* (See Ephesians 3:21.) Now, my text is one note of the song. May God help me to understand, and also make you understand it. *"He shall build the temple of the Lord, and he shall bear the glory."* We all know that the Lord Jesus Christ is here alluded to, for the context runs—"Behold the man, whose name is the Branch"—which title is ever applied to the Messiah, Jesus Christ of Nazareth. *"He grew up out of his place, and he shall build the temple of the Lord; even he shall build the temple of the Lord, and he shall bear the glory, and shall sit and rule upon his throne; and he shall be a priest upon his throne: and the counsel of peace shall be between them both."* (See Zechariah 6:12-13.)

Now we shall notice this morning:

First of all, the *temple,* that is the Church of Christ.

Second, we shall notice next, its *builder*—"He," that is Jesus, "shall build the temple."

Third, we shall stop a moment and pause to admire his *glory,*—"He shall bear the glory."

Fourth, we shall attempt, under the good hand of the Holy Spirit, to make some *practical applications of the subject.*

1. THE FIRST POINT IS THE TEMPLE.

The temple is the Church of God; and here let me begin by just observing, that when I use the term "Church of God," I use it in a very different sense from that in which it is sometimes understood. It is usual with many Church of England people, to use the term "church" as specially applying to the bishops, archdeacons, rectors, curates, and so forth: these are said to be the church and the young man who becomes a pastor of any congregation is said to "enter the church." Now I believe that such a use of the term is not scriptural. I would never for one moment grant to any man that the ministers of the gospel constitute the church. If you speak of the army, the whole of the soldiers constitute it; the officers may sometimes be spoken of first and foremost, but still the private soldier is as much a part of the army as the highest officer.

And it is so in the Church of God, all Christians constitute the Church. Any company of Christian men, gathered together in holy bonds of communion for the purpose of receiving God's ordinances, and preaching what they regard to be God's truths, is a church; and the whole of these churches gathered into one, in fact all the true believers in Christ scattered throughout the world, constitute the One true Universal Apostolic Church, built upon a rock, against which the gates of hell shall not prevail. Do not imagine, therefore, when I speak at any time of the Church, that I mean the Archbishop of Canterbury, the Bishop of London, and some twenty other dignitaries, and the whole host of ministers. No, nor when I speak of the Church do I mean the deacons, the elders, and pastors of the Baptist denomination, or any other. I mean all them that love the Lord Jesus Christ in sincerity and in truth, for these make up the one universal Church which has communion in itself with itself, not always in the outward sign, but always in the inward grace. The Church which was elect of God before the foundation of the world, which was redeemed by Christ with His own precious blood, which has been called by His Spirit, which is preserved by His grace, and which at last shall be gathered in to make the Church of the firstborn, whose names are written in Heaven.

Well, now, this Church is called the temple of God, and Christ is said to be its builder. Why is the Church called the temple? I reply very briefly, because the temple was the place where *God especially dwelt*. It was true that He did not wholly dwell in the temple made with hands, of man's building, which Solomon piled upon Mount Zion, but it is true that in a special sense the Infinite Majesty there held its tabernacle and its dwelling place. Between the wings of the overshadowing cherubim, there did shine the bright light of the Shekinah,[1] the type, the manifestation, and the proof of the special presence of Jehovah, the God of Israel. It is true He is everywhere; in the highest heavens and in the deepest hell God is to found. But He dwelt especially in His temple, so that when His people prayed, they were bidden to turn their eye towards the temple as Daniel did, when he opened his window towards Jerusalem, and offered his prayer.

Now such is the same with the Church. If you want to find God, He dwells on every hilltop, and in every valley, God is everywhere in creation; but if you want a special display of Him, if you want to know about the secret place of the tabernacle of the Host High, the inner chamber of divinity, you must go where you find the Church of true believers, for it is here He makes His continual residence known—in the hearts of the humble and contrite, who tremble at His Word.

SEEING THE CLEAREST MANIFESTATION OF GOD

Again, the temple was the place of the *clearest manifestation*. He, who wanted to see God the best of all, must see Him in His temple. I repeat, He was to be discovered everywhere. If you stood on Carmel's top, and looked towards the great sea where all the ships and the great leviathan He made are playing, there God may be discovered in His great strength. If you turned your eye on the same hill, and looked toward the Vale of Esdraelon, you would see God in every blade of grass, in every sheep feeding by the stream; God was everywhere to be discovered. But if you want to see Him, it

---

1. Glory of God.

will not be on Mount Bashan, Mount Hermon, nor Mount Tabor, for it was on Mount Zion that the Lord God loved to make a special display of himself.

GOD IS IN THE MIDST OF HIS CHURCH

It is the same with the Church. God is to be seen in the midst of her, her helper, strength, teacher, guide, deliverer, and her sanctifier. He is in Holy Communion—in the breaking of bread, pouring out of wine, holy baptism—in the immersion of believers into the Lord Jesus Christ. He is in the preaching of the Word, in the constant declaration of the great salvation of Jesus, in the lifting up of the Cross, in the high exalting of Him that died upon it, in the preaching of the Covenant, in the declaration of the grace of God—here is He to be seen, His name written in brighter letters and in clearer lines than elsewhere the wide world over.

Therefore, His Church is said to be His temple. Oh, Christian people, you know this, for God dwells in you, and walks with you; you dwell in Him, and He dwells in you—*"the secret of the Lord is with them that fear him, and he will show them his covenant."* (See Psalm 25:14.) It is your happy privilege to walk with God; He manifests himself to you, as He does not unto the world. He takes you into His inner chamber; He manifests His love; the Song of Solomon is sung in your courts, and nowhere else; it is not the song of the wide world, it is the sonnet of the inner chamber, the song of the house of wine, the music of the banquet. You understand this, for you have been brought into near acquaintance with Christ; you have been made to lean your head upon His bosom, you have been taught to look into His heart, and to see eternal thoughts of love there towards you. You know well, better than we can tell you, what it is to be the temple of the living God.

ONLY THE BELIEVER'S OFFERING WILL BE ACCEPTED BY GOD

And once more; we would fail to describe the reason why the word "temple" is used to picture the Church, if we did not observe that the Church is like the temple—*a place of worship*. There was a law passed by God that no offering should be presented to Him except upon the one altar in His temple at Jerusalem, and that law is extant to this day. No acceptable service can be offered to Christ except by His Church. Only those who believe in Christ can offer songs, and prayers, and praises that will be received of God. Whatever ordinances *you* attend to, if you are without Christ in your hearts, you contradict that ordinance and prostitute it—you do not honor God with it.

Two men go up to the temple to pray, the one a believer the other an unbeliever. He that is an unbeliever may have the gifts of oratory, the mightiest fluency of speech, but his prayer is an abomination unto God, while the feeblest utterance of the true believer is received with smiles by Him that sits upon the throne.

Two persons go to the Master's table—the one loves the ordinance in its outward sign, and reverences it with superstition, but he does not know Christ; the other believes in Christ Jesus, and knows how to eat His flesh and drink His blood as a worthy partaker in that divine ordinance. God is honored in the one; the ordinance is dishonored in the other.

Two persons come to holy Baptism: the one loves the Master, believes in His name, and trusts Him; he is baptized, he honors Christ. Another comes, perhaps an unaware nonbeliever, one who is incapable of faith; or has no faith; he dishonors God, he dishonors the ordinance in venturing to touch it if he is not one of the Church, and therefore has no right to offer the sacrifice of prayer and praise unto the Lord our God.

There is only one altar—that is, Christ; and there is only one set of priests, namely, the Church of God, the men chosen out of the world to be clothed in white robes to minister at His altar. Therefore, anyone else is only pretending to worship God, and worships Him wrongly. His offering is like that of Cain; God has no respect for his sacrifice, for without faith it is impossible to please God. We care not who it is that does the act; unless he is a believer, he cannot receive pleasure from God, nor will his sacrifice be accepted.

I have thus noted the reasons why the Church is said to be the temple. As there was only one temple, so there is only one Church. That one Church is His holy place, where God dwells, where God accepts worship, where songs of praise are daily uttered, and the smoking incense of prayer continually comes up before His nostrils with acceptance.

2. Christ is the Church's Only Builder

We have an interesting subject in the second part of our text. *"He shall build the temple of the Lord."* Now, I shall want to make a parallel between Christ's building the Church, and Solomon, as the builder of the first temple. When Solomon built the temple, the first thing he did was to obtain instructions with regard to the model upon which he should build it. Solomon was exceedingly wise, but I do not think he was his own architect. The Lord, who had shown the pattern of the old tabernacle in the wilderness to Moses, no doubt showed the pattern of the temple to Solomon, so that the pillars, and the roof, and the floor were all ordained of God and every one of them settled in Heaven.

Christ Must Be His Own Architect

Now, Christ Jesus in this is no Solomon; with this exception, that being God over all, blessed forever, He was His own architect. Christ has made the plan of His Church. You and I have made a great many plans for the building up of that Church. The Presbyterian makes his plans extremely precise. He will put an elder in every corner, and the Presbytery is the great groundwork—the pillar and the ground of the truth, and he is right in doing so to a certain extent. The Episcopalian builds his temple too. He will have a bishop at the doorpost, and he will have a priest to shut the gate. He will have everything built according to the model that was seen by Cranmer[2] in the mount, if he ever was there at all. And those of us who are of severer discipline, and have a simpler style, must have Christ's Church always built in the congregational order; every congregation distinct and separate, and governed by its own bishop, and deacons, and elders. But know this, Christ does not attend to our points of church government, for there is one part of Christ's Church that is Episcopalian, and looks as if a bishop of the Church of England had ordered it; another part is Presbyterian; another is Baptist, and another is Congregational. Yet, all these styles of architecture are somehow fused into one by the Great Architect, making that goodly structure which is called "the temple of Christ, the Church of the fiery God, the pillar and ground of truth." Christ must be His own architect. He will bring out different points of truth in different ways.

Why, I believe that different denominations are sent on purpose to set out different truths. There are some of our brethren a little too high, they bring out better than any other people, the grand old truths of sovereign grace. There are some, on the other hand, a little too low; they bring out with great clearness the great and truthful doctrines of man's responsibility. So that two truths that might have been neglected, either the one or the other, if only one form of Christianity existed, are both brought out, both made resplendent, by the different denominations of God's people, who are alike chosen of God, and precious to Him.

God forbid I should say anything that would bolster up any in their errors; nevertheless God's people, even in error, are a precious people. Even when they seem to be as earthen

---

2. Thomas Cranmer 1489-1556, leader of the English Reformation and Archbishop of Canterbury during the reign of Henry VIII.

pitchers, the work of the hands of the potter, they are still comparable to fine gold. Rest assured that the Lord has deep designs to answer, even by the divisions of His Church. We must not interfere with Christ's reasons, or with His style of architecture. Every stone that is in the temple, Jesus Christ ordained should be put where it is; even those stones that are most contemptible and unseen, were put in their places by Him.

There is not one board of cedar, one piece of burnished pinnacle, that was not foreseen and prearranged in that eternal covenant of grace which was the great plan that Christ, the Almighty Architect, drew for the building of the temple to His praise. Christ, then, is the only Architect, and He shall bear the glory, for He designed the building.

Now, you remember that when Solomon set to work to build his temple, he found a mountain ready for his purpose, Mount Moriah. The top of it was not quite broad enough; therefore he had to enlarge it, so that there might be room for the beautiful temple, the joy of the whole Earth. When Jesus Christ came to build His temple, He found no mountain on which to build it; He had no mountain in our nature, He had to find a mountain in His own, and the mountain upon which He has built His Church is the mountain of His own unchangeable affection, His own strong love, His own omnipotent grace and infallible truthfulness. It is this that constitutes the mountain upon which the Church is built, and on this the foundation has been dug, and the great stones laid in the trenches with oaths and promises and blood to make them stand secure, even though Earth would rock and all creation suffer decay.

Cedars of Lebanon Were Used in the Building of Solomon's Temple

Then after Solomon had his mountain ready and the foundation built, the next trouble he had was there were no trees near at hand: there were, however, fine trees growing in Lebanon, but his servants did not have enough skill to cut them down. Therefore, he sent for Hiram, king of Tyre, with his servants, to cut down the trees in Lebanon. After they were shaped according to the model, they were to be sent by rafts or floats to Joppa, the port nearest to Jerusalem, and there brought a short distance over land for the building of the temple. He had to do the same with the stones of the quarry; for the different stones that were needed for the building had to be hewn out of the quarry by Hiram's servants. Solomon's people assisted but lacked skill; therefore they did the more laborious and rougher part of the work. You will notice the same fact when you read the history of the building of the temple regarding the making of the vessels for the inside of the temple. It is said that Hiram cast them, and Solomon found the gold; and the molds were made in the great plain, and Solomon cast them there, with Hiram for his chief designer and director.

Christ Alone Builds His Temple— We Are His Planks of Cedar to Be Shaped

Ah, but here Solomon fails to be a type of Christ. Christ builds the temple himself. There stand the cedars of

Lebanon that the Lord has planted but they are not ready for the building; they are not cut down, shaped, nor made into those planks of cedar, whose fragrant beauty will make glad the courts of the Lord in Paradise. No; Jesus Christ must cut them down with the axe of conviction; He must cut them up with the great saw of His law, He must plane and polish them with His holy Gospel. And when He has made them fit to be pillars in the house of the Lord, they will be carried across the sea to Heaven; then shall they be placed in His temple forever. No Hiram is needed. The axe is in *His* hand, the plane is in *His* hand too. He understands well that business. Was He not a carpenter on Earth? And spiritually, He will be the same to His Church forever and ever.

WE ARE THE ROUGH STONES TO BE MADE READY

It is even the same with the stones of the temple. We are like rough stones in the quarry. Behold the hole in the pit from where we were dug, and the rock we were hewn from. But we were hewn out of that rock by no hand but Christ's. He raised up seed unto Abraham out of the stones of the pit; it was His own hammer that broke the rock in pieces, and His own arm of strength that wielded the hammer, when He broke us free from the rock of our sin. Though we are each being polished, and made ready for the temple, yet there is no one and nothing that polishes us except Christ. Afflictions cannot sanctify us, unless they are used by Christ, as His mallet and His chisel. Our joys and our efforts cannot make us ready for Heaven apart from the hand of Jesus who fashions our hearts aright, and prepares us to be partakers of the inheritance of the saints in light.

Thus you notice that Jesus Christ excels Solomon in this work, for He provides all the materials. He hews them himself; He shapes them first, and then afterwards, during life, polishes them until He makes them ready to transport them to the hill of God, where His temple is to be built. I was thinking of the beauty of the trees of Lebanon being hewn and shaped and floated to Joppa and on to Jerusalem for Solomon's temple, and what a fine symbolic representation of death it is! Is it not just so with us? Here we grow, and are at length cut down, and made ready to become pillars of the temple. Across the stream of death, we are ferried by a loving hand, and brought to the port of Jerusalem where we are safely landed, to go out no more, but to abide as eternal pillars in the temple of our Lord.

Now, you know the men of Tyre floated those rafts for Solomon's temple; but no stranger, no foreigner shall float us across the stream of death. It is remarkable that Jesus Christ always uses expressions with regard to His people, which impute their death to Him alone. You will recollect the expression in Revelation 14:15, *"Thrust in thy sickle, and reap: for the time is come for thee to reap; for the harvest of the earth is ripe."* But when He begins to reap, not the vintage, which represents the wicked that were to be crushed, but the harvest which represents the godly; then it is said in Revelation 14:14-16, *"He that sat upon the cloud thrust in the sickle."* (See Revelation 14:14-16.) He did not leave it to His angels, He did it himself. It is so with the bringing of those planks, and the moving of those stones. I say no king of Tyre and Sidon shall do it, Jesus Christ who is the death of death and hell's destruction; He himself shall pilot us across the stream, and land us safe on Canaan's side. *"He shall build the temple of the Lord."* (See Zechariah 6:12.)

MADE READY BEFOREHAND

Well, after these materials were brought for the building of Solomon's Temple, he had to employ many thousand workmen to put them in their proper places. You know that in Solomon's temple there was no sound of hammering heard, for the stones were made ready in the quarries, and brought all shaped and marked so that the masons would know the exact spot in which they were to be placed; so that no sound of iron was needed. All the planks and timbers were carried to their right places, and all the catches with which they were to be linked together were prepared, so that there might not even be the driving of a nail—everything was ready beforehand. It is the same with us. When we get to Heaven, there will be no sanctifying us there, no squaring us with affliction, no hammering us with the rod, no making us ready there. We must be made ready here; and blessed be His name, Christ will do all *that* beforehand. When we get there, we shall not need angels to put this member of the Church in one place, and that member in another. Christ, who brought the stones from the quarry and made them ready, shall himself place the people in their inheritance in paradise. For He has said, *"I go to prepare a place for you, and if I go away, I will come again and I will receive you unto myself."* (See John 14:2-3.) Christ will be His own usher, He will receive His people himself, He will stand at the gates of Heaven himself to take His own people, and put them in their allotted heritage in the land of the blessed.

Overlaid with Gold

I have no doubt you have read many times the story of Solomon's temple, and you have noticed that he overlaid the entire temple with gold. He provided much of the substance, but his father David brought him a good supply. Now Jesus will overlay all of us with gold, when He builds us in Heaven. Do not imagine we will be in Heaven looking as we are today. No, beloved, if the cedar could see itself after it had been made into a pillar, it would not know itself. If you could see yourselves as you shall be made, you would say, *"'It doth not yet appear'* how great we must be made." (See 1 John 3:2.) Nor were these pillars of cedars to be left naked and unadorned—though they had been fair and lovely then—they were overlaid with sheets of gold. So shall we be. *"It is sown in dishonor, it is raised in glory. It is sown a natural body, it is raised a spiritual body,"* plated with pure gold: no longer what it was, but precious, lustrous, glorified. (See 1 Corinthians 15:43.)

The Brazen Laver

And in the temple, we understand, there was a great brazen laver in which the priests did wash themselves, and there were other brazen lavers, in which they washed the lambs and bullocks when they were offered. In Heaven there is a great laver, in which all our souls have been washed, *"for they have washed their robes, and made them white in the blood of the lamb."* (See Revelation 7:14.) Now Christ himself prepares this sacred sea. He filled it with blood from His own veins. As for our prayers and praises, the great laver in which they are washed, was also made and filled by Christ; so that they with us are clean, and we offer acceptable sacrifices to God through Jesus Christ our Lord. I say again, before I leave this, there is no part of the great temple of the Church, which was not made by Christ. There is a great deal in the Church on Earth, that Christ had nothing to do with, but there is nothing in His true Church, and nothing especially in His glorified Church, which was not put there by Him. Therefore, we may well come to the conclusion that He shall bear all the glory, for He was the only builder of it.

3. Christ Shall Bear All the Glory

Now, what a sweet thing it is to try and glorify Christ. I am happy to have a subject that will magnify my Master. But is it not a sad thing, that when we want to magnify Christ most, our poor, failing lips refuse to speak? Oh, if you would know my Master's glory, you must see it for yourselves, for like the Queen of Sheba, the half can never be told to you, even by those who know Him most and love Him best. Half His glory never can be told.

Pause awhile, and let me endeavor to address a few loving words to you. Your Master, O you saints of the Lord, has prepared you and will build you into His temple. Speak and say, He *shall* have all the glory. Let us note, first, that the glory which He shall have will be a weighty glory. Dr. Gill[3] says, *"the expression implies, that the glory will be a weighty one, for it said, he shall bear the glory."* "They shall hang," says another expression, *"upon him all the glory of his Father's house"*;

---
3. John Gill, 1697-1771, English theologian.

and in another place, we are told, that there is *"an exceeding weight of glory,"* which is prepared for the righteous. How great then, the weight of glory which shall be given to Christ.

Oh, do not think that Christ is to be glorified in such humble measure, as He is on Earth. The songs of Heaven are nobler strains than ours. The hearts of the redeemed pay Him loftier homage than we can offer. Try not to judge the magnificence of Christ by the pomp of kings, or by the reverence paid to mighty men on Earth. His glory far surpasses all the glory of this time and space. The honor which shall be bestowed upon Him is as the brightness of the sun, the honors of Earth are but the twinkling of a fading star. Before Him, at this very day, principalities and powers bow themselves down. Ten thousand times ten thousand seraphim wait at His footstool. *"The chariots of the Lord are twenty thousand, even thousands of angels,"* and all these await His beck and command. (See Psalm 68:17.) And as for His redeemed, how do they magnify Him? By never ceasing, never changing, never wearying; they raise their shout higher, and higher, higher and louder, and louder still the strain is lifted up, and eternally it is the same. *"To him that liveth and was dead and is alive for evermore, unto him be glory, world without end."* (See Revelation 1:17-19.)

CHRIST'S GLORY IS UNDIVIDED

And note again, that this glory is *undivided* glory. In the Church of Christ in Heaven, no one is glorified but Christ. He who is honored on Earth has someone to share the honor with him, some inferior helper who labored with him in the work; but Christ has none. He is glorified, and it is all His own glory. Oh, when you get to Heaven, you children of God, will you praise any but your Master? Calvinists, today you love John Calvin; will you praise him there? Lutheran, today you love the memory of that stern reformer; will you sing the song of Luther in Heaven? Follower of Wesley, you have a reverence for that evangelist; will you in Heaven have a note for John Wesley? None, none, none! Giving up all names and all honors of men, the strain shall rise in undivided, bold, and clear unison *"unto him that loved us, that washed us from our sins in his blood, unto him be glory for ever and ever."* (See Revelation 1:5.)

CHRIST SHALL HAVE CONTINUAL GLORY

But again: He shall have *all* the glory; all that can be conceived, all that can be desired, all that can be imagined shall come to Him. Today, you praise Him, but not as you can wish; in Heaven you shall praise Him to the summit of your desire. Today you see Him magnified, but you do not see all things put under Him; in Heaven all things shall acknowledge His dominion. *There every knee shall bow before him, and every tongue confess that he is Lord.* He shall have *all* the glory. (See Romans 14:11.) But to conclude on this point, this glory is *continual* glory. It says He *shall* bear all the glory. When will this dominion become effective? When will this promise be so fulfilled that it is put away as a worn-out garment? Never,

> *"While life, and thought, and being last,*
> *Or immortality endures."*[4]

---
4. Hymn written by Isaac Watts on Psalm 146, Verse One.

We shall never cease praising Christ. We think we can almost guess how we shall feel when we get to Heaven, with regard to our Master. I think if I should ever be privileged to behold His blessed face with joy, I will want nothing but to be allowed to approach His throne, and cast what little honor I may have before His feet, and then be there and ever more adore the matchless splendor of His love and the marvels of His might. Suppose someone entering were to say to the redeemed, "Suspend your songs for a moment! You have been praising Christ, lo, these six thousand years; many of you have never ceased praising Him these many centuries! Stop your song a moment; pause and give your songs to someone else for a moment." Oh, can you conceive the scorn with which the myriad eyes of the redeemed would smite the tempter? "Stop from praising Him! No, never. Time may stop, for it shall be no more; the world may stop, for its revolutions must cease; the universe may stop its cycles and the moving of its world but for us to stop our songs—never, never!"—and it shall be said, *"Hallelujah, hallelujah, hallelujah, the Lord God Omnipotent reigneth."* (See Revelation 19:6.) He shall have all the glory, and He shall have it forever; His name shall endure forever; His name shall continue as long as the sun; men shall be blessed in Him, and all generations shall call Him blessed; therefore shall they praise Him forever and ever.

4. Making a Practical Application of Our Text

Now in conclusion, brothers and sisters, are we built upon Christ today? Can we say that we hope that we are a part of His temple; that His handiwork has been exhibited upon us, and that we are built together with Christ? If so, listen to one word of exhortation. *Let us honor Him evermore.* Oh! I think every beam of cedar, every slab of gold, and every stone of the temple, felt honored when it was raised up to be a part of the fabric for Jehovah's praise. And if that cedar and marble, could have been vocal in that day when the flame descended from Heaven, the token of Jehovah's presence, the stone, the cedar, the gold, the silver, and the brass, all would have burst out into song, and would have said, "We praise you, O God, for you have made the gold more than gold, and the cedar more than cedar, because you have consecrated us to be the temple of shine indwelling." And now, will you not do the same? O my brothers and sisters! God has highly honored you to be stones in the temple of Christ. When you think of what you were, and what you might have been. You know you might have been stones in the black dungeons of vengeance forever, dark dank stones, where the mobs, and the greed, and the slimy thing might have lived forever. You might have lived; disgraced, abandoned, cast away in the blackness of night forever. When you think of this, and then remember that you are stones in Jehovah's temple,—living stones,—oh, you must say that you will praise Him, for man is more than man, now that God dwells in him.

Daughters of Jerusalem, rejoice for you are more than women now! Sons of Israel, rejoice, for your manhood is exalted! He has made you temples of the Holy Ghost—God dwelling in you and you in Him. Go out from this place and sing His praise; go forth to honor Him, and while the silent world wants you to be its mouth, go and speak for the mountain, for the hill, for the lake, for the river, for the oak, and for the insect; speak for all things; for you are to be like the temple, the seat of the worship of all worlds. You are to be like the priests and offerers of the sacrifices of all creatures.

Let me address myself last of all to others of you. Alas my hearers, I have many here who have no portion in Israel, neither any lot in Jacob. There are many of you, who are not stones in the spiritual temple, never to be used in the building up of God's Jerusalem. Let me ask you one thing; it may seem a slight thing today to be left out of the roll call of Christ's Church,—but will it seem a slight thing to be left out when Christ calls for His people? When you are all assembled around His great white throne at last, and the books are opened, oh how dread the suspense, while name after name is read! How dreadful your suspense, when it comes to the last name and yours has been left out! That verse of our hymn has often impressed me very solemnly:

> *"I love to meet among them now,*
> *Before thy gracious feet to bow,*
> *Though vilest of them all;*
> *But can I bear the piercing thought—*
> *What if my name should be left out,*
> *When thou for them shalt call?"*[5]

Sinner imagine it! The list is read, and your name unmentioned. Laugh at religion now! Scoff at Christ now! Now that the angels are gathering for the judgment; now that the trumpet sounds exceedingly loud and long; now that the heavens are red with fire, and now that the great furnace of hell leaps over its boundary, and is about to encircle you

---

5. "When Thou, My Righteous Judge, Shall Come" Verse 2, Words written in 1700's by Countess of Huntingdon, Music by Lowell Mason 1839.

in its flame; now despise religion! Ah! No. I see you. Now your stiff knees are bending, your bold forehead is covered with the hot sweat of trembling for the first time, and your eyes that once were full of scorn are full of tears, as you look on Him whom you despised—now you are weeping over your sin. Sinner, it will be too late then, for there is no cutting of the stone after it gets to Jerusalem. Where you fall is where you will lie. When judgment ends you, there eternity shall leave you.

Time shall be no more when judgment comes, and when time is no more, change is impossible! In eternity there can be no change, no deliverance, no signing of acquittal. Once lost, lost forever; once damned, damned to all eternity. Will you choose this and despise Christ or will you have Christ and have Heaven? I charge you by Him that shall judge the quick and the dead, whose I am, and whom I serve, who is the searcher of all hearts, choose you this day whom you will serve. If sin is best serve sin, and reap its wages. If you can make your bed in hell, if you can endure eternal burnings, be honest with yourself, and look at the wages while you do the work. But if you want to have Heaven, if you want to be among the many who shall be glorified with Christ, believe on the Lord Jesus Christ; believe now. *"To day if ye will hear his voice, harden not your hearts, as in the provocation"* (Hebrews 3:15). *"Kiss the Son, lest he be angry, and ye perish from the way, when his wrath is kindled but a little"* (Psalm 2:12). Men, brethren, and fathers, believe and live; cast yourself at Jesus' feet, put your trust in Him,

> *"Renounce thy works and ways with grief, And fly to this most sure relief;"* [6] *giving up all you are*

---

6. "O Thou, My Soul, Forget No More," Verse 3, Joshua Marshman 1801.

to come to Him, to be saved by Him now, and saved eternally. O Lord, bless my weak but earnest appeal, for Christ's sake. Amen.

CHAPTER 7

CHRIST—OUR SUBSTITUTE

A Sermon
(No. 310)
Delivered on Sunday Evening, April 15, 1860,
Reverend Charles H. Spurgeon,
at New Park Street, Southwark, London, England

*"For he hath made him to be sin for us,
who knew no sin; that we might be made
the righteousness of God in him."*—2 Corinthians 5:21

Sometime ago an excellent lady sought an interview with me, with the object as she said, of enlisting my sympathy upon the question of "Anti-Capital Punishment." I heard the excellent reasons she urged against hanging men who had committed murder, and though they did not convince me, I did not seek to answer her. She proposed that when a man committed murder, he should be confined for life. My remark was, that a great many men who had been confined half their lives were not a bit the better for it, and as for her belief that they would necessarily be brought to repentance, I was afraid it was but a dream. "Ah," she said, good soul as she was, "that is because we have been all wrong about punishments. We punish people because we think they deserve to be punished. Now, we ought to show them," she said, "that we love them; that we only punish them to make them better." "Indeed, madam," I said, "I have heard that theory a great many times, and I have seen much fine writing upon the matter, but I am no believer in it. The design of punishment should be amendment, but the ground of punishment lies in the positive guilt of the offender. I believe that when a man does wrong, he ought to be punished for it, and that there is a guilt in sin which justly merits punishment."

Oh no; she could not see that. Sin was a very wrong thing, but punishment was not a proper idea. She thought that people were treated too cruelly in prison, and that they ought to be taught that we love them. If they were treated kindly in prison, and tenderly dealt with, they would grow so much better, she was sure." With a view of interpreting her own theory, I said, "I suppose, then, you would give criminals all sorts of indulgences in prison. Some great vagabond who has committed burglary dozens of times—I suppose you would let him sit in an easy chair in the evening before a nice fire, and mix him a glass of spirits and water, and give him his pipe, and make him happy, to show him how much we love him." "Well, no, she would not give him the spirits, but, still, all the rest would do him good." I thought that was a delightful picture certainly. It seemed to me to be the most prolific method of cultivating rogues which ingenuity could invent. I imagine that you could grow any number of thieves in that way; for it would be a special means of propagating all manner of roguery and wickedness. These very delightful theories to such a simple mind as mine were the source of much amusement, the idea of fondling villains, and treating their crimes as if they were the tumbles and falls of children, made me laugh heartily. I fancied I saw the government resigning its functions to these excellent persons, and the grand results of their marvelously kind experiments. The sword of the magistrate transformed into a spoon for gruel, and the jail becoming a sweet retreat for injured reputations.

SENTIMENTALISM OF THE NAMBY-PAMBY SORT

Little however, did I think I should live to see this kind of stuff taught in pulpits; I had no idea that there would come out a divinity, which would bring down God's moral government from the solemn aspect in which Scripture reveals it, to a namby-pamby sentimentalism, which adores a Deity destitute of every masculine virtue. But we never know today what may occur tomorrow. We have lived to see a certain sort of men—thank God they are not Baptists—though I am sorry to say there are a great many Baptists who are beginning to follow in their trail—who seek to teach nowadays, that God is a universal Father, and that our ideas of His dealing with the impenitent as a Judge, and not as a Father, are remnants of antiquated error. Sin, according to these men, is a disorder rather than an offence, an error rather than a crime. Love is the only attribute they can discern, and the fullness of Deity they have not known. Some of these men push their way very far into the bogs and mire of falsehood, until they inform us that eternal punishment is ridiculed as a dream. In fact, books now appear which teach us that there is no such thing as the Vicarious Sacrifice of our Lord Jesus Christ. They use the word Atonement it is true, but in regard to its meaning, they have removed the ancient landmark. They acknowledge that the Father has shown His great love to poor sinful man by sending His Son, but not that God was inflexibly just in the exhibition of His mercy, not that He punished Christ on the behalf of His people, nor that indeed God ever will punish anybody in His wrath, or that there is such a thing as justice apart from discipline.

Even *sin* and *hell* are but old words employed henceforth in a new and altered sense. Those are old-fashioned notions, and we poor souls who go on talking about election and imputed righteousness, are behind our time. Moreover, the gentlemen who bring out books on this subject, applaud Mr. Maurice[1], and Professor Scott[2], and the like, but are too cowardly to follow them, and boldly propound these sentiments. These are the new men whom God has sent down from Heaven, to tell us that the Apostle Paul was all wrong, that our faith is vain, that we have been quite mistaken, that there was no need for propitiating blood to wash away our sins; that the fact was, our sins needed discipline, but penal vengeance and righteous wrath are quite out of the question. When I speak like this, I am free to confess that such ideas are not boldly taught by a certain individual whose volume excites these remarks, but as he puffs the books of gross perversions of the truth, I am compelled to believe that he endorses such theology.

Spurgeon's Comment on the Sentimental Namby-Pamby

Well, brethren, I am happy to say that sort of stuff has not gained entrance into this pulpit. I dare say the worms will eat the wood before there will be anything of that sort sounded in this place; and may these bones be picked by vultures, and this flesh be rent in sunder by lions, and may every nerve in this body suffer pangs and tortures, before these lips shall give utterance to any such doctrines or sentiments.

---

1. Frederick Denison Maurice, 1805-1872, an English clergyman and social activist.
2. William Scott, 1813-1872, English clergyman, a leading High Church figure of his time.

We are content to remain among the vulgar souls who believe the old doctrines of grace. We are lolling still to be behind in the great march of intellect, and stand by that unmoving Cross, which, like the polestar, never advances, because it never stirs, but always abides in its place, the guide of the soul to Heaven, the one foundation other than which no man can lay, and without building upon which, no man shall ever see the face of God and live.

Thus much have I said upon a matter which just now is exciting controversy. It has been my high privilege to be associated with six of our ablest brethren in the ministry, in a letter of protest against the countenance which a certain newspaper seemed willing to lend to this modern heresy. We trust it may be the means, in the hands of God, of helping to check that downward march—that wandering from truth which seems by some singular infatuation, to have unsettled the minds of some brethren in our denomination. Now I come to address you upon the topic that is most continually assailed by those who preach another gospel *"which is not another—but there be some that trouble you, and would pervert the gospel of Christ,"* (see Galatians 1:7), namely, the doctrine of the substitution of Christ on our behalf, His actual atonement for our sins, and our positive and actual justification through His sufferings and righteousness. It seems to me that until language can mean the very reverse of what it says, until by some strange logic, God's Word can be contradicted and can be made to belief itself, the doctrine of *substitution* can never be rooted out of the words which I have selected for my text,

> *"He hath made him to be sin for us, who knew no sin, that we might be made the righteousness of God in him."* (See 2 Corinthians 5:21.)

First, the sinlessness of the substitute.

Second, the reality of the imputation of sin to Him.

Third, the glorious reality of the imputation of righteousness to us.

1. First, The Sinlessness of the Substitute.

The doctrine of Holy Scripture is this, that inasmuch as man could not keep God's law, having fallen in Adam, Christ came and fulfilled the law on the behalf of His people. That inasmuch as man had already broken the divine law and incurred the penalty of the wrath of God, Christ came and suffered in the place, and stead of His elect ones. By His enduring the full vials of wrath, they were be emptied out and not a drop ever fell upon the heads of His blood-bought people. Now, you will readily perceive that if one is to be a substitute for another before God, either to work out a righteousness or to suffer a penalty, that substitute must himself be free from sin. If he has sin of his own, all that he can suffer will be but the due reward of his own iniquity. If he has transgressed, he cannot suffer for another, because all his sufferings are already due on his own personal account.

On the other hand, it is quite clear that none but a perfect man could ever work out a spotless righteousness for us, and keep the law in our stead. For if he had dishonored the commandment in his thought, there must be a corresponding flaw in his service. If the warp and woof are speckled, how can he bring forth the robe of milk-white purity, and wrap it about our loins? He must be a spotless one who shall become the representative of his people, either to give them a passive or active righteousness, either to offer a satisfaction as the penalty of their sins, or a righteousness as the fulfillment of God's demand.

ONLY THE LORD JESUS WAS WITHOUT SIN

It is satisfactory for us to know, and to believe beyond a doubt, that our Lord Jesus was without sin. Of course, in His divine nature He could not know iniquity; and as for His human nature, it never knew the original taint of depravity. He was of the seed of the woman, but not of the tainted and infected seed of Adam. Overshadowed by the Holy Ghost as the virgin was, no corruption entered into His nativity. That *holy thing* which was born of her was neither conceived in sin nor shaped in iniquity. He was brought into this world immaculate. He was immaculately conceived and immaculately born. In Him that natural black blood which we have inherited from Adam never dwelt. His heart was upright within Him; His soul was without any bias to evil; His imagination had never been darkened. He had no infatuated mind. There was no tendency whatever in Him but to do that which was good, holy, and honorable.

And because He did not share in the original depravity, He did not share in the imputed sin of Adam which we have inherited—not, I mean, in himself personally, though He took the consequences of it as He stood as our representative. The sin of Adam had never passed over the head of the second Adam. All that were in the loins of Adam sinned in him when he touched the fruit; but Jesus was not in the loins of Adam. Though He might be thought of as being in the womb of the woman—"a new thing which the Lord created in the earth,"—He lay not in Adam when he sinned, and consequently no guilt from Adam, either of depravity of nature, or of distance from God, ever fell upon Jesus as the result of anything that Adam did. I mean upon Jesus as considered *in himself* though He certainly took the sin of Adam as He was the representative of His people.

THE PERFECT LAMB OF GOD'S PASSOVER

Again, as in His nature He was free from the corruption and condemnation of the sin of Adam, so also in His life, no sin ever corrupted His way. His eye never flashed with unhallowed anger; His lip never uttered a treacherous or deceitful word; His heart never harbored an evil imagination. Never did He wander after lust; no covetousness ever so much as glanced into His soul. He was *"holy, harmless, undefiled, separate from sinners."* (See Hebrews 7:26.) From the beginning of His life to the end, you cannot put your finger even upon a mistake, much less upon a willful error. So perfect was He, that no virtue seems to preponderate[3], or by an opposing quality give a bias to the scale of absolute rectitude.

John is distinguished for his love, Peter for his courage; but Jesus Christ is distinguished for neither one above the other, because He possesses all in such sublime unison, such heavenly harmony, that not one virtue stands out above the rest. He is meek, but He is courageous. He is loving, but He

---

3. Outweigh.

is decided; He is bold as a lion, yet He is quiet and peaceful as a lamb. He was like that fine flour which was offered before God in the burnt offering; a flour without grit, so smooth, that when you rubbed it, it was soft and pure, no particles could be discerned: so was His character fully ground, fully compounded. There was not one feature in His moral countenance which had undue preponderance above the other; but He was filled with everything that was virtuous and good. He was tempted, it is true, but He never sinned. The whirlwind came from the wilderness, and smote upon the four corners of that house, but it fell not, for it was founded upon a rock. The rains descended, Heaven afflicted Him; the winds blew, the mysterious agency of hell assailed Him; the floods came, all Earth was in arms against Him, yet He stood firm in the midst of all. Never once did He even seem to bend before the tempest; but buffeting the fury of the blast.

He bore all the temptations that could ever happen to man, which summed themselves up and consummated their fury on Him. He stood to the end, without a single flaw in His life, or a stain upon His spotless robe. Let us rejoice in this, my beloved brothers and sisters that we have such a substitute—one who is fit and proper to stand in our place, and to suffer in our stead. He had no need to offer a sacrifice for himself; no need to cry for himself, "Father, I have sinned"; no need to bend the knee of the penitent and confess His own iniquities, for He is without spot or blemish, the perfect lamb of God's Passover.

WHO KNEW NO SIN

I would have you carefully notice the particular expression of the text, for it struck me as being very beautiful and significant,—"who *knew* no sin." It does not merely say *did* none, but *knew* none. Sin was no acquaintance of His; He was acquainted with grief, but no acquaintance of sin. He had to walk in the midst of its most frequented haunts, but did not know it; not that He was ignorant of its nature, or did not know its penalty, but he did not *know it;* He was a stranger to it, He never gave it the wink or nod of familiar recognition. Of course He knew what sin was, for He was very God, but with the sin He had no communion, no fellowship, and no brotherhood. He was a perfect stranger in the presence of sin; He was a foreigner; He was not an inhabitant of that land where sin is acknowledged. He passed through the wilderness of suffering, but into the wilderness of sin He could never go. "He *knew* no sin"; remember that expression and treasure it, and when you are thinking of your substitute, and see Him hang bleeding upon the Cross, think that you see written in those lines of blood written along His blessed body, "He knew no sin." Mingled with the redness of His blood—that Rose of Sharon; behold the purity of His nature, the Lily of the Valley—"He knew no sin."

2. THE ACTUAL SUBSTITUTION OF CHRIST, AND THE REAL IMPUTATION OF SIN TO HIM

Here be careful to observe who transferred the sin. *"He made him to be sin for us."* God the Father laid on Jesus the iniquities of us all. Man could not make Christ sin. Man could not transfer his guilt to another. It is not for us to say whether Christ could or could not have made himself sin for us; it is certain, He did not take this priesthood upon himself, but He was called of God, as was Aaron. The Redeemer's vicarious position is warranted, no, rather ordained by divine authority.

"He hath made him to be sin for us." I must now beg you to notice how very explicit the term is. Some of our expositors will have it that the word "sin" used here must mean "sin-offering." "He made him to be a sin-offering for us." I thought it well to look at my Greek Testament to see whether it could be so. Of course we all know that the word here translated "sin," is very often translated "sin-offering," but it is always useful, when you have a disputed passage, to check it thoroughly, and see whether in this case the word would bear such a meaning. These commentators say it means a sin-offering,—well, I will read it: "He hath made him to be a sin-offering for us who knew no *sin-offering*." Does not that strike you as being ridiculous? But they are precisely the same words; and if it is fair to translate it "sin-offering" in one place, it must, in all reason, be fair to translate it so in the other. The fact is, while in some passages it may be rendered "sin-offering," in this passage it cannot be so, because it would be to run counter to all honesty to translate the same word in the same sentence two different ways. No; we must take them as they stand. *"He hath made him to be sin for us,"* not merely an offering, but *sin* for us.

My predecessor, Dr. Gill, edited the works of Tobias Crisp, but Tobias Crisp went further than Dr. Gill or any of us can approve; for in one place Crisp calls Christ *a sinner*, though he does not mean that He ever sinned himself. He actually calls Christ a transgressor, and justifies himself by that passage, "He was numbered with the transgressors." Martin Luther is reputed to have broadly said that, although Jesus Christ was sinless, yet He was the greatest sinner that ever lived, because all the sins of His people lay upon Him. Now, such expressions I think to be unguarded, if not profane. Certainly Christian men should take care that they not use language which, by the ignorant and uninstructed, may be translated to mean what they never intended to teach.

Jesus Knew No Sin

The fact is, brethren, that in no sense whatever—take that as I say it—in no sense whatever can Jesus Christ ever be conceived of as having been guilty. *"He knew no sin."* Not only was He not guilty of any sin which He committed himself, but He was not guilty of our sins. No guilt can possibly attach to a man who has not been guilty. He must have had complicity in the deed itself, or else no *guilt* can possibly be laid on Him. Jesus Christ stands in the midst of all the divine thunders, and suffers all the punishment, but not a drop of sin ever stained Him. In no sense is He ever a guilty man, but He is always an accepted and a holy one. What, then, is the meaning of that very forcible expression of my text?

Doctrine of Analogy

We must interpret scriptural modes of expression by the words used by the speakers. We know that our Master once himself said himself, *"This cup is the new covenant in my blood."* (See Luke 22:20.) He did not mean that the cup was the covenant. He said, *"Take, eat, this is my body"*—not one of us conceives that the bread is the literal flesh and blood of Christ. We take that bread as if it was the body, and it actually represents it. Now, we are to read a passage like this, according to the analogy of faith. Jesus Christ was made by His Father sin for us, that is, He was treated as if He had himself been sin. He was not sin; He was not sinful; He was not guilty; but, He was treated by His Father, as if He had not only been sinful, but as if He had been *sin itself*. That is a strong expression used here. Not only has God made Him to be the substitute for sin, but to be sin. God looked on Christ as if Christ had been sin; not as if He had taken up the sins of His people, or as if they were laid on Him, though that were true, but as if He himself had positively been that noxious—that God-hating—that soul-damning thing, called sin. When the Judge of all the Earth said, "Where is Sin?" Christ presented himself. He stood before His Father as if He had been the accumulation of all human guilt; as if He himself were that thing which God cannot endure, but which He must drive from His presence forever.

And now see how this making of Jesus to be sin was enacted to the fullest extent. The righteous Lord looked on Christ as being sin, and therefore Christ must be taken outside the camp. Sin cannot be borne in God's Zion, cannot be allowed to dwell in God's Jerusalem; it must be taken outside the camp, it is a leprous thing, put it away. Sin must be cast out from fellowship, from love, from pity. Take Him away, take Him away, you crowd! Hurry Him through the streets and bear Him to Calvary. Take Him outside the camp—as was the beast which was offered for sin outside the camp, so must Christ be, who was made sin for us.

GOD NOW LOOKS ON HIM AS BEING SIN

And sin must bear punishment. Christ is punished. The most fearful of deaths is exacted at His hand, and God has no pity for Him. How should He have pity on sin? God hates it. No tongue can tell, no soul can divine the terrible hatred of God to that which is evil, and He treats Christ as if He were sin. Christ prays, but Heaven shuts out His prayer; His eye to Heaven, He sees nothing there. How should He? God cannot look on sin, and sin can have no claim on God: *"My God, my God,"* He cries in Matthew 27:46, *"why hast thou forsaken me?"* O solemn necessity, how could God do anything with sin but forsake it? How could iniquity have fellowship with God? Shall divine smiles rest on sin? No, no, it must not be. Therefore, He who is made sin must bemoan desertion and terror. God cannot touch Him, cannot dwell with Him, and cannot come near Him. He is abhorred, cast away; it has pleased the Father to bruise Him; He has put Him to grief. At last He dies. God will not keep Him in life—how would He? Is it not the right thing in the world that sin should be buried? "Bury it out of my sight, hide this corruption," and lo! Jesus, as if He were sin, is put away out of the sight of God and man as a thing obnoxious. I do not know whether I have clearly uttered what I want to state, but what a grim picture that is, to conceive of sin gathered up into one mass—murder, lust, rape, adultery, and all manner of crime, all piled together in one hideous heap. We ourselves, brethren, impure though we be, could not bear this; how much less would God with His pure and holy eyes bear with that mass of sin, and yet there it is, and God looked upon Christ as if He were that mass of sin. He was not sin, but God looked upon Him as made sin for us. He stands in our place, assumes our guilt, takes on Him our iniquity, and God treats Him as if He had been sin.

OUR SINS HAVE ALL BEEN PUNISHED IN CHRIST

Now, my dear brothers and sisters, let us just lift up our hearts with gratitude for a few moments. Here we are tonight; we know that we are guilty, but our sins have all been punished years ago. Before my soul believed in Christ, the punishment of my sin had all been endured. We are not to think that Christ's blood derives its efficacy from our faith. Fact precedes faith. Christ has redeemed us; faith discovers this; but it was a fact of that finished sacrifice. Though still defiled by sin, yet who can lay anything to the charge of the man whose guilt is gone, lifted bodily from off him, and put upon Christ? How can any punishment fall on that man who ceases to possess sins, because his sin was cast on Christ eighteen hundred years ago, and Christ has suffered in his place and stead? Oh, glorious triumph of faith to be able to say, whenever I feel the guilt of sin, whenever conscience pricks me, "Yes, it is true, but my Lord is answerable for it all, for He has taken it all upon himself, and suffered in my place, and stead." How precious when I see my debts, to be able to say, "Yes, but the blood of Christ, God's dear Son, has cleansed me from all sin!" How precious, not only to see my sin dying when I believe, but to know that it was dead, it was gone; it ceased to be, eighteen hundred years ago. All the sins that you and I have ever committed, or ever shall commit, if we are heirs of mercy, and children of God, are all dead things.

> "*Our Jesus nailed them to his cross,*
> *And sung the triumph when he rose.*"

These cannot rise in judgment to condemn us; they have all been slain, shrouded, buried; they are removed from us as far as the east is from the west, because *"He hath made him to be sin for us who knew no sin."*

---

3. THAT WE MIGHT BE MADE THE RIGHTEOUSNESS OF GOD IN HIM

You see then the reality of the imputation of sin to Christ from the amazing doctrine that Christ is made sin for us. But now notice the concluding thought, upon which I must dwell a moment, but it must be very briefly, for two reasons, my time has gone, and my strength has gone too. Now, here I beg you to notice, that it does not simply say that we might be made *righteous*, but *"that we might be made the righteousness of God in him;"* as if righteousness, that lovely, glorious, God-honoring, God-delighting thing—as if we were actually made *that*. God looks on His people as being abstract righteousness, not only righteous, but righteousness. To be righteous, is as if a man should have a box covered with gold, the box would then be golden; but to be righteous*ness* is to have a box of solid gold. To be a righteous man is to have righteousness cast over me; but to be made righteousness, that is to be made solid essential righteousness in the sight of God.

Well now, this is a glorious fact and a most wonderful privilege, that we poor sinners are made *"the righteousness of God in him."* God sees no sin in any one of His people, no iniquity in Jacob, when He looks upon them in Christ. In themselves He sees nothing but filth and abomination, in Christ nothing but purity and righteousness. Is it not, and must it not ever be to the Christian, one of his most delightful privileges to know that altogether apart from anything that we have ever done, or can do, God looks upon His people as being righteous. Not just righteous, but as being righteousness, and that despite all of the sins they have ever committed, they are accepted in Him as if they had been Christ, while Christ was punished for them as if He had been sin. Why, when I stand in my own place, I am lost and ruined; my place is the place where Judas stood, the place where the devil lies in everlasting shame. But when I stand in Christ's place—and I fail to stand where faith has put me until I stand there—when I stand in Christ's place, the Father's everlastingly beloved One, the Father's accepted One, Him whom the Father delights to honor—when I stand there, I stand where faith has a right to put me, and I am in the most joyous spot that a creature of God can occupy. Oh, Christian, get up there, get yourself up into the high mountain, and stand where your Savior stands, for that is your place. Lie not there on the dunghill of fallen humanity, that is not your place now; Christ has once taken it on your behalf. *"He made him to be sin for us."*

Your place is up yonder, above the starry hosts, where *"He has raised us up together, and made us sit together in heavenly places in Him."* (See Ephesians 2:6.) Not there, at the day of judgment, where the wicked shriek for shelter, and beg for the hills to cover them, but there, where Jesus sits upon His throne—there is your place, my soul. He will make you to sit upon His throne, even as He has overcome, and has sat down with His Father upon His throne. Oh! That I could mount to the heights of this sermon tonight; it needs a seraphic[4] preacher to picture the saint in Christ, robed in Christ's righteousness, wearing Christ's nature, bearing Christ's palm of victory, sitting on Christ's throne, wearing Christ's crown. And yet this is our privilege! He wore my crown, the crown of thorns; I wear His crown, the crown of glory. He wore my dress, no, rather, He wore my nakedness when He died upon the Cross; I wear His robes, the royal robes of the King of kings. He bore my shame; I bear His honor. He endured my sufferings to this end that my joy may be full, and that His joy may be fulfilled in me. He laid in the grave that I might rise from the dead and that I may dwell in Him, and all this He comes again to give me, to make it sure to me and to all that love His appearing, to show that all His people shall enter into their inheritance.

Now, my brothers and sisters, Mr. Maurice, McLeod, Campbell, and their great admirer, Mr. Brown, may go on with their preaching as long as they like, but they will never make a convert of a man who knows what the vitality of religion is; for he who knows what substitution means, he who knows what it is to stand where Christ stands, will never care to occupy the ground on which Mr. Maurice stands. He who has been made to sit together with Christ, and once to enjoy the real preciousness of a transfer of Christ's righteousness to him and his sin to Christ, that man has eaten the bread of Heaven, and will never renounce it for husks. No, my brethren, we would lay down our lives for this truth rather than give it up. No, we cannot by any means turn aside from this glorious stability of faith, and for this good reason, that there is nothing for us in the

---

4. One who uses angelic descriptions to teach the Word of God.

doctrine which these men teach. It may suit intellectual gentlefolk, I dare say it does; but it will not suit us. We are poor sinners and nothing at all, and if Christ is not our all in all, there is nothing for us. I have often thought the best answer for all these new ideas is, that the true gospel was always preached to the poor; *"The poor have the gospel preached to them."* (See Matthew 11:5.) I am sure that the poor will never learn *the gospel* from these new divines, for they cannot make head or tail of it, nor the rich either; for after you have read through one of their volumes, you have not the least idea of what the book is about, until you have read it through eight or nine times, and then you begin to think you are a very stupid being for ever having read such inflated heresy, for it sours your temper and makes you feel angry, to see the precious truths of God trodden underfoot.

WE LAY DOWN OUR LIVES FOR THE WORD OF GOD

Some of us must stand out against these attacks on truth, although we do not love controversy. We rejoice in the liberty of our fellow men, and would have them proclaim their convictions; but if they touch these precious things, they touch the apple of our eye. We can allow a thousand opinions in the world, but that which infringes upon the precious doctrine of a covenant salvation, through the imputed righteousness of our Lord Jesus Christ,—against that we must, and will, enter our hearty and solemn protest, as long as God spares us. Take away once from us those glorious doctrines, and where are we, brethren? We may as well lay ourselves down and die, for nothing remains that is worth living for.

STAND UP FOR THE WORD OF TRUTH

We have come to the valley of the shadow of death, when we find these doctrines to be untrue. If these things which I speak to you tonight are not the verities of Christ; if they are not true, there is no comfort left for any poor man under God's sky, and it would be better for us never to have been born. I must say what Jonathan Edwards says at the end of his book, "If any man could disprove the doctrines of the gospel, he should then sit down and weep to think they were not true, for," says he, "it would be the most dreadful calamity that could happen to the world, to have a glimpse of such truths, and then for them to melt away in the thin air of fiction, as having no substantiality in them." Stand up for the truth of Christ; I would not have you be bigoted, but I would have you be decided. Do not give acceptance to any of this trash and error, which is going abroad, but stand firm. Be not turned away from your steadfastness by any pretense of intellectuality and high philosophy, but earnestly contend for the faith once delivered to the saints, and hold fast the form of sound words which you have heard of us, and have been taught, even as you have read in this sacred Book, which is the way of everlasting life.

Therefore, beloved, without gathering up my strength for the fray, or attempting to analyze the subtleties of those who would pervert the simple gospel, I speak out my mind and utter the words of my heart among you. Little enough will you concern yourself, over whom the Holy Ghost has given me the oversight, what the grievous wolves may plan, if you keep within the fold. Break not the sacred bounds wherein God has enclosed His Church. He has encircled us in the arms of covenant love. He has united us in indissoluble bonds to the Lord Jesus. He has fortified us with the assurance that the Holy Spirit shall guide us into all truth. God grant that those beyond the effectiveness of visible fellowship with us in this eternal gospel may see their danger and escape from the fowler's snare!

CHAPTER 8

CHRIST—PERFECT THROUGH SUFFERINGS

A Sermon
(No. 478)
Delivered on Sunday Morning, November 2, 1862,
By Reverend Charles H. Spurgeon,
at the Metropolitan Tabernacle, Newington,
London, England

"For it became him, for whom are all things, and by whom are all things, in bringing many sons unto glory, to make the captain of their salvation perfect through sufferings."—Hebrews 2:10

Believing that God foreknows all things, we cannot but come to the conclusion that He foreknew the fall, and that it was but an incident in the great method by which He would glorify himself. Foreknowing the fall, and foreordaining and predestinating the plan by which He would rescue His chosen out of the ruins thereof, He was pleased to make that plan a manifestation of all His attributes, and, to a very great extent, a declaration of His wisdom. You do not find in the method of salvation a single tinge of folly. The Greeks may call it folly, but they are fools themselves. The gospel is the highest refinement of wisdom, yes, even of divine wisdom, and we cannot help perceiving that not only in its main features, but in its little points, in the details and the minutiae, the wisdom of God is most clearly to be seen. Just as in the making of the tabernacle in the wilderness not a single loop or catch was left to human chance or judgment, so in the great scheme of salvation, not a single fragment was left to the human will or to the folly of the flesh. It appears to be a law of the divine action that everything *must* be according to the fitness and necessity involved in perfect wisdom—*"It behooved that Christ should suffer"*; (see Luke 24:46), and in our text we find, *"It became him, from whom are all things, and by whom are all things, in bringing many sons unto glory, that he should make the captain of their salvation perfect through sufferings."* (See Hebrews 2:10.) It seemed to be but the order of natural fitness and congruity, in accordance with the nature and character of God, that the plan of salvation should be just what it is. *Oh, how careful we should be who have to preach it never to alter it in the slightest degree.* How concerned we must be to lift our prayers to Heaven that God would give us a clear understanding, first, of what we have to teach, and then a clear method of teaching what we have learned, so that no mistake may be made here. For a mistake here would mar that express image of God which shines in the gospel, and prevent our hearers from seeing the beautiful fitness and proportion which are so adapted to reveal the perfect character of God. We say the plan *must* be what it is; it could not be otherwise so as to be in keeping with the divine character; and, therefore, it is imperative upon us that we make no alteration in it, no, not of a word, lest we should hear the Apostle's anathema hissing through the air like a thunderbolt from God—*"If we or an angel from heaven preach any other gospel than that ye have received let him be accursed!"* (See Galatians 1:8.)

Three things to consider in this text:

First, that Christ is a perfect Savior.

Second, that He became so through suffering.

Third, that His being made perfect through suffering will ennoble and dignify the whole work of grace.
"It became him"—it seemed fitting—*"that in bringing many sons unto glory he should make the captain of their salvation perfect through sufferings."*

1. CHRIST IS THE PERFECT SAVIOR

I. Let us begin with the joyous thought, so well-known to you all, but so necessary still to be repeated, that the Lord Jesus is a perfect Savior. For, He is perfectly adapted for the work of saving. The singular constitution of His nature adapts Him to His office. He is *God*. It was necessary that He should be so. Who but God could sustain the enormous weight of human guilt? What but Divinity was equal to bear the awful load of wrath which was to be carried upon His shoulders? What knowledge but Omniscience could understand all the evil, and what power but Omnipotence could undo that evil? That Christ is God must ever be a theme for grateful admiration to His people. They who reject the divinity of Christ can have but a poor foundation to rest upon; the fickle sand would seem to be more stable than the basis of their hope. It is enough for one man to work out his own obedience; more than enough for one man to bear wrath for himself; how, then, could he do it for others, and for those countless multitudes whose ruin was to be retrieved?

Christ Had to Be Both God and Man

But, beloved, we know that even if Christ had only been God, He would not have been fitted for a perfect Savior, unless He had become *man*. Man had sinned; man must suffer. It was man in whom God's purposes had been for a while defeated; it must be in man that God must triumph over His great enemy. He *must* take upon himself the seed of Abraham, so that He may stand in their room and stead, and become their federal head. An angel, we believe, could not have suffered on the tree; it would not have been possible for an angelic nature to have borne those agonies which the wrath of God demanded as an expiation for guilt. But when we see the Lord Jesus before us, being verily the Son of Man, and as certainly the Son of God, we perceive that now Job's desire is granted; we have a *daysman*[1] that can lay His hand on both, and touch humanity in its weakness, and divinity in its strength; can make a ladder between Earth and Heaven; can bridge the distance which separates fallen manhood from the perfection of the eternal God. No nature but one so complex as that of Jesus of Nazareth, the Son of God, would have been perfectly adapted for the work of salvation.

And as He was adapted in His nature, so, beloved, it is very clear to us that He was also adapted by His *experience*. A physician should have some acquaintance with disease; how shall he know the remedy if he is ignorant of the malady. Our Savior knew all because *"he took our*

---

1. Mediator.

infirmities and he bare our sicknesses. (See Mathew 8:17.) He was tempted in all points, like as we are." (See Hebrews 4:15.) He looked not at sin from the distance of Heaven but He walked, and lived in the midst of it. He did not pass hurriedly through the world as one might hastily walk through a hospital without clearly understanding the disease, but He lived His more than thirty years in the very center of it, seeing sin in all its shapes; yes, seeing it in shapes that you and I have not yet seen. He saw it in demoniac forms, for hell was let loose for a season, that the combat might be the more terrible and the victory the more glorious. He saw sin carried to its most aggravated extent, when it crucified God himself, and nailed Jesus, the heir of Heaven, to the accursed tree. He understood the disease; He was no *empiric*[2]*; He had studied the whole case through; deceitful as the human heart is, Jesus knew it; fickle as it is in its various appearances— Protean* [3]*as it is in its constantly varying shapes, Christ knew and understood it all.*

His lifelong walking of the hospital of human nature had taught Him the disease. He knew the *subjects, too, upon whom to operate.* He knew man, and what was in man; yes, better than the most skilled surgeon can know by experiment. He knew by experience. He himself took our infirmities and bare our sorrows. He was himself the patient, himself the medicine. He took upon himself the nature of the race He came to save, and so every feeling made Him perfect in His work; every pang instructed Him; every throb of anguish made Him wise, and rendered Him the more accomplished to work out the purposes of God in the bringing of the many sons unto glory. If you will add to His perfect experience *His*

---

2. Charlatan or quack.
3. Variable.

marvelous character, you will see how completely adapted He was to the work.

Christ, Perfect Love, Perfect Power, Perfect Zeal, Perfect Savior

For a Savior, we need one who is full of love, whose love will make Him firm to His purpose, whose love will constrain Him to yoke every power and talent that He has to the great work. We want one with zeal so flaming, that it will eat Him up; of courage so indomitable, that He will face every adversary rather than forego His end. We want one, at the same time, who will blend with this brass of courage the gold of meekness and of gentleness; we want one who will be determined to deal fearlessly with His adversaries, who will put on zeal as a cloak, and will deal tenderly and compassionately with the disease of sin-sick men, such an one we have in Christ. No man can read the character of Christ with any sort of understanding without saying, "That is *the man* I want as my friend." The argument which Christ used was a very powerful one—*"Take my yoke upon you, and learn of me."* Why? *"For I am meek and lowly in heart"* (Matthew 11:29). The character of Christ qualifies Him to be the world's Savior, and there is something in His character, when properly understood, which is so attractive, that we may well say:

> *"His worth if all the nations knew,*[4]
> *Sure the whole world would love him too."*

---

4. A Famous Isaac Watts quote.

If we had to make a Savior ourselves, and it were left to a parliament of the wisest senators of the race to form an ideal personage who would just meet man's case, if the Divine One had lent us His own wisdom for the occasion, we could only have desired just such a person as Christ is. In character, we would have needed just such traits of nature and of spirit as we see in Jesus of Nazareth, the Son of God. We think, therefore, we may safely say to every unconverted man, Christ is adapted to be a Savior to you. We know that the saints, without our saying it, will respond, "Yes, and He is just fitted to be a Savior to us." Man, yet God; bone of our bone, and yet counting it no robbery to be equal with God; sufferer like ourselves, bearer of all the ills of manhood, and yet, unlike us, free from sin, holy, harmless, undefiled: qualified in all respects to undertake and accomplish the great work; O Jesus, you are a perfect Savior to us.

II. Furthermore, as Christ is thus perfectly adapted, *He is also perfectly able to be a Savior.* He is a perfect Savior by reason of ability. He is now able to meet *all the needs* of sinners. That need is very great. The sinner needs *everything.* The beggar at the door of Christ, asks not for crumbs or *groats*[5], but needs all that Christ can give. Nothing short of all-sufficiency can ever meet the needs of a poor son of Adam fallen by sin. Christ Jesus has all fullness dwelling in himself. "More than all in Christ we find": pardon in His blood; justification in His righteousness; wisdom in His teaching; sanctification in His Spirit. He is the God of all grace to us. Deep as our miseries and boundless as our sins may be, the mines of His unfathomable love, His grace, and His power, exceeds them still. Send a spirit throughout all

---

5. A silver coin of England worth four pennies, but no longer in use.

nations to hunt up the most abject of all races; discover, at last, a tribe of men degenerated as low as the beasts; select out of these the vilest, one who has been a cannibal; bring before us one lost to all sense of morality, one who has put bitter for sweet and sweet for bitter, light for darkness and darkness for light; let that man be red with murder, let him be black with lust; let villainies infest his heart as innumerable and detestable as the frogs of Egypt's plague—yet Christ is able to meet that man's case.

It is impossible for us to produce an exaggeration of the work of sin and the devil, which Christ would not be able to overcome by the plenitude of His power. *"He is able to save unto the uttermost them that come unto God by Him."* (See Hebrews 7:25.) That divine Word which made Heaven and Earth, is able to make a new creature in Christ Jesus; and that power which never can be exhausted, which after making ten thousand times ten thousand worlds could make as many more is all in Christ, and is linked with the virtue of His merit and the prevalence of His blood, and therefore He has all power in Heaven and in Earth to save souls. As He has this power to meet all needs, so He can meet all need *in all cases*.

WHAT IS YOUR CASE?

There has never been brought to Christ a man whom He could not heal. If born blind, a touch of His finger has given sight; if lame He has made him leap like a hart; yes, and though dead, the voice of Christ has made Lazarus come forth from His tomb. Some troubled consciences think their case is not in the list of possible cures, let us assure them it must be. I would like to know who is the vilest sinner, for if I knew him I would feel delighted to behold him, since I would see a platform upon which my Lord's grace might stand to be the more gloriously resplendent in the eyes of men. Are you the vilest of the vile this morning? Do you feel so? Does Satan say you are so? Then I pray you do my Master the honor to believe that He is still able to meet your case, and that He can save even you. Though you think yourselves the ends of the Earth, the useless threads of the garment of manhood, yet *"look unto him and be ye saved, all ye ends of the earth, for he is God, and besides him there is none else."* (See Isaiah 45:22.) As He can meet all cases, so He can meet all cases *at all times*. One villainous act of hell is to tell sinners that it is too late. While the lamp continues to burn, the vilest sinner that returns shall find mercy in Him. At the eleventh hour He saved the thief; let this not be a reason for your procrastination—that is ungrateful; let it, however, be a cause for hope—that is reasonable.

SALVATION CAN BE YOURS THIS VERY MOMENT

He is able to save you *now*. Now, at this hour, at this very moment, if you trust Him You are saved. If now, without an hour's delay to go to your room, without even five minutes' time elapsing in which to prepare your soul for Him, if now you can believe that Christ can save you, He will do it, do it at this moment. His cures are instantaneous; a word, and it is done. Swift as the lightning's flash is the accomplishment of His purpose of grace. *"As the lightning flashes from the west even to the east, so shall the coming of the Son of Man be"* at His last great advent; and so is it in His marvelous advent into the hearts of sinners whom He ordains to save. (See Matthew 24:27.)

The Wickedness of Unbelief and Doubt

Christ is able to meet all cases, and able to meet them at this very hour. Sinner, Christ is perfectly able to save you, and to save you perfectly. I know the will and wit of man want to be doing something to begin salvation. Oh, how wicked is this! Christ is Alpha, why would you take His place and be an Alpha to yourselves? This week I have had two cases in which I have had to hold a solemn argument with troubled souls about this matter. Oh! the "ifs" and "buts" they put forth; the "perhaps," and "and," and "peradventures," and "Oh, I don't feel this," and "I don't feel that!" Oh, that is wicked questioning of Christ! While talking with them, endeavoring to comfort them, and I hope not unsuccessfully, I was led to feel in my own mind what an awful crime it is to doubt God, to doubt Him that speaks from above, to doubt Him when He hangs bleeding on the tree. While it seemed to me to be such a hard thing to bring a sinner to trust Christ, yet it did seem, on the other hand, such a sin of sins, such a masterpiece of iniquity that we do not trust Christ at once. Here is the plan of salvation—trust Christ and He will save you.

Perfect Trust

But they say "I do not feel enough"; or else "I have been such a sinner"; or else "I cannot feel the joy I want"; or else "I cannot pray as I would." Then I put it to them. Do you trust Christ? "Yes," they will say, "I do trust Christ, and yet am not saved." Now, this makes God a liar, for He says, *"He that believeth on him is not condemned: and he that believeth on him hath everlasting life."* (See John 3:16-18.) When a soul professes to trust Christ, and yet says "I am afraid He will not save me," what is this but telling the Eternal God to His face that He is false? Can you imagine a grosser infamy than this? Oh! that men were wise, that they would take God at His Word, and believe that Christ is a perfect Savior, not asking Him to help them to believe first, but able to begin with them just where they are, and to lift them up from all the hardness of their hearts and the blackness of their souls to the very gates of Heaven. He is a perfect Savior, soul, and a perfect Savior for you.

LOOK AND LIVE

You know the old story in Numbers 21:8 of the brazen serpent. There may have been some very wise persons who, when the brazen serpent was lifted up, would say "I cannot look there and be healed, for, you see, I do not feel the venom in my veins as my next door neighbor does." The man is bitten, and his veins are swelling, but he says he does not feel the pain so acutely as his neighbor, and he does not feel the joy of those who are healed, or else he would look. "If some angel would come," he says, "and tell me that the brazen serpent was set up on purpose for me, and that I am ordained to be healed by it, then I would look." There is a poor ignorant man over there that asks no questions but does just as he is told. Moses cries "Look, look, ye dying; look and live!" and, asking no questions about what he has felt, or what he was, or what he should feel, that poor soul yonder just looks and the deed is done; the flush of health runs through him, and he is restored. While the questioner, the wise man in his awful conceit, too wise indeed, to do as he is told, perishes through his own folly, a victim to the serpents, but yet more a victim to his own conceit. Christ is a perfect Savior to begin His work in you, and He will also be a perfect Savior to carry on the work. He will never want your help; He is a perfect Savior to finish the work. He will bring you at last to His right hand, and enthroned with Him in light you shall bless and praise the name of God that He provided a perfect Savior for men.

Salvation Work Completed

III. Once more, let me remind you *that Christ is a perfectly successful Savior.* I mean by this that, in one sense, *He has already finished the work of salvation.* All that has to be done to save a soul Christ has done already. There is no more ransom to be paid; to the last drachma He has counted down the price. There is no more righteousness to be wrought out; to the last stitch He has finished the garment. There is nothing to be done to reconcile God to sinners; He has reconciled us unto God by His blood. There is nothing needed to clear the way to the mercy seat; we have a new and living way through the veil that was rent, even the body of Christ. There is no need of any preparation for our reception on the part of God. "It is finished," was the voice from Calvary; it meant what it said, *"It is finished"* (John 19:30). Christ has finished transgression, made an end of sin, and brought in everlasting righteousness.

And, as He has been successful in doing all the work for us, so, *in every case where that work has been applied, perfect success has followed.* Produce a single case where an application has been made to Christ without success. Find a single soul in whom Christ has begun His work, and then left it. You do hear of some who fall from grace: produce them. We are told of some who are children of God today and children of the devil tomorrow: produce them. We are told that one whom He loves, He may leave; produce those whom He has ever left. Let them be seen. Hold them up to the gaze of men and devils—the patients in whom Christ's medicine did work awhile, but failed to produce a lasting cure. Heaven would be clothed in sackcloth if such a discovery were made, for if He has failed to keep on Earth, why not in Heaven? Hell would be echoing with infernal laughter if one such instance were found, for where would be the honor of God's Word and promise? We challenge you, you princes of darkness, and you who make the vast assembly of the damned in hell, we challenge you to produce in all your ranks a single case of one who trusted in Christ that He delivered, and yet Christ cast him away. Or one in whom the new spirit was infused, regeneration wrought, and who yet, after all fell and perished like the rest. Lift up your eyes to Heaven; innumerable as the stars are the spirits redeemed by blood; as many as there are, they are all witnesses to the fact that Christ is a perfect Savior. He is not one who professes, but does not perform, for He has carried them all there, and as we gaze upon them we can say, "You have redeemed them unto God by your blood; you can save, and perfectly save, O Lord Jesus Christ."

All Things Are Made for His Glory

Now I have thus dwelt upon the perfect adaptation, the perfect ability, and the perfect success of Christ, our text tells us in Hebrews 2:10, that it became him, for whom are all things, that he should give us such a Savior. "For whom are all things," says the Apostle; that is, all things are made for His glory. Now, it could not have been for God's glory to give us an imperfect Savior; to send us one who would mock us with hopes which could not be fulfilled. It would have been a tantalizing of human hope, which I do not hesitate to pronounce an awful cruelty, if any but a complete and perfect Savior had been presented to us. If it had been partly works and partly grace, there would have been no grace in it. If it had been needful for us to do something to make Christ's atonement efficacious, it would have been no atonement for us. We would have gone down to the pit of hell with this as an aggravation, that a God who professed to be a God of mercy had offered us a religion of which we could not avail ourselves; a hope which did but delude us, and make our darkness the blacker.

I want to know what some of my brethren in the ministry, who preach such very high doctrine, do with their God's character. They are told to preach the gospel to every creature, but they very wisely do not do it, because they feel that the gospel they preach is not a gospel suitable to every creature; so they neglect their Master's mandate, and single out a few. I bless my Master that I have an available gospel, one that is available to you always, for *"whosoever believeth in him shall not perish, but have everlasting life,"* and I hold that it would be inconsistent with the character of Him "for whom are all things," and that it would be derogatory to His honor if He would have sent you a salvation that would not meet your need; and if He would have sent me to preach a gospel to you which could not completely save. But, glory be to God, the salvation preached here, the salvation taught in this Book, brings all to you, and asks nothing from you.

"HIM BY WHOM ARE ALL THINGS. . ."

Moreover, Paul calls our God—*"him by whom are all things."* It would be inconsistent with the character of Him by whom are all things if He had sent a partial Savior; a part for us to do ourselves, and for Christ to do the rest. Look at the sun. God wills for the sun to light the Earth; does He ask the earth's darkness to contribute to the light? Does He question night, and ask it whether it has in its somber shades something which it may contribute to the brightness of noon? No, my brethren, up rises the sun in the morning, like a giant to run his race, and the

Earth is made bright. And shall God turn to the dark sinner, and ask him whether there is anything in him that may contribute to eternal light? No; up rises the face of Jesus, like the Sun of Righteousness, with healing beneath His wings, and darkness is, at His coming, light. See, too, the showers. When the Earth is thirsty and cracking, does the Lord say unto the clouds, "Wait until the Earth can help you, and can minister unto its own fertility?" No, truly, the wind blows and the clouds cover the sky, and upon the thirsty Earth the refreshing showers come down. So it is with Christ; waiting not for man, and tarrying not for the Son of Man; asking nothing from us, He gives us of His own rich grace, and is a complete and perfect Savior.

Thus we have completed our first point; I wish we had more time for our second point; so we will pass to it at once.

2. CHRIST WAS MADE A PERFECT SAVIOR THROUGH SUFFERING

He was not made perfect in character by His suffering, for He was always perfect—perfect God, perfect man; but He was made officially perfect, perfect as the captain of our salvation through His sufferings, and that in four ways.

I. By His sufferings He became perfect as a Savior *from having offered a complete expiation for sin.* Sin could not have been put away by holiness. The best performance of a non-suffering being could not have removed the guilt of man. Suffering was absolutely necessary, for suffering was the penalty of sin. *"In the day thou eatest thereof,"* said God to Adam, *"thou shalt surely die."* (See Genesis 2: 17.) Die then He must. Nothing short of death could meet the case. Christ must go to the Cross; He must suffer there; and He must bow His head and give up the ghost, or else no atonement for sin would be possible. The curse came upon us as the result of sin. *"Cursed is every one that continueth not in all things written in the book of the law to do them."* (See Galatians 3:10.) Now had Christ not been perfect, and had He not suffered, He never could have taken our curse. *"Cursed is every one that hangeth on the tree"* (see Galatians 3:13), but without the tree, without the Cross, Christ could not have been our substitute, and all He did would have been of no use to us.

CHRIST THE PERFECT EXPIATION FOR OUR SIN

Being crucified He became accursed; being crucified He died, and thus He could make perfect expiation for sin. Sin demanded punishment; punishment must consist of loss and pain. Christ lost everything, even to the stripping of His garment; His glory was taken from Him; they made nothing of Him; they spat in His face; they bowed the knee, and mocked Him with bitter irony. There must be pain, too, and He endured it; in His body there were the wounds and the fever which the wounds produced, and in His soul there was an exceeding heaviness even unto death, and an agony which no tongue can tell, for we have no words in which to speak of it. We believe that this agony was commensurate with the agonies of the lost in hell; not the same agony, but an equivalent for it. And remember, not the equivalent for the agony of one, but an equivalent for the hells of all that innumerable host of souls whose sins He bore, condensed into one black draft to be drained in a few hours. The miseries of an eternity without an end, miseries caused by a God infinitely angry because of an awful rebellion, and these miseries multiplied by the millions for whom the man Christ Jesus stood as covenant head.

What a bitter cup that was, men and brethren! It might have staggered even Him! And yet, He drained that cup, drained it to its utmost dregs not a drop was left. For you, my soul, no flames of hell; for Christ the *Paschal*[6] lamb has been roasted in that fire. For you, my soul, no torments of

---
6. Refers to the Lamb of God. (See John 1:29.)

the damned, for Christ has been condemned in your stead. For you, my spirit, no desertion of your God, for He was forsaken of God for you. "It is done, it is finished, and by your sufferings, Lord Jesus, you have become perfect as the expiator of your people's sins." Remember, my brethren, remember that your sins are perfectly expiated. Do not let them trouble you as to punishment; the punishment has gone. Sins cannot lie in two places at one time; they were put on Christ, and they cannot be on you. In fact, your sins are not to be found; the scapegoat has gone, and your sins will never be found again. Your sins, if they were searched for, could not be discovered, nor can the piercing eye of God find a single blemish in you. So far as the punishment of the law is concerned it is finished, and Christ is a perfect Savior.

II. I repeat, if Christ had not suffered He could not have been perfect as a Savior, *because He could not have brought in a perfect righteousness*. It is not enough to expiate sin. God requires perfect obedience of man, if man wants to be in Heaven he must be perfectly obedient. Christ, because He took away our guilt, has supplied us with a matchless righteousness. His works are our works; His doings are, by imputation, our doings. But a part of obedience is a patient endurance of God's will. Patience is no small part of the full obedience of a sincere soul. Christ must therefore suffer hunger, and cold, and nakedness throughout life, so that He may be capable of the virtue of patience.

An obedience even unto death is now the only perfect form of obedience. The man who wants to keep the law of God perfectly must not turn back even at martyrdom. *"Thou shalt love the Lord thy God with all thy heart, with all thy soul, and with all thy strength,"* would now require death to consummate it. (See Luke 10:27.) It was not possible for the

Master to have made the robe, woven from the top throughout without seam, unless the scarlet thread of crucifixion had run along its edge. But now, my soul, Christ is your perfect Savior, for He presents you with a perfect righteousness. There is nothing more to do. Neither my living nor my dying can make my righteousness more complete. No doing, no laboring, no denying, no suffering, are needed to finish that which Christ began. "It is finished." Put on your robe, O Christian; walk ever in it; let it be your wedding dress. Angels admire you; God himself accepts you; and as you come into His wedding feast He sees you with this garment on, and He asks you not how you have come, but bids you sit down and feast forever, for you are such that even He can keep company with in His glory.

> III. *Yet, it was necessary that Christ should suffer to make Him a perfect Savior so far as His sympathy goes.* After sin is washed away, and righteousness imputed, we yet want a friend, for we are in a land of troubles and sorrows. Now, if Christ had not suffered He could not have been a faithful high priest, made like unto His brethren. We would never have had that sweet text—"He was tempted in all points, like as we are, yet without sin," if He had not suffered. (See Hebrews 4:15.) But now He knows all kinds of suffering. It is not possible that even out of the thousands now in this house there could be one heart whose need Christ cannot meet.

> "In every pang that rends the heart
> The man of sorrows had a part."[7]

---
7. Hymn # 451, "Where High the Heavenly Temple Stands" Verse 1, Written by Michael Praetorius.

Disease, sickness of body, poverty, need, friendlessness, hopelessness, desertion—He knows all these. You cannot cast human suffering into any shape that is new to Christ. *"In all their affliction he was afflicted"* (Isaiah 63:9.). If you feel a thorn in your foot, remember that it once pierced His head. If you have a trouble or a difficulty, you may see there the mark of His hands, for He has climbed that way before. The whole path of sorrow has His blood-sprinkled footsteps all along, for the Man of Sorrows has been there, and He can now have sympathy with you. "Yes," I hear one say, "but my sorrows are the result of sin." So were His; though not His own, yet the result of sin they were. "Yes," you say, "but I am slandered, and I cannot bear it." They called Him a drunken man, and a wine-bibber. Why, when you once think of the sufferings of Christ, yours are not worth a thought. Like the small dust of a balance that may be blown away with the breath of an infant, such are our agonies and our trials when compared with His. Drink your little cup; then see what a cup He drained. The little vinegar and gall that are your share you should gladly receive, for these light afflictions, which are but for a moment, are not worthy to be compared to the sufferings through which He passed.

CHRIST BECAME PERFECT AS AN EXAMPLE FOR US

Finally, upon this point; He therefore, became perfect *as our example*. This, too, was necessary in bringing many sons unto glory, for we come to Heaven by following the example of Christ, as well as by being washed in His blood. *"Without holiness no man shall see the Lord"*; (see Hebrews 12:14), and that holiness is best of all promoted by an investigation of Christ's character, and a studious imitation of all its points. Now had Christ not suffered He could not have been an example to us. We should have said, "Yes, yes, He may be an example to angels who don't suffer, but not to men who have to tread the hot coals of the furnace." He could have afforded no example of patience if He had never suffered; He could never have taught us to forgive if He had never felt injuries; He could not have trained us to have holy courage if He had never fought a battle; and He could never have shown us the way to make tribulation work experience, and experience hope, if He had not waded through tribulation to get to His throne.

We do not want an example taken from princes to be applied to peasants. We need a poor man to be an example for the poor; we want a man who lives in private to teach us how to live in retirement; we want one who fears not the face of crowds to show us how to walk in our public ways. If we want to meet the needs of fallen humanity, we need a man just like the Savior, who has passed through all the various phases of life, was in all companies, was shot at from all quarters, was tempted in all points like as we are, and this could not have been if He had been led in quiet ways along a path of joy. He must do business on the tempestuous deeps; His ship must rock, His anchor drag, the thick darkness and the lightning must gather round Him; as they did, therefore, the captain of our salvation was made perfect *through suffering,* as an example for our imitation. I wish that we might each know Him in the efficacy of His blood, in the glory of His righteousness, in the sweetness of His sympathy, and in the perfection of His example, for then we would know Him to the joy of our hearts forever.

3. CHRIST BEING MADE PERFECT THROUGH SUFFERING WILL ENNOBLE AND DIGNIFY THE WHOLE WORK OF GRACE

"It became him for whom are all things and by whom are all things, in bringing many sons unto glory"—that is the great work—*"to make the captain of their salvation perfect through suffering."* The whole thing will work for His glory. Oh, my brethren, how this will glorify God at the end, that Christ, the man, would be made perfect through suffering! How this will glorify Him in the eyes of *devils!* Looking upwards from their beds of fire where they bite their iron bands in vain, now they will see the wisdom and power of God as more than a match for the wisdom and might of their leader! It was in man that they defeated God; and in man God destroys them. They trampled on man's heel; man has broken their head. They took away from man the transient crown of his Eden-glory; man now wears the unfading crown of immortality. Man, even man, sits upon the throne of the Godhead, and that man crowned with light and glory everlasting was a man who encountered Satan; who met him, too, on fair grounds; not a man shielded from pain; not a man who had an immunity from internal or external distress; but a man full of weakness, full of infirmity, like other men, and yet, through God in alliance with His manhood, more than a conqueror, and now reigning forever and ever.

Milton[8], I think it is, supposes that this may have been the reason for Satan's first rebellion, because he could not bear

---
8. John Milton, poet and author of *Paradise Lost*.

that an inferior race would be lifted up to be set above him on God's throne. Whether this is so or not, it must certainly be an aggravation to the misery of that proud arch-traitor, that now the man, the man, the man in whose image God was defeated, is heir of all things, King of kings, and Lord of lords. How greatly God will be exalted that day in the eyes of lost spirits. Ah, you that shall perish—God grant there may be none such here!—if you would ever perish in hell, you would have to glorify God as you see Christ, who was made perfect through suffering, reigning there. You will not be able to say, "My damnation lies at God's door," for you will see in Christ a suitable Savior. You will have to look up and say, "Yes, He who was preached to me on Sabbath-days was God; He could save me. He whom I was bidden to trust in was man, and could sympathize with me, but I would not come unto Him that I might have life."

LETTERS OF FIRE

In letters of fire you will see it written, "You knew your duty, but you did not do it"; and even your moans and groans as you suffer will be but an utterance of this awful truth—"Great God, you are just, no, you are doubly just. Just first in damning me for sin, just second, in trampling me underfoot, because I trampled underfoot the blood of the Son of God and counted His covenant an unholy thing." Your weeping and wailing shall be but the deep bass of the awful praise which the whole universe, willingly or unwillingly, must give to Him who has provided a perfect Savior, and made Him perfect through suffering.

The Delight of the Redeemed

Oh, my brethren, what delight and transport will seize *the minds of those who are redeemed!* How God will be glorified then! Why, every wound of Christ will cause an everlasting song. As we circle His throne, rejoicing, will this not be the very summit of all our harmony—*"Thou wast slain, and hast redeemed us unto God by thy blood."* (See Revelation 5:9.) We must not say what God could do or could not do, but it does seem to me that by no process of creation could He have ever made such beings as we shall be when we are brought to Heaven; for if He had made us perfect at that time, we would have stood through our own holiness; or if He had forgiven us without an atonement then we would never have seen His justice, or His amazing love. In Heaven we shall be creatures who feel that we have everything but deserve nothing; creatures that have been the objects of the most wonderful love, and so mightily attached to our Lord, it would be impossible for a thousand Satans to ever lead us astray. I repeat, we shall be such servants as even the angels cannot be, for we shall feel under deeper obligation to God than them. They are created happy; we shall be redeemed by the blood of God's dear Son, and I am sure, brethren, day after day, after day, with no night ever again, we shall circle God's throne rejoicing, having more happiness than the angels, for they do not know what evil is, but we shall have known it to the full, and yet shall be perfectly free from it. They do not know what pain is, but we shall have known pain, and grief, and death, and yet shall be immortal. They do not know what it is to fall, but we shall look down to the depths of hell and remember that these were our portion.

Oh! how we will sing, how we will chant His praise, and this, I say again, shall be the highest note, that we owe all to that bright one, that Lamb in the midst of the throne. We will tell it over, and over, and over again, and find it an inexhaustible theme for melodious joy and song that He became man, that He sweat great drops of blood, that He died, and that He rose again. While the angels are singing "Hallelujah! Hallelujah! Hallelujah! Hallelujah!" we will bid them stop the song a moment, while we say, "He whom you thus adore was once covered with bloody sweat." As we cast our crowns at His feet, we will say, *"And he was once despised and rejected of men."* (See Isaiah 53:3.) Lifting up our eyes and saluting Him as God over all, blessed forever, we will remember the reed, the sponge, the vinegar, and the nails; and as we come to Him and have fellowship with Him. He shall lead us beside the living fountains of water, and we will remember the black brook of Kedron of which He drank, and the awful depths of the grave into which He descended. Amid all the splendors of Heaven, we shall never forget the agony, misery, and dishonor of Earth. And even when they sing the loudest sonnets of God's love, power, and grace, we will sing this after all, and before all, and above all, that Jesus the Son of God died for us, and this shall be our everlasting song—*"He loved us and gave himself for us, and we have washed our robes, and made them white in the blood of the Lamb."* (See Revelation 7:14.)

CHAPTER 9

CHRIST IS GLORIOUS—
LET US MAKE HIM KNOWN

A Sermon
(No. 560)
Delivered on Sunday Morning, March 20, 1864,
by Reverend Charles H. Spurgeon,
at the Metropolitan Tabernacle, Newington,
London, England

"And he shall stand and feed in the strength of the Lord, in the majesty of the name of the Lord his God; and they shall abide: for now shall he be great unto the ends of the earth."—Micah 5:4

You have a very vivid idea of the sufferings of Christ. Your faith has seen Him sweating great drops of blood in the Garden of Gethsemane. You have looked on with amazement while He gave His back to those who smote Him, and His cheeks to them who plucked off the hair, and hid not His face from shame and spitting. With sorrowful sympathy you have followed Him through the streets of Jerusalem, weeping and bewailing Him with the women. You have sat down to watch Him when He was nailed to the tree; you have wept at His bitter complaint in Matthew 27:46—*"My God, my God, why hast thou forsaken me?"* and you have rejoiced in His shout of victory in John 19:30—*"It is finished!"* With Magdalene and Nicodemus, you have followed His dead body to the tomb, and seen it wrapped about with spices, and left to its lonely sleep. Are your perceptions quite as keen concerning the glory which *did* follow and *is* following? Can you see Him quite as distinctly when on the third morning the Conqueror rises, bursting the bonds of death with which He could not be held? Can you clearly view Him ascending up on high, leading captivity captive? Can you hear the ring of angelic clarions, as with dyed garments from Bozrah the Victor returns from the battle, dragging death and hell at His chariot wheels? Do you plainly perceive Him as He takes His seat at the right hand of the Father, henceforth expecting until His enemies are made His footstool?

And can you be as clear this morning about the reigning Christ as you have been about the suffering Christ? Look, my brethren, "the Lion of the tribe of Judah, the Root of David, *has* prevailed to open the book, and to loose the seven seals thereof!" At this hour He goes forth, riding upon His white horse, conquering and to conquer. Look! at His girdle swing the keys of Heaven, and death, and hell, for *"the government shall be upon his shoulder: and his name shall be called Wonderful, Counsellor, The mighty God, The everlasting Father, The Prince of Peace."* (See Isaiah 9:6.) *"God also hath highly exalted him, and given him a name which is above every name: that at the name of Jesus every knee should bow."* (See Philippians 2:9-10.)

Behold Him in His Glory

Behold Him, my brethren, in His present plenitude[1] of glory, and endeavor to get as clear a perception of it as you

---

1. Full supply.

have had of His shame. Not only weep at His burial, but rejoice at His resurrection; not only sorrow at His Cross, but worship at His throne. Do not merely think of the nails and of the spear, but behold the imperial purple which hangs so nobly upon His royal shoulders, and of the divine crown which He wears upon His majestic brow.

I want to conduct you in such a frame of mind through the glories of my text:

First, bidding you observe *the perpetual reign of Christ*: *"He shall stand and feed in the strength of the Lord, in the majesty of the name of the Lord his God"*; then I shall beg you to observe that flowing from this is:

Second, the *perpetual continuance of His church: "and they shall abide"*; and then proceeding both from His continued reign and from the Church's consequent perpetual existence comes:

Third, the *greatness of our King: "for now shall he be great unto the ends of the earth"* (Micah 5:4).

1. The Perpetual Reign of Christ

At the outset, observe carefully *the perpetual reign of Christ*. He lives, He reigns, and He is king over His people. Notice first, that His reign is *shepherd-like in its nature*. The kings of the Gentiles exercise lordship over them, but our Master washed His disciples' feet. Earthly monarchs are often tyrants; their yoke is heavy, and their language domineering; but it is not so with our King; *his yoke is easy, and his burden is light, for he is meek and lowly of heart.* (See Matthew 11:29-30.) He is a shepherd-king. He has supremacy, but it is the superiority of a wise and tender shepherd over His needy and loving flock; He commands and receives obedience, but it is the willing obedience of the well-cared-for sheep, rendered joyfully to their beloved Shepherd, whose voice they know so well. He rules by the force of love and the energy of goodness. His power lies not in imperious threatening, but in imperial loving-kindness. Let the children of Zion be joyful in their King, *for "men shall be blessed in him: all nations shall call him blessed."* (See Psalm 72:17.)

Never have people had such a king before. His service is perfect freedom; to be His subject is to be a king; to serve Him is to reign. Blessed are the people who are the sheep of His pasture; if they follow in His footsteps their road is safe; if they sleep at His feet no lion can disturb their peace; if they are fed from His hand they shall lie down in green pastures, and know no lack; if they abide close to His person they shall drink of rivers of delight. Righteousness and peace are the stability of His throne; joy and gladness are the ornaments of His reign. Oh, how happy are we who belong to such a prince. O King in Jeshurun, we pay you homage with loyal hearts; *we come into your presence with thanksgiving, and into your courts with praise,* for thou art our God, and we are the people of thy pasture, and the sheep of thy hand. (See Psalm 100:3-4.)

HE SHEPHERDS US

Notice that the reign of Jesus is *practical in its character.* It is said *"he shall stand and feed."* The great Head of the Church is actively engaged in providing for His people. He does not sit down upon the throne in an empty state, or hold a scepter without wielding it in government. No, He stands and feeds. The expression "feed," in the original is like an analogous one in the Greek, which means to shepherd, to do everything expected of a shepherd: to guide, to watch, to preserve, to tend, as well as to feed. Our Lord Jesus Christ, the great Head of the Church, is always actively engaged for the Church's good. Through Him the Spirit of God constantly descends upon the members of the Church; by Him ministers are given in due season, and all Church officers in their proper place.

> *When he ascended up on high he received gifts for men (see Psalm 68:18.):* "And he gave some, apostles; and some, prophets; and some, evangelists; and some, pastors and teachers; or the perfecting of the saints, for the work of the ministry, for the edifying of the body of Christ." (See Ephesians 4:11-12.)

Our Lord does not close His eyes to the state of His Church. Beloved, He is not a listless spectator of our needs. This very day, He is standing and feeding His people. They are scattered, I know, wide as the poles asunder, but our mighty Shepherd can see every sheep and lamb of His flock, and He gives them all their portion of meat in due season. He it is that like a mighty breaker goes forth at the head of His flock, and they follow where He clears the way: *"He shall stand and feed."* Oh, blessed carefulness and divine activity of our gracious King, always fighting against our enemies, and at the same time shedding His *benignant*[2] influences upon His friends.

CHRIST'S REIGN IS CONTINUAL

Consider again, for it is in our text, that this active reign is *continual in its duration*. It is said, *"He shall stand* and feed"; not "He shall feed now and then, and then leave His position"; not, "He shall one day grant a revival, and then next day leave His Church to barrenness." Beloved, there is no such pastor as Christ. "I know my sheep," He can say, in a very high and peculiar sense. He knows them through and through; he feels with them; in all their afflictions He is afflicted; He is one with them eternally.

There is no such wakeful watchman as the Lord Jesus. Is it not written, *"I the Lord do keep it; I will water it every moment: lest any hurt it, I will keep it night and day."* (See Isaiah 27:3.) Those eyes never slumber, and those hands never rest; that heart never ceases to beat with love, and those shoulders are never weary of carrying His people's burdens. The Church may go through her dark ages, but Christ is with her in the midnight. She may pass through her fiery furnace, but Christ is in the midst of the flame with her. Her whole history through, wherever you find the Church, there shall you find the Church's Lord. The head is never severed from the body, nor is the watchful care of this gracious husband

---

2. Gracious.

towards His spouse suspended for an instant.

I beseech you labor to realize the noble picture. Here are His sheep in these pastures this morning, and here is our great Shepherd with the crown upon His head, standing and feeding us all; no, not *us* alone, but dispensing His tender mercies to all the multitudes of His elect throughout the whole world. He is at this moment King in Zion, ruling, and overruling, present everywhere, and everywhere showing himself strong in the defense of His saints. I wish that our Churches could be more influenced by a belief in the abiding power, presence, and pre-eminence of their living and reigning Lord. He is no dead King whose memory we are bidden to embalm, but a living Leader and Commander whose commands we must obey, whose honor we must defend.

Do not fail to discern that the empire of Christ in His Church is *effectually powerful in its action;* "*He shall feed in the strength of Jehovah.*" Wherever Christ is, there is God; and whatever Christ does is the act of the Most High. Oh! it is a joyful truth to consider that He who redeemed us was none other than God himself, He who led our captivity captive was Jehovah-Jesus; He who stands today representing the interests of His people is very God of very God, He who has sworn that every one of His people whom He has redeemed by blood shall be brought safe to His Father's right hand, is himself essential Deity. O my brethren, we rest upon a sure foundation when we build upon the Incarnate God; and O you saints of God, the interests of each one of you, and of the one great Church, must be safe, because our champion is God; Jehovah is our Judge, Jehovah is our Lawgiver, Jehovah is our King, and He will save us. How can He fail or be discouraged? When He makes bare His arm, who shall stand against Him?

Let us rehearse the mighty deeds of the Lord and tell of His wonders of old. Remember how He got victory upon Pharaoh and the pride of Egypt! Pharaoh said, *"Who is the Lord, that I should obey his voice to let Israel go?"* (See Exodus 5:2.) Ten plagues of terrible majesty taught the boaster that the Lord was not to be despised, and the humbled tyrant bade the people go their way. With a high hand and an outstretched arm did the Lord bring forth His people from the house of bondage. When the proud, high, heart of Egypt's king again rose against the Most High, the Lord knew how to lay His adversary lower than the dust. I think I see the hosts of Mizraim, with their horses and their chariots, hurrying after the Lord's fugitives. Their mouths are foaming with rage. *"The enemy said, I will pursue, I will overtake, I will divide the spoil; my lust shall be satisfied upon them"* (Exodus 15:9).

See how they ride in all their pompous glory, swallowing the Earth in their fury. O Israel, where shall your defense be? How will you escape from your tyrant master? Be still, O you seed of Jacob; you sons of Abraham, rest yourselves patiently, for these Egyptians whom you see today, you shall see no more forever. With their horses and their chariots the fierce foemen descended into the depths of the sea, but the Lord looked upon them, and troubled them. *"Thou didst blow with thy wind, the sea covered them: they sank as lead in the mighty waters"* (Exodus 15:10). The depths have covered them; they sank into the bottom like a stone. *"Let us sing unto the Lord, for he hath triumphed gloriously; the horse and his rider hath he thrown into the sea"* (Exodus 15:1). Surely it shall be so at the last with Jesus our King, and all His saints; we also shall sing "the song of Moses, the servant of God, and of the Lamb," in that day when the archenemy shall be overthrown, and the hosts of evil shall be consumed, and they who hate the Lord shall become as the fat of rams, into smoke shall they consume, yes, into smoke they shall consume away.

THE LORD'S KINGDOM IS MAJESTIC

One other word remains; our Lord's kingdom *is most majestic in its aspect.* You will observe it is written by the prophet—*"He shall feed in the majesty of the name of the Lord his God."* Jesus Christ is greatly to be reverenced; the familiarity with which we approach Him is always to be tempered with the deepest and most reverent adoration. He is our brother, bone of our bone, and flesh of our flesh, but still *"he counteth it not robbery to be equal with God."* (See Philippians 2:6.) I know He made himself of no reputation, and took upon Him the form of a servant, and he calls himself today our husband, and makes us to be members of His body, of His flesh, and of His bones; but yet we must never forget that it is written in Hebrews 1:6, *"Let all the angels of God worship him,"* and

> *"At the name of Jesus every knee shall bow, of things in heaven, and things in earth, and things under the earth; and that every tongue should confess that Jesus Christ is Lord, to the glory of God the Father"* (Philippians 2:10-11).

Yes, Christ is majestic in His Church. I wish, brethren, we always thought of this. There is a glory and a majesty about all the laws of Christ, and all His commands, so that whether we baptize at His command, break bread in remembrance of Him, or lift up His Cross in ministry—in whatever we do, in

His name, which is in fact, what He does through us, there is an attendant majesty which should make our minds feel perpetually reverent before Him. O that the world could see the glory of Christ in the Church! O that the world did but know who it is that is in the midst of the few, the feeble, the weak, the foolish as they call them. O Philistia, if you did but know who is our champion, Your Goliath of Gath would soon hide his diminished head. O Assyria, if you knew that the ancient might of Him who smote Sennacherib, still abides with us, your hosts would turn their backs and yield us an easy victory. There is a true and mysterious presence of Christ with His people, according to the promise in Matthew 28:20, *"Lo, I am with you always, even unto the end of the world"*; it is because the world ignores this that she despises and sneers at the Church of God. Therein is our comfort and our glory. We have a majesty about us if we are the people of God, which is not to be *gainsaid*[3]; angels see it and wonder—a majesty of indwelling Godhead, for the Lord is in the midst of us for a glory and around us for a defense.

2. THE CONSEQUENT PERPETUITY OF THE CHURCH

Because of the unseen but most certain presence of Christ as King in the midst of His people, His Church *abides*—so says the text. Here remember first that a Church *exists*. What a wonder this is! It is perhaps, the greatest miracle of all ages that God has a Church in the world. You who are conversant with human history will hear me out when I say that the whole history of the Church is a series of miracles,

---

3. Not to be challenged.

a long stream of wonders! A little spark kindled in the midst of oceans, and yet all her boisterous waves cannot quench it! Here is the great wonder which John saw in vision, and which history reveals in solemn, sober fact. A woman,

> *"being with child, cried, travailing in birth, and pained to be delivered. And there appeared another wonder in heaven; and behold a great red dragon . . . stood before the woman which was ready to be delivered, for to devour her child as soon as it was born."* (See Revelation 12:2-34.)

The man-child, who is to rule all nations with a rod of iron, was brought forth and caught up to God and to His throne. As for the woman, the Church, she fled as on eagles' wings to her wilderness-shelter prepared of God, until, in great wrath, the dragon pursued and persecuted her. Apt enough is that metaphor,

> *"The serpent cast out of his mouth water as a flood after the woman, that he might cause her to be carried away of the flood . . . And the dragon was wroth with the woman, and went to make war with the remnant of her seed, which keep the commandments of God, and have the testimony of Jesus Christ."* (See Revelation 12:15-17.)

Yet, my brethren, as surely as that glorious man-child, the Lord Jesus, lives and sits upon the throne, so surely shall the woman, the poor afflicted Church, live on until the dragon's time is over, and the King shall reign upon the Earth.

Trials Upon the Church

To what trials, my brethren, has not the Church of God been subjected? What new invention can Satan bring forth? The fire, the rack, imprisonment, banishment, confiscation, slander, all these have been tried, and in them all the Church has been more than conqueror through Him who loved her. False doctrine without, heresy and schism within, hypocrisy, formalism, fanaticism, pretenses of high spirituality, worldliness, these have all done their worst. I marvel at the wondrous ingenuity of the great enemy of the Church, but think his devices must nearly have come to an end. Can he invent anything further?

We have been astounded in these ages by the prodigy of an infidel bishop; we have been struck dumb with sorrow and amazement at a decree which declares that a Church professing to be a Church of Christ must permit men to be her ministers who deny the inspiration of Holy Scripture. This is a new thing under the sun. Popery and infidelity are to be both legalized and fostered in a Church professing to be Christian and Protestant. What next? and what next? But what of all this? *The* Church, I mean the company of the Lord's called and faithful and chosen still exists; the Lord has His elect people who still hold forth the Word of truth, and in the most reprobate Church still He may say, *"I have yet a few names even in Sardis which have not defiled their garments; and they shall walk with me in white: for they are worthy."* (See Revelation 3:4.)

Observe, the text says, "she abides," which means, not that she exists now and then by starts and spasms, but *she exists always.* This is wonderful! Always a Church! When the full force of the pagan emperors came like a thundering avalanche upon her, she shook off the stupendous load as a man shakes the flakes of snow from his garment, and she lived on uninjured. When papal Rome vented its malice yet more furiously and ingeniously; when cruel murderers hunted the saints among the Alps, or troubled them in the low country; when *Albigenses*[4] *and Waldenses*[5] poured out their blood in rivers, and dyed the snow with crimson, she lived still, and never was in a healthier state than when she was immersed in her own gore. When after a partial reformation in this country, the pretenders to religion determined that the truly spiritual should be troubled and harassed until they left the land, God's Church did not sleep or suspend her career of life or service. Let the covenant signed in blood witness to the vigor of the persecuted saints.

WHERE IS THE CHURCH?

Hearken to her psalm amidst the brown heath-clad hills of Scotland, and her prayer in the secret meetinghouses of England. Hear the voices of *Cargil*[6] *and Cameron*, Scotland thundering among the mountains against a false king and an apostate people; hear the testimony of John Bunyan and his peers who would sooner rot in dungeons than bow the knee to Baal. Ask me "Where is the Church?" and I can find her at any and every period from the day when first in the upper room the Holy Ghost came down even until now. In one unbroken line our apostolic succession runs;

---

4. A religious movement in the Middle Ages.
5. A religious movement during the 12th century in France.
6. Cargil and Cameron are towns in Scotland.

not through the Church of Rome; not from the superstitious hands of priest-made popes, or king-created bishops, (what a varnished lie is the apostolic succession of those who boast so proudly of it!) but through the blood of good men and true, who never forsook the testimony of Jesus; through the loins of true pastors, laborious evangelists, faithful martyrs, and honorable men of God, we trace our pedigree up to the fishermen of Galilee and glory that we perpetuate by God's grace that true and faithful Church of the living God, in whom Christ did abide and will abide until the world's crash.

THE ABIDING CHURCH

Observe, dear friends, that in the use of the term *"Abide,"* we have not only existence, and continued existence, but the idea of *quiet, calm, uninjured duration*. It does not say she lingers, hunted, tempted, and worried, but she abides. Oh, the calmness of the Church of God under the attacks of her most malicious foes. Cruel adversary, the virgin daughter of Zion has shaken her head at you and laughed you to scorn! She abides in peace when the world rages against her. It is most noteworthy how in most instances the Church of God still keeps her foothold where she has been most savagely persecuted.

In modern times we find in Madagascar, after years of exterminating persecution, the Church of God rises from her ashes, like the phoenix from the flames. The chief wonder is that she abides *perfect*. Not one of God's elect has gone back; not one of the blood-bought has denied the faith. Not one single soul that was effectually called could be made to deny Christ, even though his flesh was pulled from his bones by hot pincers, or his tormented body flung to the jaws of wild beasts. All the enemy has done has been of no avail against the Church. The old rock has been washed, and washed, and washed again by stormy waves, and submerged a thousand times in the floods of tempest, but even her angles and corners abide unaltered and unalterable. We may say of the Lord's tabernacle, not one of her stakes has been removed, nor one of her cords been broken. The house of the Lord from foundation to pinnacle is perfect still: *"The rain descended, and the floods came, and the winds blew, and beat upon that house; and it fell not:"* nay, nor a single stone of it *"for it was founded upon a rock"* (Matthew 7:25).

But why all this, dear friends, why is it that we have seen the Church endure to this day? How is it that we are confident that even should worse times arrive, the Church would weather the storm and abide until moons shall cease to shine and set? Why this security? Only because Christ is in the midst of her. You do not believe, I hope, in the preservation of orthodoxy by legal instruments and trust deeds. This is what too many dissenters have relied upon. We certainly cannot depend upon creeds; they are good enough in their way, as trust deeds are too, but they are as broken reeds if we rely upon them. We cannot depend upon parliament, or kings, or queens. We may draw up the most express and distinct form of doctrine, but we shall find that the next generation will depart from the truth unless God is pleased to give it renewed grace from on high. You cannot, by presbytery, or independency, or episcopacy, secure the life of the Church—I find the Church of God has existed under an episcopacy—a form of government not without its virtues and its faults. I find the Church of God flourished under a presbytery, and decayed under it too.

I know it can be successful under an Independent form of Church government and can decline into *Arianism*[7] quite as easily. The fact is that forms of government have very little to do with the vital principle of the Church. The reason why the Church of God exists is not her ecclesiastical regulations, her organization, her formularies, her ministers, or her creeds, but the presence of the Lord in the midst of her. Therefore, while Christ lives, and Christ reigns, and stands and feeds His Church, she is safe; but if He were gone, she would be quite powerless, as it is with you and me when the Spirit of God has departed from us; we become weak as other men.

3. The Greatness of Our King

But now, thirdly, flowing from both these, from the perpetual presence of Christ and from the continued existence of His Church, is the greatness of our King. *"Now shall he be great unto the ends of the earth"* (Micah 5:4). Christ is great in His Church, and O how great He is in our hearts where He reigns supreme! My heart leaps at the sound of His name:

> *"Jesus, the very thought of thee,*[8]
> *With rapture fills my breast."*

O for crowns, for golden crowns! Let us crown Him King in Zion! O for a well-tuned harp and for David's feet, to dance before the ark at the very mention of Jesus'

---
7. A theological doctrine developed around 320 A.D. in Egypt.
8. "Jesus the Very Thought of Thee" a poem by Reverend E. Caswall.

name! Now shall He be great indeed in our hearts! But He is to be great to the ends of the Earth. That is a promise, of which we will say it is *accomplished in a measure even now.*

Christ is made great until the conversion of every sinner. When the supplicating penitent sinner cries, "God be merciful to me a sinner," and the peace-speaking blood comes dropping upon the troubled conscience, and the soul bows meekly to accept the finished righteousness, then is Christ great. And He is great in the consecration of every one of His blood-bought saints; when they live for Him; when in their prayers they make mention of Him; when they give Him their heart's music, their life's light, and their lips' testimony; when they feel that tribulation is joyous if endured for Him, and the sternest toil a dear delight when undertaken for His sake— then Christ is great.

Think, my brethren, this morning, how many ships are now furrowing the blue sea in which there are hearts that love the name of Jesus. Listen—across the waves of the Atlantic and the Pacific I hear the sound of prayer and praise from many a vessel bearing the British flag. From many an island of the sea the song is borne upon the breeze. And there across the waters in the land of our American brethren, now so sadly chastened with war, multitudes of hearts beat as high as ours at the mention of the Savior's name. Here across the narrow Channel, in Holland, Sweden, Germany, Switzerland, and even in France and Italy, how many live in His name and praise Him this day!

We speak of our Queen's dominions and say that the sun never sets upon them. We may in truth say this of our Lord Jesus; men of all colors trust in His blood; they who look upward to the Southern Cross and they who follow the polar star, alike worship His dear name. And when England ceases her strain of joy, in the hush of night, Australia takes up the song, and so from land to land, and from shore to shore, a sacrifice of a pure offering is brought to His shrine. It is accomplished, in some degree, but oh, how small the degree when we think of the thick darkness which covers the multitude of the people.

Again, it is a promise which is *guaranteed as to its fulfillment in the fullest sense.* Courage brethren, courage! The night is not forever, the morning comes! Watchman, what do you say? Are there not streaks reddening the east? Has not the God of day, the Lord Jesus, begun to shoot His divine arrows of light upwards into the thick darkness? It is even so. As I think of the signs of the times, I would fondly hope that we shall live to see brighter and better days. "*Now,*" says the text, "*shall he be great unto the ends of the earth.*" Prophet, I wish that your "now" were true this day. Now, even now, let Him reign! Why does He tarry? Why are His chariots so long in coming? Will it be, my brethren, that Christ will come before the world is converted? If so, welcome Jesus. Or will the world be converted first? If so, welcome the mercy three times. But whether or not, this we do know, He shall have dominion from sea to sea, and from the river even unto the ends of the Earth. They who dwell in the wilderness shall bow before Him, and His enemies shall lick the dust. The day shall come when the *Fifth Great Monarchy*[9] shall be coextensive with the world's bounds, and everywhere the Great Shepherd shall reign.

---

9. An extremist group in the 1600's.

PROMISES MUST STILL BE LIFTED IN PRAYER FOR FULFILLMENT

But remember, dear friends, that while this promise is thus guaranteed as to its fulfillment, it is to be *prayed for as to its accomplishment*. *"I will yet for this be enquired of by the house of Israel, to do it for them"* (Ezekiel 36:37). The mountain of the Lord shall be in the latter days, but remember, though there be no sound of trowel or a hammer, there will be heard the sound of prayer and praise, as upward the mountain of God's house shall ascend. You know the picture and story. The prophet had seen the Lord's house standing, as it were, in a valley, and as he looked upon it, presently it became a little hill; the ground began to heave; and by-and-by it had swollen from a little hill into a lofty mountain. Up and up it rose, and grew more great before his eyes, until even the Alps were dwarfed and the Himalayas were stunted, and up it still went, not the house only, but the mountain too, until infinitely it was higher than the projected Tower of Babel, which man meant to be the world's center. The house stood out clear and sharp above the clouds, having pinnacles high up in God's Heaven, and yet deep foundations in man's Earth, and all nations began to flow to it as to the great center. What a dream! What a vision! Yet such shall it be. The Church is, as it were, in a plain just now; she begins to move. Oh stupendous movement! She begins to rise, her mountains swell and grow; she attracts observers; she cannot be held down. Who can attempt to restrain the swelling mass? Who shall prevent the gigantic birth? Up rises the mountain, as though swollen by some inward fire, up and up it swells, and swells, and swells, until Earth touches

Heaven, and God communes with men. Then shall be heard the great hallelujah, *"The tabernacle of God is with men, and he will dwell with them."* (See Revelation 21:3.)

Christ Must Be Glorified by the Body of Christ

But then, and this is the conclusion, and I hope God may help me to press it on your hearts. *All this is to be labored for* as well as prayed after. My soul pants and pines to see Christ glorious in the eyes of men. Lives there a Christian here with soul so dead that he does not desire the extension of his Master's kingdom? Sirs, is there one among you who counts it little to see Jesus Christ lifted up in men's hearts? I know I speak to a people—and the Lord knows that is the dearest of which is beloved, the fairest among ten thousand, and the altogether lovely. Now, if Christ is to be glorified, He must be glorified by you; if His kingdom is to come, it must come through you. God works, but God works by means. He works in you *"to will and to do of his own good pleasure."* (See Philippians 2:13.)

The Church Must Run the Race

Souls are to be saved, but they are not saved without instruments. The feast is to be furnished with guests, but you are to go into the highways and hedges, and compel them to come in. I know my Master is to have many crowns, but they are to be crowns for which you race, and which you have fought, which you have won through His grace that you will place at His feet, that He may honor you by wearing them upon His brow. Now we, as a people, have been greatly blessed and helped of God, and I believe the Master has a very high claim upon us. We, above all the churches in the world are indebted to the grace and mercy of God, and we ought to be doing something for the extension of the Savior's kingdom.

We cannot boast of wealth; we cannot profess to build all over London a multitude of churches as the Bishop hopes to do. Any scheme of raising three millions of money by us must be looked upon as being entirely a dream; we cannot attempt such a thing; if London is to be converted by money we must give up the task. We have no mitered bishops, no queens to subscribe, and no nobles and dukes, and the like to add their thousands and their tens of thousands of pounds. We are a feeble folk; what then can we do for God? Why, do as much as the strong! What can we do for God? Do as much as the mighty! No, my brethren, our very weakness and want of power shall be our adaptation to God's work; and he, who lives by the sword of Saul, and the armor of the son of Kish, will use David, and his sling and his stone, and smite Goliath's brow with it.

Gideon and the Winepress

I have been musing all this week upon that celebrated scene in ancient history, which seems to me to be so much like the state of our Church just now; the story of Gideon, the son of Joash, threshing wheat in the winepress, because he was afraid to be seen; the Midianites had conquered the land.

Now we, as Baptists, have generally been too much afraid to be seen; we have threshed our corn somewhere away in the winepress—up a back court—down a narrow street; any dirty hole would do to build a chapel in; so long as people could not find it then the site was thought advantageous; and if nobody could ever see it that was the place for our fathers, and for some who still linger among us. Joash was threshing wheat in the winepress, to hide it from the enemy.

Well now, I think the time has come that we should not be afraid of these Midianites any longer. Long has the Church of God been oppressed and kept back; she has been content to let the world devour her increase. There have been few additions to the churches; they remain very much what they were twenty or thirty years ago; but, my brethren, some of us think that we have seen our fleece wet with dew, while all around was dry; and we believe the Lord has said to us, *"The Lord is with thee, thou mighty man of valor"* (Judges 6:12). We think we have had the Lord's commission, "Go in this thy strength."

We do not expect all of you to go with us, for the people are too many. We expect that there are many of the trembling and faint-hearted who will step back from the battle; men who are look out for their families, and must provide for them; men who are saving up money, and grudge their sovereigns, and so on—these of course will stand back, and let them; for such men encumber our march. We fear that you are not all men who run to the battle; but we have a few who care very little for the ease and repose of life, who snatch a hasty draught as they run, and with heat, and zeal, and passionate earnestness run to meet the adversary. Now, these we expect to go with us to the fray. In the name of the Lord, I proclaim a new crusade against the sin and vice of this huge city. What are we to do? The hosts of Midian are to be counted by millions. Here in this great city we have three million people, and what if I were to say, two-and-half million of them do not know their right hand from their left in matters of religion. I believe I should speak too charitably; for if I could believe there were half a million of true believers in London, I would have vastly greater hopes of it than I have now. But, alas, that is not the case. Millions and millions are gathered in the valley of indecision that are not upon the Lord's side.

WE CAN DO NOTHING OF OURSELVES

What can you and I do? We can do nothing of ourselves, but we can do everything by the help of our God. Where Christ is there is might and where God is there is strength; let us therefore in God's name determine to plant new churches wherever openings occur. Like Gideon's men let us rally around our church officers, and follow where a warm heart leads the way. Gideon took his men, and bade them do two things; covering up a torch in an earthen pitcher, he bade them, at an appointed signal, break the pitcher and let the light shine, and then sound with their trumpets, crying, *"The sword of the Lord and of Gideon! the sword of the Lord and of Gideon!"* (See Judges 7:18.)

This is just what all Christians must do. First, *you must shine;* break the pitcher which conceals you; throw aside the bushel which has been hiding your candle, and shine. *"Let your light shine before men; let your good works be such,* that when they look upon you, they shall know that you have been with Jesus. (See Matthew 5:16.) There is much good done by the shining. Then *there must be the sound,* the blowing of the trumpet. O dear friends, the great mass of London will never hear the gospel, unless you go and blow the trumpet in their ears. Many who are members of this church never heard a gospel sermon, until they heard some of you preaching in the street.

"Why," said one "I never went to a place of worship; but I went down a street, and there stood a young man at the corner; I listened to him, and God was pleased to send an arrow to my conscience, and I came into the house of God afterwards." Take the gospel to them; carry it to their door; put it in their way; do not allow them to escape it; blow the trumpet right against their ears. In the name of God, I pray you do this. Remember that the true war cry of the Church is Gideon's war-cry, *"The sword of the Lord!"* God must do it, it is God's work.

THE CHURCH MUST CRY OUT "THE SWORD OF THE LORD AND OF GIDEON"

But we are not to be idle; instrumentality is to be used—"The sword of the Lord *and of Gideon!"* Remember this, if we only cry, *"The sword of the Lord!"* we shall be guilty of an idle presumption, and shall be tempting God to depart from His fixed rule of procedure. This is the cry of every lazy lie-n-bed. What good ever comes of saying, "The Lord will do His own work, let us sit still?" Nor must it be *"The sword of Gideon"* alone, for that would be idolatrous reliance on an arm of flesh; we can do nothing of ourselves. Not "The sword of the Lord" only, that would be idleness; but the two together, *"The sword of the Lord and of Gideon."*

O my brethren, God help you to learn this lesson well, and then you will go forth shining and sounding, living and teaching, testifying and living out the truth! You shall most assuredly make the Kingdom of Christ come, and His name shall be honored if you will do this. It seems to me that now is a glorious opportunity. There is a spirit of hearing upon the people.

Almost anyone may get a hearing who is willing to preach Christ. Now or never! Sons of Jacob! You are to be like a lion among the flock of sheep, and will you lie down and slumber? Up and every man to the prey! Sons of Jacob! You are to be as dew upon the grass, and will you tarry for men and wait for the sons of men? No. In God's name, go forward, and let something be done for God, and for His Christ, for a perishing age, for a dark world, for Heaven's glory, and for hell's defeat. Up! You who know the Lord; you swordsmen of our Israel, up and at them, and God give you a great victory and deliverance!

I want you to make some practical point of these things today. God has been pleased to put a sword into my hand, and to give me my lamp and my pitcher; my college [Pastor's College founded by Spurgeon in 1856] of young men is now become in the Lord's hands a marvelous power for good. A blessing greater than I could have expected rests on this work. We are continually sending them out, and God owns them in the conversion of souls. I have never seen any agency more blessed to the conversion of souls, than the agency of our college. Without saying anything to depreciate other efforts, I do believe God has conferred on our Institution a crowning and special blessing, and will continue to do so yet more and more. I want you all, both hearers and readers of my sermons, to feel that this is your work, and to help me in it while I continue to cry, *"The sword of the Lord and of Gideon!* God works, and therefore we work; God is with us, and therefore we are with God, and stand on His side.

Inasmuch as many of these men raise churches, we want you to help to build the places where the new congregations can be accommodated afterwards; and to that end we have striven to raise a fund of five-thousand pounds, to be lent out to these new churches on loan to be repaid by installments without interest. It is but a small sum, but it is as much as I think we can do, and frugal care will turn it to good account. Some three-thousand pounds have been promised by our seven shepherds and principal men; but there are many who have not promised anything yet, and we shall be glad if they will come forward, for otherwise this useful fund cannot be raised.

When this is done with, once for all, we will go on and do something else for Jesus. Do break this pitcher; get this done, and let your light of this thing shine. We must be doing something for God. I speak to you now upon the practical point, and come to it at once. If *you* are content to live without serving God, *I am not*; and if you are willing to let these hours roll by without doing something to extend the kingdom of Jesus, let me be gone from you; let me be gone from you to those of warmer spirits and of holier aspirations, for I must fight for God! There must be victories won for Him! We must extend the range of the gospel; we must find places where souls can be brought to hear the Word.

Hell shall not forever laugh at our inactivity, and Heaven shall not eternally weep at our sloth! Let us be up and doing, and let this thing be done by the many, the few have already done their parts. Promises reaching over five years are asked of you, you can all do something. And then, every one of you, when you have done your share in this, go out personally and serve with your flaming torch of holy example, and with your trumpet tones of earnest declaration and testimony serve your Lord, and God shall be with you, and Midian shall be put to confusion, and the Lord of hosts shall reign forever and ever. *"He that believeth and is baptized shall be saved; but he that believeth not shall be damned"* (Mark 16:16). Hear you that note, O dead souls, and live.

CHAPTER 10

Christ the Conqueror of Satan

A Sermon
(No. 1326)
Delivered on Sunday Morning, November 26, 1876,
by Reverend Charles H. Spurgeon,
at the Metropolitan Tabernacle, Newington,
London, England

"And I will put enmity between thee and the woman, and between thy seed and her seed; it shall bruise thy head, and thou shalt bruise his heel."—Genesis 3:15

This is the first gospel sermon that was ever delivered upon the surface of this Earth. It was memorable discourse indeed, with Jehovah himself for the preacher, and the whole human race and the Prince of Darkness for the audience. It is worthy of our heartiest attention.

Is it not remarkable that this great gospel promise should have been delivered so soon after the transgression? As yet no sentence had been pronounced upon either of the two human offenders, but the promise was given under the form of a sentence pronounced upon the serpent. Not yet had the woman been condemned to painful travail, or the man to exhausting labor, or even the soil to the curse of thorn and thistle. Truly "mercy rejoices against judgment." Before the

Lord had said in Genesis 3:19, *"dust thou art, and unto dust shalt thou return.* "He was pleased to say that the seed of the woman would bruise the serpent's head. Let us rejoice, then, in the swift mercy of God, which in the early watches of the night of sin came with comfortable words unto us.

These words were not directly spoken to Adam and Eve, but they were directed distinctly to the serpent himself, and that by punishment to him for what he had done. It was a day of cruel triumph to him, such joy as his dark mind is capable of had filled him, for he had indulged his malice, and gratified his spite. He had in the worst sense destroyed a part of God's works, he had introduced sin into the new world, he had stamped the human race with his own image, and gained new forces to promote rebellion and multiply transgression, and therefore he felt that sort of gladness which a fiend can know who bears a hell within him. But now God comes in, takes up the quarrel personally, and causes him to be disgraced on the very battlefield upon which he had gained a temporary success.

He tells the dragon that He will undertake to deal with him; this quarrel shall not be between the serpent and man, but between God and the serpent. God saith, in solemn Words, *"I will put enmity between thee and the woman, between thy seed and her seed,"* and He promised that there shall rise in the fullness of time a champion, who, though He suffer, shall smite in a vital part the power of evil, and bruise the serpent's head. It seems to me this was more of a comfortable message of mercy to Adam and Eve, because they would feel sure that the tempter would be punished, and as that punishment would involve blessing for them, the vengeance due to the serpent would be the guarantee of mercy to themselves.

Perhaps, however, by thus obliquely giving the promise, the Lord meant to say, "Not for your sakes do I this, O fallen man and woman, nor for the sake of your descendants; but for my own name and honor's sake, that it be not profaned and blasphemed amongst the fallen spirits. I undertake to repair the mischief which has been caused by the tempter, that my name and my glory may not be diminished among the immortal spirits who look down upon the scene." All this would be very humbling, yet consolatory to our parents if they thought of it, seeing that mercy given for God's sake is always to our troubled apprehension more sure than any favor which could be promised to us for our own sake. The divine sovereignty and glory afford us a stronger foundation of hope than merit, even if merit can be supposed to exist.

Effects of the First Gospel Sermon

Now we must note concerning this first gospel sermon that on it the earliest believers relied on and trusted in. This was all that Adam had by way of revelation, and all that Abel had received. This one lone star shone in Abel's sky; he looked up to it and he believed. By its light he learned of sacrifice and obeyed by bringing the firstlings of his flock and laid them on the altar, thereby proving, in his own person, how the seed of the serpent hated the seed of the woman, for his brother slew him for his testimony.

Although Enoch the seventh from Adam prophesied concerning the Second Advent, he does not appear to have uttered anything new concerning the first coming, so this one promise remained as man's sole word of hope. The torch that flamed within the gates of Eden just before man was driven forth lit up the world to all believers until the Lord was pleased to give more light, and to renew and enlarge the revelation of His covenant, when He spoke to His servant Noah. Those aged fathers who lived before the flood rejoiced in the mysterious language of our text, and resting on it, they died in faith.

Now, my brethren, you must not think of this as a small revelation, for if you consider it carefully you will see it is wonderfully full of meaning. If it had been on my heart to handle it doctrinally this morning, I think I could have shown you that it contains the entire gospel. There lay within it, as an oak lies within an acorn, all the great truths which make up the Gospel of Jesus Christ. Observe that here is the grand mystery of Incarnation. Christ is that seed of the woman who is spoken of here; and there is a hint not darkly given as to how that Incarnation would be effected. Jesus was not shadowed of the Holy Ghost, and "the holy thing" which was born of her was as to His humanity the seed of the woman only; as it is written, *"Behold, a virgin shall conceive, and bear a son, and shall call his name Immanuel"* (Isaiah 7:14).

DOCTRINE OF THE TWO SEEDS— GOD'S PROMISE

The promise plainly teaches that the deliverer would be born of a woman, and carefully viewed; it also foreshadows the divine method of the Redeemer's conception and birth. So also is the doctrine of the two seeds plainly taught here—*"I will put enmity between thee and the woman, and between thy seed and her seed"* (Genesis 3:15). There was evidently to be in the world a seed of the woman on God's side against the serpent, and a seed of the serpent that would always be upon the evil side even as it is unto this day. The Church of God and the synagogue of Satan both exist. We see an Abel and a Cain, an Isaac and an Ishmael, a Jacob and an Esau; those that are born after the flesh, being the children of their father the devil, for his works they do. But those that are born again—being born after the Spirit, after the power of the life of Christ, are thus in Christ Jesus the seed of the woman, and contend earnestly against the dragon and his seed.

CHRIST'S SORROWS

Here, too, the great fact of the sufferings of Christ is clearly foretold—*"Thou shalt bruise his heel."* (Genesis 3:15b). Within the compass of those words we find the whole story of our Lord's sorrows from Bethlehem to Calvary. *"It shall bruise thy head"*:

- there is the breaking of Satan's regal power,
- there is the clearing away of sin,
- there is the destruction of death by resurrection,
- there is the leading of captivity captive in the ascension,
- there is the victory of truth in the world through the descent of the Spirit,
- there is the latter-day glory in which Satan shall be bound, and lastly
- there is the casting of the evil one and all his followers into the lake of fire.

The conflict and the conquest are both encompassed within these few fruitful words. They may not have been fully understood by those who first heard them, but to us they are now full of light. The text at first looks like a flint, hard and cold; but sparks fly from it plentifully, for hidden fires of infinite love and grace lie concealed within. Therefore, we should be rejoicing exceedingly over this promise of God. We do not know what our first parents understood by it, but we may be certain that they gathered a great amount of comfort from it.

They must have understood that they were not then and there to be destroyed, because the Lord had spoken of a "seed." They would argue that it must be needful that Eve should live if there would be a seed from her. They understood, too, that if that seed was to overcome the serpent and bruise his head, it must bring good to themselves: they could not fail to see that there was some great and mysterious benefit to be conferred upon them by the victory which their seed would achieve over the instigator of their ruin. They went on in faith upon this, and were comforted in travail and in toil, and I do not doubt that both Adam and Eve in their faith entered into everlasting rest.

This morning I intend to handle this text in three ways.

First, We shall notice *its facts*.

Second, We shall consider *the experience within the heart of each believer which tallies to those facts*.

Third, The *encouragement* which the text and its connection as a whole afford to us.

1. THE FACTS

The facts are four, and I call your earnest attention to them. The first is *Enmity was excited*. The text begins, *"I will put enmity between thee and the woman."* They had been very friendly; the woman and the serpent had conversed together. She thought at the time that the serpent was her friend; and she was so much his friend that she took his advice in the teeth of God's precept, and was willing to believe bad things of the great Creator, because this wicked, crafty serpent insinuated the same. Now, at the moment when God spoke, that friendship between the woman and the serpent had already in a measure come to an end, for she had accused the serpent to God, and said in Genesis 3:13, *"The serpent beguiled me, and I did eat."* So far, so good.

The friendship of sinners does not last long; they have already begun to quarrel, and now the Lord comes in and graciously takes advantage of the quarrel which had commenced, and says, "I will carry this disagreement a great deal further, *I will put enmity between thee and the woman"* (Genesis 3:15). Satan counted on man's descendants being his confederates, but God would break up this covenant with hell, and raise up a seed that would war against the satanic power. Thus we have here God's first declaration that He will set up a rival kingdom to oppose the tyranny of sin and Satan, that He will create in the hearts of a chosen seed an enmity against evil, so that they shall fight against it, and with many a struggle and pain shall overcome the Prince of Darkness.

The divine Spirit has abundantly achieved this plan

and purpose of the Lord, combating the fallen angel by a glorious man: making man to be Satan's foe and conqueror. Henceforth the woman was to hate the evil one, and I do not doubt that she did so. She had abundant cause for so doing, and as often as she thought of him it would be with infinite regret that she could have listened to his malicious and deceitful talk. The woman's seed has also evermore had enmity against the evil one. I mean not the carnal seed, for Paul tells us in Romans 9:8, *"They which are the children of the flesh, these are not the children of God: but the children of the promise are counted for the seed."* The carnal seed of the man and the woman are not meant, but the spiritual seed, even Christ Jesus and those who are in Him. Wherever you meet these, they hate the serpent with a perfect hatred. We would if we could destroy from our souls every work of Satan, and out of this poor afflicted world of ours we would root up every evil which he has planted.

That seed of the woman, that glorious *One*,—for He speaks not of seeds as of many but of seed that is one,—you know how He abhorred the devil and all his devices. There was enmity between Christ and Satan, for He came to destroy the works of the devil and to deliver those who are under bondage to him. For that purpose He was born; for that purpose He did live; for that purpose He did die; for that purpose He has gone into the glory, and for that purpose He will come again, that everywhere He may find His adversary and utterly destroy Him and his works from amongst the sons of men. This putting of the enmity between the two seeds was the beginning of the plan of mercy, the first act in the program of grace. Of the woman's seed it was henceforth said, *"Thou lovest righteousness, and hatest wickedness: therefore God, thy God, hath anointed thee with the oil of gladness above thy fellows"* (Psalm 45:7).

Then comes the second prophecy, which has also turned into a fact, namely *the coming of the champion*. The seed of the woman by promise is to champion the cause, and oppose the dragon. That seed is the Lord Jesus Christ. The prophet Micah saith:

> *"But thou, Bethlehem Ephratah, though thou be little among the thousands of Judah, yet out of thee shall he come forth unto me that is to be ruler in Israel; whose goings forth have been from of old, from everlasting. Therefore will he give them up, until the time that she which travaileth hath brought forth" (Micah 5:2-3).*

To none other than the babe which was born in Bethlehem of the blessed Virgin can the words of the prophecy refer. She it was who did conceive and bear a son, and it is concerning her son that we sing, *"Unto us a child is born, unto us a son is given: . . . and his name shall be called Wonderful, Counsellor, The mighty God, the everlasting Father, the Prince of Peace"* (Isaiah 9:6). On the memorable night at Bethlehem, when angels sang in Heaven, the seed of the woman appeared, and as soon as he saw the light the old serpent, the devil, entered into the heart of Herod if possible to slay Him, but the Father preserved Him, and suffered none to lay hands on Him.

As soon as he publicly came forward upon the stage of action, thirty years after, Satan met Him foot to foot. You know the story of the temptation in the wilderness, and how there the woman's seed fought with him who was a liar from the beginning. The devil assailed Him three times with all the artillery of flattery, malice, craft and falsehood, but the peerless champion stood unwounded, and chased His foeman from the field. Then our Lord set up His kingdom, and called one and another unto Him, and carried the war into the enemy's country. In divers places He cast out devils. He spoke to the wicked and unclean spirit in Mark 9:25 and said, *"I charge thee, come out of him,"* and the demon was expelled. Legions of devils flew before Him: they sought to hide themselves in swine to escape from the terror of His presence. *"Art thou come. . . to torment us before the time?"* (Matthew 8:29) was their cry when the wonderworking Christ dislodged them from the bodies which they tormented.

He made His own disciples mighty against the evil one, for in His name they cast out devils, until Jesus said, *"I beheld Satan as lightning fall from heaven"* (Luke 10:18). Then there came a second personal conflict, for I take it that Gethsemane's sorrows were to a great degree caused by a personal assault of Satan, for our Master said, *"This is your hour, and the power of darkness"* (Luke 22:53). He said also, *"The prince of this world cometh"* (John 14:30). What a struggle it was. Though Satan had nothing in Christ, yet he sought if possible to lead Him away from completing His great sacrifice, and there our Master did sweat as it were great drops of blood, falling to the ground, in the agony which it cost Him to contend with the fiend. It was then that our Champion began the last fight of all and won it to the bruising of the serpent's head. Nor did He end until He had spoiled principalities and powers and made a show of them openly.

> *"Now is the hour of darkness past,*
> *Christ has assumed his reigning power;*
> *Behold the great accuser cast*
> *Down from his seat to reign no more."*

The conflict our glorious Lord continues in His seed. We preach Christ crucified, and every sermon shakes the gates of hell. We bring sinners to Jesus by the Spirit's power, and every convert is a stone torn down from the wall of Satan's mighty castle. Oh yes, and the day shall come when everywhere the evil one shall be overcome, and the words of John in the Revelation shall be fulfilled.

> *"And the great dragon was cast out, that old serpent, called the Devil, and Satan, which deceiveth the whole world: he was cast out into the earth, and his angels were cast out with him. And I heard a loud voice saying in heaven, Now is come salvation, and strength, and the kingdom of our God, and the power of his Christ: for the accuser of our brethren is cast down, which accused them before our God day and night"* (Revelation 12:9-10).

Thus did the Lord God in the Words of our text promise a champion who would be the seed of the woman, between whom and Satan there would be war forever and ever: that champion has come, the man-child has been born, and though the dragon is filled with wrath with the woman, and made war with the remnant of her seed which keep the testimony of Jesus Christ, yet the battle is the Lord's, and the victory falls unto Him whose name is Faithful and True, who judges in righteousness and makes war.

The third fact which comes out in the text, though not quite in that order, is that *our Champion's heel should be bruised*. Do you need me to explain this? You know how all His life His heel, that is His lower part, His human nature, was perpetually being made to suffer. He carried our sicknesses and sorrows. But the bruising came mainly when both in body and in mind His whole human nature was made to agonize; when His soul was exceedingly sorrowful even unto death, and His enemies pierced His hands and His feet, and He endured the shame and pain of death by crucifixion.

Look at your Master and your King upon the Cross, all disdained with blood and dust! There was His heel most cruelly bruised. When they take down that precious body and wrap it in fair white linen and spices, and lay it in Joseph's tomb, they weep as they handle the casket in which the Deity had dwelt, for there again Satan had bruised His heel. It was not merely that God had bruised Him, *"though it pleased the Father to bruise him"* (see Isaiah 53:10) but the devil had let loose Herod, and Pilate, and Caiaphas, and the Jews, and the Romans, all of them his tools, upon Him whom he knew to be the Christ, so that He was bruised of the old serpent. That is all, however! It is only His heel, not His head, which is bruised! For lo, the Champion rises again; the bruise was neither mortal nor continual. Though He dies, yet still so brief is the interval in which He slumbers in the tomb that His holy body has not seen corruption, and He comes forth perfect and lovely in His manhood, rising from His grave as from a refreshing sleep after so long a day of restless toil! Oh the triumph of that hour! As Jacob only halted on his thigh when he overcame the angel, so did Jesus only retain a scar in His heel, and that He bears to the skies as His glory and beauty. Before the throne He looks like a lamb that has been slain, but in the power of an endless life He lives unto God.

Then comes the fourth fact, namely, that while his heel was being bruised, *he was to bruise the serpent's head.* The figure represents the dragon as inflicting an injury upon the champion's heel, but at the same moment the champion himself with that heel crushes in the head of the serpent with fatal effect. By His sufferings Christ has overthrown Satan; by the heel that was bruised He has trodden upon the head which devised the bruising.

> *"Lo, by the sons of hell he dies;[1]*
> *But as he hangs 'twixt earth and skies,*
> *He gives their prince a fatal blow,*
> *And triumphs o'er the powers below"*

Though Satan is not dead, my brethren, I was about to say, I pray to God he were, and though he is not converted, and never will be, nor will the malice of his heart ever be driven from him, yet Christ has so broken his head that he has missed his mark altogether. He intended to make the human race the captives of his power, but they are redeemed from his iron yoke. God has delivered many of them, and the day shall come when He will cleanse the whole Earth from the serpent's slimy trail, so that the entire world shall be full of the praises of God.

Satan thought that this world would be the arena of his victory over God and good, instead of which it is already the grandest theater of divine wisdom, love, grace, and power. Even Heaven itself is not as resplendent with mercy as the Earth is, for here it is the Savior poured out His blood, which cannot be said even of the courts of paradise above. Moreover Satan thought, no doubt, that when he had led our race astray and brought death upon them, he had effectually marred the Lord's work. He rejoiced that they would all pass under the cold seal of death, and that their bodies would rot in the sepulchre. Had he not spoiled the handiwork of

---
1. Poem by Isaac Watts.

his great Lord? God may make man as a curious creature with intertwined veins and blood and nerves, and sinews and muscles, and He may put into his nostrils the breath of life; but, "Ah," said Satan, "I have infused a poison into him which will make him return to the dust from which he was taken."

But now, behold, our Champion whose heel was bruised has risen from the dead, and given us a pledge that all His followers shall rise from the dead also. Thus is Satan foiled, for death shall not retain a bone, or a piece of a bone, of one of those who belonged to the woman's seed. At the trump of the archangel from the Earth and from the sea they shall arise, and this shall be their shout, *"O death, where is thy sting? O grave, where is thy victory?"* (1Corinthians 15:55). Satan, knowing this, feels already that by the resurrection his head is broken. Glory be to the Christ of God for this!

In multitudes of other ways the devil has been vanquished by our Lord Jesus, and so shall he ever be until he shall be cast into the lake of fire.

2. Our Experience as it Tallies with These Facts

Now, brothers and sisters, those of us who have been saved were by nature the heirs of wrath even as the unsaved are now. It does not matter how godly our parents were, the first birth brought us no spiritual life, for the promise is not to them which are born of blood, or of the will of the flesh, or of the will of man, but only to those who are born of God, *"That which is born of the flesh is flesh"* (John 3:6);

you cannot make anything else and there it abides, and the flesh, or carnal mind, abides in death; it is not reconciled to God, neither indeed can be. He who is born into this world but once, and knows nothing of the new birth, must place himself among the seed of the serpent, for only by regeneration can we know ourselves to be the true seed. How does God deal with us who are His called and chosen ones? He means to save us, and how does He work to that end?

THE FIRST WORK OF GRACE

The first thing He does is, is to come to us in mercy, and "put enmity between us and the serpent." That is the very first work of grace. There was peace between us and Satan once; when he tempted we yielded; whatever he taught us we believed; we were his willing slaves. But perhaps you, my brethren, can recollect when you first began to feel uneasy and dissatisfied; the world's pleasures no longer pleased you; all the juice seemed to have been taken out of the apple, and you had nothing at all. Then you suddenly perceived that you were living in sin, and you were miserable about it, and though you could not get rid of sin you hated it, and sighed over it, and cried, and groaned.

In your heart of hearts you remained no longer on the side of evil, for you began to cry, "*O wretched man that I am! who shall deliver me from the body of this death?*" (Romans 7:24). You were already ordained to be the woman's seed from the covenant of grace, and now the decree began to discover itself in life bestowed upon you and working in you. The Lord in infinite mercy dropped the divine life into your soul. You did not know it, but there it was, a spark of the celestial fire, the living and incorruptible seed which abides forever. You began to hate sin, and you groaned under it as under a galling yoke; more and more it burdened you, you could not bear it. That is the way it was with you: is it so now? Is there still enmity between you and the serpent? Indeed you are more and more the sworn enemies of evil and you willingly acknowledge it.

Then came the champion: that is to say, *"Christ was formed in you the hope of glory."* (See Colossians 1:27.) You heard of Him and you understood the truth about Him, and it seemed a wonderful thing that He should be your substitute and stand in your place and stead, and bear your sin and all its curse and punishment, and that He should give His righteousness, His very self to you that you might be saved. Ah, then you saw how sin could be overthrown, did you not? As soon as your heart understood Christ then you saw that what the law could not do, in that it was weak through the flesh, Christ was able to accomplish, and that the power of sin and Satan under which you had been in bondage, and which you now loathed, could and would be broken and destroyed because Christ had come into the world to overcome it.

Next, do you remember how you were led to see *the bruising of Christ's heel* and to stand in wonder and observe what the enmity of the serpent had wrought in Him? Did you not begin to feel the bruised heel yourself? Did not sin torment you? Did not the very thought of it vex you? Did not your own heart become a plague to you? Did not Satan begin to tempt you? Did he not inject blasphemous thoughts, and urge you on to desperate measures; did he not teach you to doubt the existence of God, and the mercy of God, and the possibility of your salvation, and so on? This was his nibbling at your heel. He is at his old tricks still. He worries whom he can't devour with a malicious joy.

Did not your worldly friends begin to annoy you? Did they not give you the cold shoulder because they saw something about you so strange and foreign to their tastes? Did they not impute your conduct to fanaticism, pride, obstinacy, bigotry, and the like? Ah, this persecution is the serpent's seed beginning to discover the woman's seed, and to carry on the old war. What does Paul say? *"But as then he that was born after the flesh persecuted him that was born after the Spirit, even so it is now"* (Galatians 4:29). True godliness is an unnatural and strange thing to them, and they hate it. Though there are now no stakes in Smithfield, nor racks in the Tower, yet the enmity of the human heart towards Christ and His seed is just the same, and very often shows itself in *"trials of cruel mockings"* which to the tender hearts are very hard to bear. (See Hebrews 11:36.) Well, this is your heel being bruised in sympathy with the bruising of the heel of the glorious seed of the woman.

WE CONQUER. . . .

But, brethren, do you know something of the other fact, namely, that *we conquer, for the serpent's head is broken in us*. Now what do you say? How say you? Is not the power and dominion of sin broken in you? Do you not feel that you cannot sin because you are born of God? Some sins which were masters of you once, do not trouble you now. I have known a man guilty of profane swearing, and from the moment of his conversion he has never had any difficulty in the matter. We have known a man snatched from drunkenness, and the cure by divine grace has been very wonderful and complete. We have known persons delivered from unclean living, and they have at once become chaste and pure, because Christ has smitten the old dragon such blows that he could not have power over them in that respect. The chosen seed sin and mourn it, but they are not slaves to sin; though their heart goes not after it they sometimes have to say "the thing I do," but they are wretched when it is so. They consent with their heart to the law of God that it is good, and they sigh and cry that they may be helped to obey it, for they are no longer under the slavery of sin; the serpent's reigning power and dominion is broken in them.

Guilt Is Gone

It is broken next in this way; the guilt of sin is gone. The great power of the serpent lies in unpardoned sin. He cries, "I have made you guilty: I brought you under the curse." "No," we say, "we are delivered from the curse and are now blessed, for it is written, *'Blessed is the man whose transgression is forgiven, whose sin is covered.'"* (See Psalm 32:1.) We are no longer guilty, for *"who shall lay any thing to the charge of God's elect?"* (Romans 8:33). Since Christ has justified, who is he that condemns? Here is a swinging blow to the old dragon's head, such as he never will recover.

Oftentimes the Lord also grants us to know what it is to overcome temptation and to break the head of the fiend; Satan allures us with many types of bait; he has studied our points well, he knows the weakness of the flesh: but many and many a time blessed be God, we have foiled him completely to his eternal shame! The devil must have felt himself of little consequence that day when he tried to overthrow Job, dragged him down to a dunghill, robbed him of everything, covered him with sores, and yet could not make him yield. Job conquered Satan when he cried out to God *"Though he slay me, yet will I trust in him"* (Job 13:15). A feeble man had vanquished a devil that could raise the wind and blow down a house, and destroy the family who were feasting in it. Devil as he is, and crowned prince of the power of the air, yet the poor bereaved patriarch sitting on the dunghill covered with sores, being one of the woman's seed, through the strength of the inner life won the victory over Satan.

> *"Ye sons of God oppose his rage.*[2]
> *Resist, and he'll be gone:*
> *Thus did our dearest Lord engage*
> *And vanquish him alone."*

Under Our Feet

Moreover, dear brethren, we have this hope that the very being of sin in us will be destroyed. The day will come when we shall be without spot or wrinkle or any such thing; and we shall stand before the throne of God, having suffered no injury whatever from the fall and from all the machinations of Satan, for as it written in Revelation 14:5, *"they are without fault before the throne of God."* What triumph that will be! The Lord will tread Satan under your feet shortly. When He has made you perfect and free from all sin, as He will do, then you will have bruised the serpent's head indeed.

---

[2]. A hymn by Isaac Watts.

After Our Resurrection

The time of your resurrection, too, when Satan shall see you come up from the grave like one that has been perfumed in a bath of spices, when he shall see you arise in the image of Christ, with the same body which was sown in corruption and weakness raised in incorruption and power, then will he feel an infinite chagrin, and know that his head is bruised by the woman's seed. I ought to add that every time any one of us is made useful in saving souls we repeat the bruising of the serpent's head.

Sunday School Teachers

When you go, dear sister, among those poor children, and pick them up from the gutters, where they are Satan's prey, where he finds the raw material for thieves and criminals, and when through your means, by the grace of God, the little wanderers become children of the living God, then you in your measure bruise the old serpent's head. I pray you do not spare him.

Ministers

When we by preaching the gospel turn sinners from the error of their ways, so that they escape from the power of darkness, again we bruise the serpent's head.

The Body of Christ

Whenever in any shape or way you are blessed to the aiding of the cause of truth and righteousness in the world, you, too, who were once beneath his power, and even now have sometimes to suffer from his nibbling at your heel, you tread upon his head. In all deliverances and victories you overcome, and prove the promise true,—*"Thou shalt tread upon the lion and adder: the young lion and the dragon shalt thou trample under feet. Because he hath set his love upon me, therefore will I deliver him: I will set him on high, because he hath known my name"* (Psalm 91:13-14).

3. The Encouragement

Let us speak awhile upon the encouragement that our text and the context yields to us; for it seems to me to abound. Brethren, I want you to exercise faith in the promise and be comforted. The text evidently encouraged Adam very much. I do not think we have attached enough importance to the conduct of Adam after the Lord had spoken to him. Notice the simple but conclusive proof which he gave of his faith. Sometimes an action may be very small and unimportant, and yet, as a straw shows which way the wind blows, when thought about carefully it may display at once the whole state of the man's mind.

ADAM'S ACT OF FAITH

Adam acted in faith upon what God had said, for we read, *"And Adam called his wife's name Eve* [or Life]; *because she was the mother of all living"* (Genesis 3:20). She was not a mother at all, but as the life was to come through her by virtue of the promised seed, Adam marks his full conviction of the truth of the promise though at the time the woman had borne no children. There stood Adam, fresh from the awful presence of God; what more could he say? He might have said with the Prophet in Psalm 119:120, *"My flesh trembleth for fear of thee,"* but even then he turns around to his fellow-culprit as she stands there trembling too, and he calls her Eve, mother of the life that is yet to be. It was grandly spoken by Father Adam: it makes him rise in our esteem.

Had he been left to himself he would have murmured or at least despaired, but no, his faith in the new promise gave him hope. He uttered no word of repining against the condemnation to till with toil the unthankful ground, nor on Eve's part was there a word of repining over the appointed sorrows of motherhood; they each accept the well-deserved sentence with the silence which denotes the perfection of their resignation; their only word is full of simple faith. There was no child on whom to set their hopes, nor would the true seed be born for an age; still Eve is to be the mother of all living, and he calls her so.

Exercise like faith, my brother, on the far wider revelation which God has given to you, and always extract the utmost comfort from it. Make a point; whenever you receive a promise from God, to get all you can out of it; if you carry out that rule, it is wonderful what comfort you will gain. Some go on the principle of getting as little as possible out of God's Word. I believe that such a plan is the proper way with a man's word; always understand it at the minimum, because that is what he means; but God's Word is to be understood at the maximum, for He will do exceeding abundantly above what you ask or even think.

THE FIRST BLOOD SACRIFICE

Notice by way of further encouragement that we may regard our reception of Christ's righteousness as an installment of the final overthrow of the devil. The twenty-first verse says, *"Unto Adam also and to his wife did the Lord God make coats of skins, and clothed them"* (Genesis 3:21). A very condescending, thoughtful, and instructive deed of divine love! God heard what Adam said to his wife, and saw that he was a believer, and so he comes and gives him the type of the perfect righteousness, which is the believer's portion—he covered him with lasting raiment.

No more fig leaves, which were a mere mockery, but a close fitting garment which had been procured through the death of a victim; the Lord brings that and puts it on him, and Adam could no more say, "I am naked." How could he, for God had clothed him. Now, beloved, let us take out of the promise that is given us concerning our Lord's conquest over the devil this one item and rejoice in it, for Christ has delivered us from the power of the serpent who opened our eyes and told us we were naked, by covering us from head to foot with a righteousness which adorns and protects us, so that we are comfortable in heart, and beautiful in the sight of God, and are no more ashamed.

Next, by way of encouragement in pursuing the Christian life, I would say to young people, expect to be assailed. If you have fallen into trouble through being a Christian, be encouraged by it; do not regret or fear it, but rejoice in that day, and leap for joy, for this is the constant token of the covenant. There is enmity between the seed of the woman and the seed of the serpent still, and if you did not experience any of it you might begin to fear that you were on the wrong side. Now that you smart under the sneer of sarcasm and oppression rejoice and triumph, for now are you partakers with the glorious seed of the woman in the bruising of his head.

Still further encouragement comes from this. Your suffering as a Christian is not brought upon you for your own sake; you are partners with the great seed of the woman, you are confederates with Christ. You must not think the devil cares much about you: the battle is against Christ in you. When you were not in Christ, the devil would never trouble you. When you were without Christ in the world you might have sinned as you like, your relatives and workmates would not have been at all grieved with you, they would rather have joined you in it; but now the serpent's seed hates Christ in you. This exalts the sufferings of persecution to a position far above all common afflictions. I have heard of a woman who was condemned to death in the days of the *Marian Persecutions*[3], and before her time came to be burned a child was born to her, and she cried out in her sorrow. A wicked adversary, who stood by said, "How will you bear to die

---

3. Persecution of the Protestants beginning in 1555 by Queen Mary of England.

for your religion if you make such ado?" "Ah," she said, "Now I suffer in my own person as a woman, but then I shall not suffer, but Christ in me." Nor were these idle words, for she bore her martyrdom with exemplary patience, and rose in her chariot of fire in holy triumph to Heaven. If Christ be in you, nothing will dismay you, but you will overcome the world, the flesh, and the devil by faith.

Resist the Devil...

Last of all; let us resist the devil always with this belief that he has received a broken head. I am inclined to think that Luther's way of laughing at the devil was a very good one, for he is worthy of shame and everlasting contempt. Luther once threw an inkstand at the devil's head when he was tempting him very sorely, and though the act itself appears absurd enough, yet it was a true type of what that greater reformer was all through his life, for the books he wrote were truly a flinging of the inkstand at the head of the fiend. That is what we have to do: we are to resist him by all means.

Let us do this bravely and tell him to his teeth that we are not afraid of him. Tell him to recollect his bruised head, which he tries to cover with a crown of pride, or with a popish cowl, or with an infidel doctor's hood. We know him, and see the deadly wound he bears. His power is gone; he is fighting a lost battle; he is contending against omnipotence. He has set himself against the oath of the Father; against the blood of the incarnate Son; against the eternal power and Godhead of the blessed Spirit, all of which are engaged in the defiance of the seed of the woman in the day of battle.

Therefore, brethren, be steadfast in resisting the evil one being strong in faith, giving glory to God.

> "Tis by thy blood, immortal Lamb,
> Thine armies tread the tempter down;
> "tis by thy word and powerful name
> They gain the battle and renown.
> "Rejoice ye heavens; let every star
> Shine with new glories round the sky;
> Saints, while ye sing the heavenly war,
> Raise your Deliverer's name on high."[4]

---

4. "T'was By Thy Blood Immortal Lamb." Written by Isaac Watts in 1674.

CHAPTER 11

Christ's Resurrection and Our Newness of Life

A Sermon
(No. 2197)
Delivered on Sunday Morning, March 29, 1891,
by Reverend Charles H. Spurgeon,
at the Metropolitan Tabernacle, Newington,
London, England

"Therefore we are buried with him by baptism into death: that like as Christ was raised up from the dead by the glory of the Father, even so we also should walk in newness of life."—Romans 6:4

I have preached on this entire verse before, so this morning I shall take the liberty to dwell chiefly upon the latter part of it—*"Like as Christ was raised up from the dead by the glory of the Father, even so we also should walk in newness of life."*

The idea that the grace of God should lead us to licentiousness is utterly loathsome to every Christian man. We cannot endure it. The notion that the doctrines of grace give license to sin, comes from the devil, and we explore it with a detestation more deep than words can express. *"How shall we, that are dead to sin, live any longer therein?"* (Romans 6:2).

On our first entrance upon a Christian profession, we are met by the ordinance of baptism, which teaches the necessity of purification. Baptism is, in its very form, a washing, and its teaching requires cleansing of the most thorough kind. It is a burial, in which the man is viewed as dead with Christ to sin, and is regarded as rising again as a new man. Baptism sets forth, as in a picture, the union of the believer with the Lord Jesus in His baptism of suffering, and in His death, burial, and resurrection. By submitting to that sacred ordinance, we declare that we believe ourselves to be dead with Him, because of His endurance of the death penalty, and dead to the world and to the dominion of sin by His Spirit; at the same time, we also profess our faith in our Lord's resurrection, and that we ourselves are raised up in union with Him, and have come forth through faith into newness of life. It is a very impressive and vivid symbol, but it is without meaning unless we rise to purity of life.

Union

The basis of this confession lies in the union of every believer with Christ Jesus. We are dead with Him, because we are one with Him. We are risen with Him, because we are one with Him. Every believer is, in the purpose of divine grace, identified with Jesus. He was given to the Lord Jesus from before the foundation of the world, and placed under His covenant headship. The Lord Jesus suffered for the believer as his substitute, and virtually every saved person died in Christ, who represented him. The believer rose in Christ by virtue of the eternal union which exists between the saint and His Savior. Therefore the believer continues to live, for the Lord has said, *"Because I live, ye shall live also"* (John 14:19).

Our destiny is identified with that of our covenant Head. His life is the model of our experience: He makes us to be conformed to His image now, and *"we shall be like him; for we shall see him as he is"* (1 John 3:2). O my hearer, if you are not in Christ you have nothing. Out of Christ you are in the wilderness: with Him you are in a paradise. In Christ believers possess all the treasures of wisdom, knowledge, grace, power, and love. All things are yours, if you are Christ's. From our union to Christ follows our sanctification: we cannot follow after sin, for Christ does not follow after it. He died unto sin once, and we are henceforth dead to it. He is risen by the glory of the Father, and we are risen with Him into righteousness, acceptance, and joy.

1. THE RESURRECTION OF OUR LORD WAS ATTENDED WITH GLORY

Follow me in the text, taking as your first thought the fact that He was *"raised up from the dead by the glory of the Father"* (Romans 6:4). Christ's resurrection is linked with the fullness of eternal glory. *In itself it was a great marvel.* Our Lord was assuredly dead: the Roman guards at the Cross took care that no condemned person escaped the death penalty; in our Lord's case His heart was pierced with the spear to make sure that no life remained in Him. Joseph begged for His body, and by the loving hands of those who were sure that He was dead He was wrapped in spices and fine linen, and laid in the rocky tomb. There lay our Lord, in the grave, with a stone rolled at the cave's mouth, and a seal set upon it by those in authority, whose envy made them take double precautions. As when a prince lies slumbering in his pavilion he is watched by a guard, so was our Lord's sepulcher watched by a guard of Roman soldiers, that no man might steal His body. There He lay in the heart of the Earth, for a portion of three days and nights.

He was really dead, and in the grave He wore all the marks of decease: a napkin was bound about His head, and the fragrant spice-filled linen cloths encircled His body. On the morning of the third day it was truly said, in Luke 24:34, *"The Lord is risen indeed"*; for He actually, literally, and in very fact awoke to life, unbound the napkin and laid it by itself, leisurely folded His grave clothes, and when the angel had rolled away the stone from the mouth of the sepulcher, the First-begotten from the dead came forth in a material body to live among His disciples for forty days. During the time of His sojourn, His resurrection was established by many infallible proofs: He was seen, heard, touched, and handled. One of His disciples put his finger into the print of the nails, and thrust his hand into His side. He possessed a real body, for He ate a piece of a broiled fish and of a honeycomb before them all.

It was Jesus of Nazareth, and none other than He, who met His disciples at Galilee. On this firm basis of fact we build our holy faith; but, certain as it is, it is nonetheless a marvel. All glory be to Him *"that brought again from the dead our Lord Jesus, that great Shepherd of the sheep, through the blood of the everlasting covenant"* (Hebrews 13:20).

Glorious Resurrection

The resurrection of our Lord is glorious in contrast with His humiliation. It has in it sufficient of glory to redeem His passion from the shame which gathered about it. We read in Matthew 20:18-19 how He was to be betrayed, condemned to death, delivered to the Gentiles, mocked, scourged, and crucified; but we note that all the gloom of that dread tragedy is removed by the few words with which our Lord ended the story: *"And the third day he shall rise again"* (Matthew 20:19). The blaze of resurrection lights up the whole length of the Valley of the Shadow. His death wears no dishonor on its brow, for His rising again has set a diadem thereon. We celebrate Gethsemane and Calvary, and find no bitterness in all their grief, because death is swallowed up in the victory of resurrection. The whole earthly life of Jesus with its poverty, its slander, its sorrow, its scourging, its spitting, its crucifixion, is raised above all trace of dishonor by His glorious resurrection.

Glorious in the Effects

His resurrection is glorious in its effects. He was "delivered for our offenses," but "he was raised again for our justification." In death He discharged our debt: in resurrection He exhibited the receipt of all our liabilities. He was surety for us, and therefore He smarted and went down to the prison of the grave; but by death He discharged His *suretyship* [1] and was

---

1. The state of being surety, the obligation of a person to answer

set free. Our Lord has risen, and therefore we shall rise in the day of His appearing. The *"breaker"*[2] leads the way, and behind the mighty champion the whole company of His redeemed pass through the portals of the tomb in the power of His resurrection. The stone is rolled away for them as well as for Him. They cannot be held in the bonds of death, for He could not be detained a captive. What a glory there is in our Lord's resurrection, when we further remember that *"he ever liveth to make intercession for us"* therefore, He is able to save them to the uttermost that come unto God by him!" (See Hebrews 7:25.) The fullness of salvation comes to us because He has risen from the dead, and is now making intercession for the transgressors. O brethren, the resurrection of Jesus is bright as the sun with glory! Faith in it thrills our hearts. Well might we end each line of our hymns with a "hallelujah!" When we say one to another, "The Lord is risen indeed," we feel like singing all the time, for now our faith is not in vain, we are not in our sins, and those who have fallen asleep have not perished.

GLORIOUS TO THE CAUSE

Our Lord's resurrection was glorious as to its cause, for it was a display of the glory of the Father. For "glory" you may read "power," if you please; for it was a great work of power to raise Jesus from the dead. But it was more than a miracle of power, for all the attributes of God united their glory in the resurrection of Christ. God's love came there, and opened those closed eyes; His delight adorned those

---

for the debt, default or miscarriage of another.
2. A wave that crests into foam as it hits the shoreline.

deadly wounds; His wisdom set in motion that pierced heart. Divine justice claimed His loosing from the grave, and mercy smiled as she lit up His face with an immortal smile. There and then did Jehovah make all His glory to pass before us, and He proclaimed the name of the Lord.

If you ask where God's glory most is seen, I will not point to creation, nor to providence, but to the raising of Jesus from the dead. It is true that in the silence of the tomb there were no spectators, but God himself was there. After the deed was done, there were many who beheld His glory; and when at the close of His sojourn below He ascended beyond the clouds, and all Heaven came forth to meet Him, and to behold the conqueror of death and hell. In His resurrection the glory of God was laid bare. The veil which concealed the sacred presence was rent from top to bottom; and the glory of the Lord was seen in the resurrection of Christ from the dead.

GLORIOUS BECAUSE HE SUFFERED ONCE FOR ALL

That resurrection is glorious, because of its sequel in reference to our Lord. Of this I have already spoken in measure; only let me remind you that He rose to die no more. Once has He suffered, but it is once for all. His victory is final. Like Samson, the fierce lion of death roared upon him in the vineyard. The monster had hitherto overcome everyone whom he assailed; but this time he met his match. Our greater Samson rent him as though he were a kid; and though our deliverer fell in the act of victory, He rose from the death struggle with fullness of life.

Behold, He comes to us today, bearing handfuls of honey, on which He bids us feed. He has taken it from the carcass of the lion which He slew. Now death is a store of sweets, rather than a cup of gall. To the child of God, death furnishes a couch of rest, and is no longer a dark and noisome prison cell. Death is the refining pot for this poor flesh and blood: the body is sown in corruption, but it is raised in incorruption and immortality. We shall with these eyes behold our Lord when He shall stand in the latter day upon the Earth.

O glorious resurrection, which has turned our poison into medicine! O miracle of love, which has made death to be the gate of life! When you were singing the Easter hymn just now, it seemed to me as if we filled the whole Earth with silver bells; and when you came to the last verse, you were so fully getting into the music of the truth, that I had half a mind to cry, "Let us begin again." In the rising of Jesus, death itself is shut up in prison, and ten thousand Hallelujahs come flying down from Heaven to teach us how to sing—

> *"Vain the watch, the stone, the seal*
> *Christ has burst the gates of hell;*
> *Death in vain forbids him rise,*
> *Christ hath open'd paradise."*[3]

---

3. The hymn "Christ the Lord Is Risen Today" written by Charles Wesley in 1779.

2. THE PARALLEL IN OUR EXPERIENCE IS ALSO FULL OF GLORY

When the time of love had fully come, we also rose as to our spirits; that *"like as Christ was raised up from the dead by the glory of the Father, even so we also should walk in newness of life."* (Romans 6:4). Partakers of His death, we are also partakers of His resurrection. This body of ours will have its share in that blessing of adoption in due time. As yet, it remains subject to pain, weakness, and death; for it is as the apostle puts it, *"If Christ be in you, the body is dead because of sin; but the Spirit is life because of righteousness"* (Romans 8:10). The spirit has its resurrection even now; but we are *"waiting for the adoption, to wit, the redemption of our body"* (Romans 8:23). At the second coming of the Lord the dead shall be raised incorruptible, and the living shall be changed. We have the first fruits of the Spirit, inasmuch as we are spiritually risen from the dead; and the rest will follow in due course.

QUICKENING

It is a blessed thing that we should be made alive in Christ. As many of you as have believed in the Lord Jesus have been raised from among the dead. You were once without faith and without feeling. You had no sense of sin; you had no desire after holiness; you had no confidence in Christ; you had no love for the Father: but *"you hath he quickened, who were dead in trespasses and sins"* (Ephesians 2:1). You live now even as Jesus lived when He was *"declared to be the*

Son of God with power, according to the spirit of holiness, by the resurrection from the dead" (Romans 1:4). Why should the Lord of life have raised you from your death? Multitudes around you are still dead. You could not have made yourselves alive; for it is clear that the dead cannot rise by their own power. You were like the dry bones of Ezekiel's valley, without even the form or the moisture of life. You were more difficult to quicken than your Savior's body; for *"he saw no corruption,"* but you were corrupt of heart. (See Acts 13:37.) Ah, how much you saw of corruption! In you has Jehovah repeated the miracle which He performed on His beloved Son.

Remember that *quickening is a needful part of the process of sanctification.* Sanctification, in its operation upon our character, consists of three things.

- First, we die unto sin. A wondrous death! By this Jesus strikes at the heart of evil. The death of Christ makes us die to sin.

- After this comes burial. We are buried with Christ, and of this burial baptism is the type and token. Covered up to be forgotten, we are to sin as a dead shepherd to his flock. As the sheep pass over the dead shepherd's grave, or even feed thereon, he regards them not; it is the same when our old sins and habits come about us, but we, as dead men, know them no more. We are buried to them.

- To complete our actual sanctification we receive heavenly quickening. *"If we be dead with Christ, we believe that we shall also live with him"* (Romans 6:8).

Yes, we do live in Him, and by Him, for *"he that believeth in him hath everlasting life."* (See John 3:16.) I trust you know what this means. Therefore, are you dead and buried in Christ? Are you now quickened in the likeness of His resurrection? This is your joyful privilege, if you are indeed believers in Christ, and joined unto the Lord in one spirit.

NEW LIFE

Being thus quickened *you are partakers of a new life.* You are not like Lazarus, who, when he was raised from the dead, had the same life restored to him. True, you have that same old life around you. Alas, that you should have it! For it will be your burden and plague. But your true life has come to you by your being born again from above.

> *"This is the record, that God hath given to us eternal life, and this life is in his Son. He that hath the Son hath life" (1 John 5:11-12a). The Holy Ghost hath wrought in us a higher life than nature possessed. "We know that whosoever is born of God sinneth not; but he that is begotten of God keepeth himself, and that wicked one toucheth him not". (1 John 5:18). We have received "a living and incorruptible seed which liveth and abideth for ever." (See 1 Peter 1:23.)*

THE MIRACLE OF NEW LIFE

In this there is a striking display of the glory of God. As in the resurrection of Christ we see all the glorious attributes of God, so there is in every believer's spiritual quickening a manifestation of the divine presence. I know not how much there is of God in the regeneration of each new-born soul; but I know this, that God likens it to a new creation, and to the resurrection; and therefore we may be sure that it is one of the highest displays of divine power. We talk of conversion, but how lightly do we estimate the full meaning of conversion! Do you not know that regeneration is one of the greatest miracles that God himself can perform? To be begotten *"again unto a lively hope"* is a mass of wonders. (See 1 Peter 1:3.) We, who before our new birth lay under spiritual death, have become possessors of a heavenly life; who shall fully comprehend this? This is a miracle indeed; and we ourselves are the subjects of it. Surely, we do not think highly enough of the notable deed which has been wrought upon our impotent selves.

Lazarus raised from the dead was the object of wonder to everybody. The Jews came to Bethany, not to see Jesus only, but to see Lazarus, who was raised from the dead. What must Lazarus have thought of being brought back from the land of darkness to visit again the haunts of men? Lazarus must have felt himself a strange and singular man; even his sisters, Mary and Martha, could not understand his experience. Christian man, you have felt what you can never tell; you have received what you can never explain, you possess a secret something which can never be set forth in words. God help you to show it by your life!

BEING BROUGHT TO PERFECTION

In this parallel of our history with the story of Christ, in our being spiritually raised from the dead, *we have a preeminent security for future perfection.* "He that hath wrought us for the selfsame thing is God, who also hath *given unto us the earnest of the Spirit"* (2 Corinthians 5:5). If He raised us up when we were dead in sin, will He not keep us alive now that we live unto Him? If He called us out of our graves when we were under the bondage of death, will He not preserve us now by the life of Him that dies no more? If the life of God has really been infused into us, who shall destroy it? Has not our Master said, *"I give unto my sheep eternal life; and they shall never perish, neither shall any man pluck them out of my hand"*? (See John 10:28.)

He would not have given us this life unless He had intended to bring it to perfection. As surely as you live by the Father, you live as Jesus does, beyond the range of further death. *"Sin shall not have dominion over you: for ye are not under the law, but under grace"* (Romans 6:14). Do you tremblingly ask me, "What if I go back unto sin?" Listen to this. It is written in the covenant, *"I will put my fear in their hearts, that they shall not depart from me"* (Jeremiah 32:40b). The life which is in you springs up unto eternal life.

You shall surely behold His face whose life is already within your breast. What a blessed thing this is! I cannot declare to you the measureless glory of God which I perceive in this quickening of souls unto God; and yet that which I perceive is the bare fringe of the glory. He could have left us to our corruptions, and then at the last He would have said, "Bury my dead out of my sight." *"Depart from me, ye cursed, into everlasting fire, prepared for the devil and his angels"* (Matthew 25:41). But instead of that, in His free love He has come in the person of His dear Son and died for us that we might die in Him, and He has quickened His Son that we should live in Him.

Soon He will say, *"Come, ye blessed of my Father, inherit*

the kingdom prepared for you from the foundation of the world" (Matthew 25:34). Wondrous grace! "He that sitteth on the throne saith, Behold, I make all things new"(see Revelation 21:5); and never is He to our hearts more truly on the throne than in this new creation of which we are this day the happy subjects.

> "Raised from the dead, we live anew;
> And, justified by grace,
> We shall appear in glory too,
> And see our Father's face."[4]

If I gave you only those two things to dwell upon, you might, by God's blessing, find a good Sabbath's meal in them. God sanctify this teaching to all our hearts!

3. THE LIFE THEN GIVEN IS EMPHATICALLY NEW

Now I want your special attention while I speak on this topic. Read our text: *"Like as Christ was raised from the dead by the glory of the Father"*—I expected that we would then read, "even so we also should be raised by the glory of the Father"; but it is not so. Paul sometimes takes great leaps of thought. It is in his mind that we are raised together with Christ; but his thought has gone further, even to the activity which comes of life; and we read,

> *"that . . . we also should walk in newness of life"* (Romans 6:4). As much as to say, "I need not

---

4. Verse 6 of the hymn: "Lord We Confess Our Numerous Faults" by Isaac Watts 1674-1748.

tell you that you have been quickened as Christ was; but since you have been made alive, you must show it by your walk and conduct." But He reminds us that this life has much newness about it.

"Newness of life"—what does it mean? It means this. When we are born again, and believe in the Lord Jesus Christ—which takes place at the same time—we receive *a life that we never before possessed.* We begin to feel, to think, and to act as we never did before. The new life is something foreign to our fallen nature: an exotic, a plant of another clime. The carnal mind knows nothing of spiritual things. The man who is not born again cannot understand what the new birth means. Spiritual things are *spiritually discerned*, and the carnal man cannot understand them. In your quickening you received a light which had never before shone in your bosom—a life that came not from men, nor by men. It is not a development of something which was hidden in our constitution; it is not the evolution of a principle that already exists but is hampered and hindered.

No: it is not written, "You has He fostered, who had the germs of dormant life"; but, *"You hath he quickened, who were dead in trespasses and sins"* (Ephesians 2:1). You had no life; you had nothing out of which life could come. Fostered you might have been; but all the fostering possible would only have developed your corrupt nature, and caused the evil within to grow at a greater rate. No seeds of eternal life lie buried in the dunghill of fallen nature. Eternal life is the gift of God.

New Principles

This novel life is new in its principles. The old life at its very best only said, "I must do right that I may win a reward." Wage-earning is the principle of the old legal life when it tries to be obedient. Now you are moved by gratitude, and not by a mercenary motive. I hear you sing:

> *Loved of my God, for him again*
> *With love intense I burn:*
> *Chosen of him ere time began,*
> *I choose him in return.*[5]

Now, you serve not as a hired servant, but as a loving child. Grace reigns. The love of Christ constrains you. It is your joy to obey out of love, and not from slavish fear.

New Motives

This life is *swayed by new motives*. You live now to please God; before you lived to please yourself, or to please your neighbors. Once you lived for what you could get for yourself; you lived for the passing pleasures of a fleeting life; but now you have launched upon eternal seas. Eternity holds your treasures; eternity excites your efforts; eternity elevates your desires. You live as seeing Him who is invisible, and your conduct is controlled, not by the judgment of fallible men, but by the rule of the heart-searching God.

---

5. "The Chiefest Among Ten Thousand." Verse 4, Hymn written by Augustus Toplady.

New Objects

Your new life has *new objects*. You aim higher; yes, you aim at the highest of all; for you live for the glory of God, and *"let your light so shine before men, that they may see your good works, and glorify your Father which is in heaven"* (Matthew 5:16). The will of God has now become your law. You count yourself only happy as you may fulfill His purposes, honor His name, and extend His Kingdom.

New Emotions

Your inner life has made you conscious of *new emotions*. You feel now as you did not to feel before. Your fears are new, your hopes are new; your sorrows are new, and your joys are new. If you were to meet your old self you would not wish to strike up an acquaintance with him, but would rather walk on the other side of the street. When I meet my former self I always quarrel with him, and he with me. I grieve to confess that I find another law in my members warring against the law of my mind, and seeking to bring me again into captivity. Behold, all things are new to us. One lady said to me, when I asked her what kind of change she had undergone—"Either the world is quite altered, or else I am." Yes friends, the light is changed, because our eyes are opened to it. We feel the very opposite of what we felt by nature.

New Hopes

Now are we cheered by *new hopes:* we have a hope of immortality; a hope so glorious, that it causes us to purify ourselves in preparation for its realization. We wait for the glorious appearing of our Lord. We look for new heavens and a new Earth. We have a lively hope which defies death.

New Possessions

Now have we *new possessions.* We used to wonder what the Christian meant when he spoke of *"possessing all things."* (See 2 Corinthians 6:10.) We know now. God has made us "rich in faith," and He has given us greater riches than all the treasures of Egypt. When the Lord lifts up His countenance upon us, we no longer cry for corn and wine and oil. Though flocks die, and crops fail, our estate is entailed; our bread shall be given us, and our waters shall be sure. Instead of groaning that life is not worth having, we bless God for our being, because of our well-being in Christ. Behold the desert now rejoices and blossoms as the rose. Where we heard only the hooting of the owl and the cry of the dragon, we hear music as of a song which has just begun, which is every moment swelling and increasing, and shall soon burst into a thunder of hallelujahs which shall never end. We are happy creatures now. Once we were doleful enough, save when we were in our cups and inflamed with a delirious mirth; but now we have peace like a river, and a secret joy which no man takes from us. We drink of a well which none can dry up: we have bread to eat that the world knows not of. Truly our fellowship is with the Father; and this, even to ourselves, is so vast a joy that it overwhelms us. When we are nearest to God, and are absorbed in Him, we cannot comprehend our own delight.

NEW WORLD

We have come into a new world altogether; a world far more grand than that which nature reveals. I often compare myself to a chick, which aforetime was imprisoned in the dark, narrow, and uncomfortable prison of its natural shell. In that condition I neither knew myself, nor of that around me, but was in a chaos, as one unborn. Do I not remember when the shell was broken and I came out into the open? Then, like a young bird, I was weak and strange, and full of wonderment at the life into which I had come. How strange was it to my soul to have the Godhead consciously perceived, and Christ and His redemption blessedly enjoyed! That young life begins to feel its wings and try them a little. It also moves with trembling footsteps, attempting a new walk. It sees things it never dreamed of when shut up in the darkness.

The new-born soul beholds *"new heavens and a new earth, wherein dwelleth righteousness"* (2 Peter 3:13). That text has come true to some of us: *"Ye shall go out with joy, and be led forth with peace: the mountains and the hills shall break forth before you into singing, and all the trees of the field shall clap their hands"* (Isaiah 55:12). It is a wonderful thing, this new life. I beg to press home the inquiry, *Do you know it?* Do you enjoy it? Do not boast that you are being educated. Educate the old life as you will, it will remain natural, and cannot become spiritual. You have been, you say, religious from your childhood. Be it so; but even to you I must say, *"Ye must be born again"* (John 3:7). There must be a passing from death unto life.

Does all I am talking about seem to be a confused maze? So far it will do you good to know that you do not understand the things of God. To know that you are a stranger to the inward life may be a blessing to you. It may be that a prayer will spring up in your heart, "Lord, implant in me this life." The Lord and giver of life is willing to bestow it. It is to be had through Jesus; for to *"as many as received him, to them gave he power to become the sons of God, even to them that believe on his name: Which were born, not of blood, nor of the will of the flesh, nor of the will of man, but of God"* (John 1:12-13). May you be born this very day into this newness of life!

The Walk Which Comes Out of This Life Is New

I must close, though the subject is sweetly absorbing, and one would like to go further into it. Our fourth point is this—the walk which comes out of this life is new. You were dead, but you have been raised from among the dead, and now you walk in "newness of life."

THE NEW LIFE THAT GOD GIVES US IS EXCEEDINGLY ACTIVE.

I have never read that we are to lie down and sleep in the newness of life. It is true I have met with persons who professed to have been saved, and therefore they took matters easily, and made themselves religiously comfortable in idleness. I greatly question whether you have new life if you do not walk. God's children are not of a sluggish race. There is vigor and fervency about them. They cannot sleep, as do others. The new life is akin to the life of angels, and angels do not spend the day in slumber or sloth. I never heard of sluggish angels. They are as flames of fire. The new life in a Christian is quick, energetic, and forceful. The new life produces a holy walk as soon as it is created. If you have been born unto God, you have cast off your lethargy, and are ready to run the race set before you. You may happen to be dull and sleepy occasionally through disease; but you will not choose this. When in spiritual health, you will glow with divine ardor and burn with holy fervency, delighting yourself in serving the Lord.

This activity of life induces progress. If we are really quickened, we are to *walk* in newness of life: that is to say, we shall move on. We are not to take the goose-step in newness of life; but to march on, going from strength to strength. We are not at the end yet; we must advance. All that we have already attained is to lead on to the beyond. It is true we have the new life in us, but we have not yet obtained everything: we must climb higher, and go further. The new life grows.

This walk is to be in newness of life. We are not to act or grow in the energy of the old life, but in newness of life. The conduct of a Christian is in newness of life: and therefore others cannot understand him because he acts so differently from them. But, alas, all professors of Christianity are not of this sort! I see a Christian man coming back one evening from a place of questionable amusement. Did he go there in newness of life? The old man used to go in that direction. When a man is doubtfully honest, and has made a bargain which will not bear the light; is that done in newness of life? When an employer grinds down the workman to the last farthing; is that done in the newness of life? Surely, you will see what I am aiming at.

Brethren, have done with the things of the flesh. Put off the old man. If Christ has quickened you, walk in newness of life. Say to the old man, "Down with you, sir! I am done with walking in your way." Let the new man come to the front, and follow his guidance. Say in your soul, "O life of God within me, be supreme. Take the upper hand, and let every thought be captive to your power." Let us not live in oldness of spiritual death, but in newness of spiritual life. What a change is wrought by the perception and possession of better things! Dr. Chalmers[6], in his Exposition of Romans, pictures a man engaged with full and earnest ambition on some humble walk of retail merchandise.

He cares about petty things, and makes great account of his little stock-taking. His hopes and fears range within his circumscribed trading; and he aspires to nothing more than to reach a few shillings a week to retire upon. Then a splendid property is willed to him, or he is introduced into a sublime

---

6. Thomas Chalmers, writer of "Exposition of Romans." Born 1780—Died 1847.

walk of high and honorable adventure. Henceforth everything is made new. The man's cares, hopes, habits, tastes, desires, are all new. His expenditure alters; his valuation of money alters; his fear about the state of the stock disappears; his joy in the prospect of a small competency is no more before his eyes. He has risen to a different level altogether. New conditions have silently changed all things. The whole man is built on a bigger scale: his house, his table, his garments, his company, and his speech, are all of another sort.

In the same way the Lord, by all that He has done for us, and in us, has changed everything. No point is unaffected. Newness of life affects our manhood from head to foot. The Lord has made us rich in himself, by the gift of Jesus, and by the work of His Spirit, and He would not have us grieving and fretting about the little matters which once were so exceedingly great to us. *"After all these things do the Gentiles seek"* (Matthew 6:32). Let us have higher cares and diviner aspirations. Let us seek to live the life of Heaven on Earth. We are called unto righteousness; let us not follow after mammon. We are new creatures; may the Lord renew us day by day! Let us quit the old; for the time we have spent in it may well suffice. Our soul aspires to a nobler destiny now.

JOY IS OUR STRENGTH

The Christian life should be one of *joyful vivacity*. We cannot always be what we should like to be, especially if we have a sluggish liver or an aching head; but I am speaking of our normal condition. The Christian man, living in newness of life, should find the freshness of the new life around him.

Our inner man is renewed day by day. A healthy Christian is one of the liveliest creatures on Earth. When he is at work you may hear him sing. He cannot help it; do not blame him for a little noise. Let him sing, and laugh until he cries. Sometimes he cannot help it; he will burst if his soul does not have vent. When he begins to talk about his Lord his eyes flash fire. Some people hint that he is out of his mind; but those who know best assure us that he was never before as sane as now.

Of course, the world thinks religion is such poor stuff that nobody could grow excited about it. To my mind, cold religion is the nastiest dish ever brought to table. True godliness is served up hot. Newness of life means a soul aglow with love to God, and therefore earnest, zealous, happy. Let the believing man have space for his larger life, and sing for his grander joy. No, do not gag him; let him sing his new song. If any man out of Heaven has a right to be happy, it is the man who lives in newness of life. Come, beloved, I want you to go home today with the resolve that the newness of life will be more apparent in your walk. Do not live the old life over again. Why should you? What good would come of it?

Come, my soul, if Christ has raised you from the dead, do not live after the fashion of the dark grave you have left behind. I am not so drawn by the sepulcher as to return to it. Walk after the fashion of the new life, and it will conduct you to God from whence it came. Live a God-like life; let the divine in you sit on the throne, and tread the animal beneath its feet. "It is easier said than done", cries one. That depends upon the life within. Life is full of power. I have seen an iron bar bent by the growth of a tree. Have you never heard of great paving-stones being lifted by fungi, which had pushed up beneath them? Life is a mighty thing, especially the divine life. If you choose to contract your souls by a sort of spiritual tight-lacing, or if you choose to bend yourselves down in a sorrow which never looks up, you may hinder your life and its walk; but give your life full scope, and what a walk you will have! Yield yourselves fully to God, and you will see. There is a happiness to be enjoyed by truly wholehearted believers that even some of God's own children would think to be impossible.

WHOLEHEARTEDNESS

Let me finish by a picture, which will show you what I mean by wholeheartedness. I have seen boys bathing in a river in the morning. One of them has just dipped his toes in the water, and he cries out, as he shivers, "Oh, it's so cold!" Another has gone in up to his ankles, and he also declares that it is fearfully chilly. But look, another runs to the bank, and dives in headfirst! He rises to the surface and seems to fairly glow. All his blood is circulating, and he cries, "Delicious! What a beautiful morning! I feel alive and glowing all over. The water is splendid!" That is the boy truly enjoying his bath! Now, you Christian people who are paddling about in the shallows of religion, and just dipping your toes into it—you stand shivering in the cold air of the world which you are afraid to leave. Oh, if you would only plunge into the river of life! How it would brace you! What tone it would give you! Do it, young man! Do it! Be a Christian, out and out. Serve the Lord with your whole being. Give yourself wholly to Him who bought you with His blood. Plunge into the sacred flood by grace, and you will exclaim—

"Oh, this is life! Oh, this is joy,
My God, to find thee so!
Thy face to see, thy voice to hear,
And all thy love to know."[7]
May we thus walk in newness of life! Amen.

Hymns from "Our Own Hymn Book"
—307, 309, 318.

---

7. "I Would Commune With Thee, My God" Hymn # 318 from *Our Own Hymn Book* written by G.B. Bubier and J.E. Jones.

Study Guide

Chapter One:

Name the three areas Spurgeon discusses in this chapter?

1. _____

2. _____

3. _____

What part of the Scripture text does each area relate to?

1. _____

2. _____

3. _____

What did you learn from this chapter regarding man's wisdom versus God's wisdom?

_____

_____

_____

Chapter Two:

What significance and similarities does the Israelites' Passover lamb, in the Old Covenant, have with Christ Jesus' the Lamb of God, in the New Covenant?

1. _____

_____

_____

What does the blood of the lamb sprinkled on the lintel and doorpost of Israelites' homes in the Old Covenant have to do with the shed blood of Christ Jesus in the New Covenant?

2. _____

_____

_____

3. Complete this Scripture: *"But if we walk in the light, as he is in the light, we have fellowship one with another, and the blood of Jesus Christ his Son _____ us from _____ _____"* 1 John 1:7.

CHAPTER THREE:

In what sense is Jesus Christ the property of every believer?

1. _____

_____

2. He that _____ not his own Son, but _____ him up for us all, how shall he not with him also freely _____ _____ things?

What is the precept that Spurgeon teaches us in part three of chapter five?

3. _____

_____

CHAPTER FOUR:

This chapter teaches about Christ being the power and wisdom of God. Fill in the blanks in the following Scripture references that prove this statement from 1 Corinthians 1: 23-24.

1. But we preach Christ _____, unto the Jews a _____, and unto the Greeks foolishness; But unto them which are _____, both Jews and Greeks, Christ the _____ of God, and the _____ of God.

STUDY GUIDE

Fill in the blanks in the following Scriptures from the Old Covenant and the New Covenant that speak of Christ being the power and wisdom of God.

2. John 1:1, "The _____ was with God, and the _____ was God."

3. John 1:3, "All _____ were made by him; and without him was not _____ made that was made."

Explain the meaning of the word "intrinsic" as used in the following question. "How could Christ's gospel have been established in this world as it was, if it did not have in itself intrinsic might?"

4. _____

_____

_____

"The fear of the Lord is the beginning of wisdom: and right understanding have they who keep his commandments" (see Psalm 111:10). Fill in the blanks in the sentence below that Spurgeon uses to explain the difference between wisdom and knowledge.

But wis_____ is not know_____ ; and we must not confound the two. Wisdom is the right use of _____ ; and Christ's gospel helps us, by teaching us the right use of knowledge.

CHAPTER FIVE:

The Scripture reference for this text is from John 12:32: "And I, if I be lifted up, will draw all men unto me." In this chapter, Spurgeon teaches the importance of the first part of that Scripture, "If I be lifted up," by explaining why, and who should be lifting Him up. What are the three things Spurgeon wanted the reader to particularly notice in this Scripture according to his text?

1. Christ crucified, Christ's g_____.
2. Christ crucified, the m_____ theme.
3. Christ crucified, the h_____ attraction.

How was the Cross Christ's glory?
4. _____
_____
_____
_____

How was the crucifixion the completion of all His work?
5. _____
_____
_____
_____

Explain why Christ's crucifixion is to be the theme of every minister's teaching?
6. _____
_____
_____
_____

When Christ and His crucifixion is preached what is the effect upon the hearer?
7. _____
_____
_____
_____

Study Guide

Chapter Six:

The title of chapter six is "Christ glorified as the builder of His Church." What is the Church comprised of?

1. _____
_____
_____

When Solomon built the temple he used rough cedar planks and stones that had to be cut and shaped. How does that relate spiritually to the Body of Christ and the Church Christ is building?

2. _____
_____
_____

Chapter Seven:

In chapter seven, Spurgeon teaches that Christ is our substitute. Write down the Scripture reference he uses in the beginning of his text?

1. _____
_____
_____

What three points does Spurgeon teach in chapter seven?

1. _____
_____

2. _____
_____

3. _____
_____

Chapter Eight:

How did Christ become the "perfect Savior?"
1. _____

2. Fill in the blanks, God imputed our s_____ to Christ Jesus and imputed Christ's r_____ to us.

Chapter Nine:

Spurgeon endeavors to move the readers' focus from the crucified Jesus to the resurrected and glorious King Christ Jesus. Spurgeon refers to Him as the Shepherd-King in chapter nine. Explain what the term shepherd-like in nature means as referring to Christ.
1. _____

Christ's reign is "perpetual." What does that mean?
2. _____

What benefit does Christ's perpetuity have for the Church?
3. _____

CHAPTER 10:

In Genesis 3:15, God spoke these Words to Satan in the Garden of Eden:
"And I will put enmity between thee and the woman, and between thy seed and her seed; it shall bruise thy head, and thou shalt bruise his heel." At what point in God's Word was this Scripture fulfilled?

1. _____

Explain the Doctrine of the Two Seeds?

2. _____

When was the first blood sacrifice? Who performed it and why?

3. _____

CHAPTER 11:

Christ was raised up by the glory of the Father according to Romans 6:4. How does this enable Christians to walk in newness of life here on Earth?

1. _____

_____

_____

What does union with Christ mean?

2. _____

_____

_____

Sanctification is a process. What does Spurgeon teach regarding the three-fold process of sanctification within our character?

3a. _____

_____

3b. _____

_____

3c. _____

_____

4. Joy is the Christian's st_____h.

Pure Gold Classics
Timeless Truth in a Distinctive, Best-Selling Collection

Reader Benefits 6

- Illustrations
- Detailed index
- Author biography
- In-depth Bible study
- Expanding Collection—40-plus titles
- Sensitively Revised in Modern English

An Expanding Collection of the Best-Loved Christian Classics of All Time.

AVAILABLE AT FINE BOOKSTORES.
FOR MORE INFORMATION, VISIT WWW.BRIDGELOGOS.COM

The Holy Spirit Power	John Wesley
The Holy Catholic Church	John Calvin
Humility	Andrew Murray
The Imitation of Christ	Thomas à Kempis
In His Steps	Charles M. Sheldon
Interior Castle	Teresa of Avila
Jewels from E.M. Bounds	E.M. Bounds
The Kneeling Christian	An Unknown Christian
Madame Jeanne Guyon	
Morning by Morning	Charles H. Spurgeon
Obtaining the Grace of Christ	John Calvin
The Overcoming Life	D.L. Moody
The Pilgrim's Progress in Modern English	John Bunyan
Power, Passion & Prayer	Charles G. Finney
The Practice of the Presence of God	Brother Lawrence
Secret Power	D.L. Moody
A Serious Call to a Devout & Holy Life	William Law
The Sermon on the Mount	John Wesley
Sinners in the Hands of an Angry God	Jonathan Edwards
The Sovereignty of God	A.W. Pink
Spurgeon on God	Charles Spurgeon
Spurgeon on the Holy Spirit	Charles H. Spurgeon
Spurgeon on Prayer	Charles H. Spurgeon
Table Talk	Martin Luther
Torrey on Prayer	
Tozer: Fellowship of the Burning Heart	
Tozer: Mystery of the Holy Spirit	A.W. Tozer
Walking with God	Andrew Murray Trilogy on Sanctification
William Wilberforce Greatest Works	
With Christ in the School of Prayer	Andrew Murray

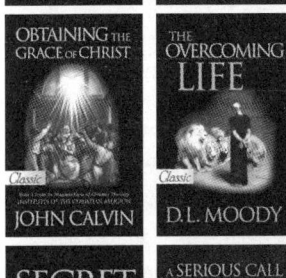

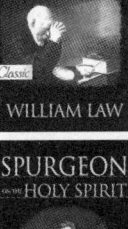

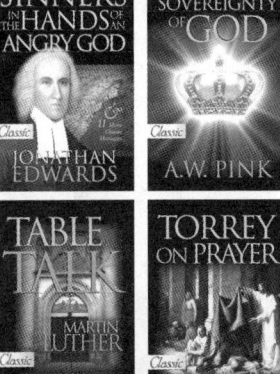

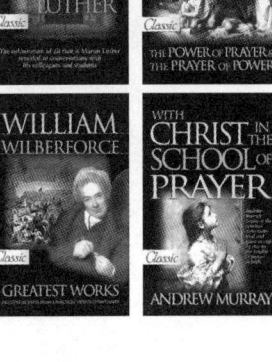